DUCHESSES

LIVING IN 21ST CENTURY BRITAIN

D1342645

ABOUT THE AUTHOR

After graduating, Jane Dismore taught English Literature to A-level in secondary schools and wrote for magazines on a freelance basis. A complete change of lifestyle saw her running private yachts in the Mediterranean for several years, which she combined with writing. She had a regular radio slot, presenting her features on the British Forces Broadcasting Service. After returning to England she qualified as a solicitor and worked in private practice for 19 years. In 2013, her first non-fiction book, *The Voice From the Garden*, was long-listed for the New Angle Prize for Literature. She now writes full-time.

DUCHESSES

LIVING IN 21ST CENTURY BRITAIN

Jane Dismore

BLINK

bringing you closer

BLINK
bringing you closer

Published by Blink Publishing

Deepdene Lodge

Deepdene Avenue

Dorking RH5 4AT, UK

www.blinkpublishing.co.uk

www.facebook.com/blinkpublishing

twitter.com/blinkpublishing

ISBN: 978-1-90582-585-1

A CIP catalogue record of this book is available from the British Library.

Design by www.envydesign.co.uk

Printed and Bound in Slovenia by Svet Print

Colour reproduction by Aylesbury Studios Ltd.

1 3 5 7 9 10 8 6 4 2

Papers used by Blink Publishing are natural, recyclable products made from wood grown in sustainable forests. The manufacturing processes conform to the environmental regulations of the country of origin.

Blink Publishing is an imprint of the Bonnier Publishing Group www.bonnierpublishing.co.uk

In memory of my mother, who knew of the concept of this book
but did not have the chance to read it.

TAKE YOUR *DUCHESSES* EXPERIENCE BEYOND THE PRINTED PAGE...

Jane Dismore
introduces
Duchesses

Step back in time with the Duchesses app and download exclusive videos, histories and family trees. Access the free app from iTunes or Google Play, point your device at the pages that display the special icon, and the videos will be revealed on screen. Here you will get the chance to watch videos of some of the wonderful duchesses included in this book, as well as an exclusive interview with the book's author, Jane Dismore. The app also includes a fantastic collection of the coats of arms for every duchess and their family trees.

The Duchesses app requires an Internet connection to be downloaded, and can be used on iPhone, iPad or Android devices. For direct links to download the app and further information, visit www.blinkpublishing.co.uk.

CONTENTS
THE DUCHESSES FEATURE IN ORDER OF THE CREATION OF THE DUKEDOMS

ACKNOWLEDGEMENTS

I am deeply grateful to those duchesses who agreed to be part of this book. In doing so, Their Graces have enabled the publication of what I believe is the first composite record of any of Britain's living, non-royal duchesses. They have been unstintingly generous with their time, their hospitality and their patience; they gave me access to their family archives and to material for those historical duchesses that each has chosen as her favourite. Their Graces have made the experience enriching, fascinating and sometimes humbling.

I am also very grateful to those dukes who have contributed by accepting their duchess's inclusion in the book and by checking historical facts. I had the great pleasure of meeting Their Graces the Dukes of Montrose, Buccleuch and Abercorn, and thank them also for their kindness and hospitality. It is with regret that I did not have the opportunity to meet the others.

Warm thanks must also go to the duchesses' personal assistants who were hugely helpful in facilitating communication: Emma Adler, Jodie Fossey, Sarah Darling, Kerry Willcox and Helen Shepherd, and commercial director Dawn Adams. Staff whose names I never knew, who also greatly assisted the process, include family archivists and historians, who patiently checked the historical content and provided photographs and further information. Dr William Roulston of the Ulster Historical Foundation was extremely helpful on the Abercorn chapters, and I am also very grateful to Gareth Fitzpatrick MBE of the Buccleuch Living Heritage Trust. Thanks also go to my agent, Andrew Lownie of the Andrew Lownie Literary Agency Ltd.

Finally, I am very grateful to my husband for his tireless practical and moral support, and to my family and friends for their encouragement.

The Duchess from *Alice in Wonderland* by Lewis Carroll.

SECRET GRACES:
INTRODUCING THE DUCHESSES

There are Britain's well-known royal duchesses, whose husbands are dukes as members of the Royal Family. Then there is a tiny group of women who sit at the top of the aristocratic tree with their dukes, just one branch down from royalty. These non-royal duchesses are just as much a part of Britain's heritage, the dukedoms having been awarded by monarchs since the 16th century, but they are a dying breed. It is unlikely that any more dukedoms will be created outside the Royal Family and without a duke there is seldom a duchess: history has shown how rare it is for a duchess to be created in her own right.

Ten of these duchesses form the basis of this book. Not only is it the first time Their Graces have been featured together but in many cases it is the first time they have talked publicly about themselves and their role. Each has also selected a favourite duchess in her title from the past, which provides a fascinating gallery from the 17th to the early 20th century and a comparison with today – for what does it mean to be a duchess in the 21st century?

Although the title of duchess has long been part of Britain's history, it can evoke mixed images. It is associated with the grandeur of stately homes that many love to visit, but also with unearned privilege. There is the intoxicating combination of glamour, vulnerability and cleverness of characters such as the 18th-century Georgiana, Duchess of Devonshire, while the racy notoriety of others from history has evoked both fascination and contempt for the perceived futility of their pampered existences. In literature, Lewis Carroll's Duchess in *Alice in Wonderland* is a slightly sinister, larger-than-life figure, the author's parody of the upper classes in Victorian Britain. 'Duchess' was sometimes applied in a derogatory way to those who wished to better themselves beyond their social station. Perhaps, above all, the term feels like the aged title it is, one whose shelf life has expired.

But in April 2011, when the eldest son of

The Duke and Duchess of Cambridge and Prince George.

the heir to the British throne married a pretty, middle-class woman called Catherine Middleton, the title was taken out of its antechamber, dusted off and deposited firmly in the high street and on the Internet. Giving an old title to someone as modern as the Duchess of Cambridge was to make it topical, even desirable again. She even caused the centuries-old rule of male primogeniture to be changed so that females now have equality with males in succession to the throne. The same is not true of her non-royal equivalents, who find equality still has a long way to go.

Although the Queen gave her grandson Prince William a dukedom, putting him among the handful of royal dukes today, the future for non-royal dukes is limited; there are only 24 left in Britain and, for reasons of death or divorce, fewer duchesses. Of those who agreed to contribute to this book, five may be recognised in the context of their stately homes open to the public. Interviews given by those duchesses are usually to promote the family estate: they do not generally talk about themselves personally. For the others, giving an interview of any kind is a rare occurrence: however old and illustrious the title, they and their families prefer to maintain their privacy, so they responded to requests with caution.

To be granted an interview with any of the duchesses was therefore a privilege. Each is very different: there is no such thing as a typical duchess. None shares the same role, riches or concerns. But what they all have in common is their marriage into families whose ancestors helped shape Britain's history: families which, even when some members were less illustrious, endowed it with the fops and the tarts and the grotesques and the romantics who make it so fabulously entertaining.

Above all, the duchesses are women who occupy a unique position within the nobility, a place some have not always found easy in an age of recession when privilege is not a popular concept. And while the Succession to the Crown Act 2013 removed the gender rule, the rules that govern the succession of other hereditary titles mean that the pressure on non-royal duchesses (and other titled women) to produce a male heir is as great as it was centuries ago. Steps are, however, finally being taken towards the inheritance of titles by women. In March 2014, Lord Lucas's Equality (Titles) Bill – known as the *Downton Abbey* Bill after the popular television series – was progressing through the House of Lords after its introduction in May 2013, although there was still some way to go. The question of inheritance by women is one on which the duchesses here give their views, sometimes with surprising results.

To consider duchesses today, it is necessary to look back at where they have come from. Historically, they are dependent beings. With very rare exceptions, a duchess cannot exist without her duke. A duke represents the highest level of peerage, next in precedence to the monarch. For that reason, there have always been very few of them. Of all the titles bestowed by a monarch, that of duke has been granted the least often:* the recognition of devoted service was hard earned.

There are those who hold much older titles, such as earls and barons, but dukes are the only ones entitled to be addressed by the monarch as 'right trusty and entirely beloved cousins'. To everyone else, they are 'Your Grace'.

The highest-ranking duke is always royal and always the heir apparent: the sovereign's eldest son, who inherits the title of Duke of Cornwall. That was the first English dukedom, created in 1337 by Edward III for his son, the Black Prince. Its current holder is Prince Charles, who is also the Duke of Rothesay, the secondary title of the sovereign's heir apparent in Scotland. The creation of dukedoms for members of the Royal Family remains, as always, in the hands of the sovereign, so neither the survival of royal dukes nor their number can ever be guaranteed.

With non-royal dukes, their titles are more

Prince Charles, Duke of Cornwall and Duke of Rothesay.

---

* Titles in descending order of rank are: Duke, Marquess (or Marquis), Earl, Viscount, Baron.

likely to die out than be created. Like all hereditary titles, that of duke is granted with a 'remainder', or instruction as to whom the title must pass when the original holder dies. Many titles have become extinct through lack of a successor. In the history of the realm, 162 separate non-royal ducal titles have been created. The most that ever existed at any one time was 40, which was at the end of George I's reign in 1727. By 1930, that number was down to 31 and it now stands at 24. No titles have been created for non-royal dukes since Fife in 1900; a later offer was made by the Queen to Winston Churchill, who declined.

Anyone who has a preconceived idea of what it is like to be a non-royal duchess today, or perhaps even seeks to become one, may be surprised by some revelations. For centuries, all dukes and other hereditary peers enjoyed tremendous power and privilege, including the right to sit in the House of Lords. Today, there is no political power left in the husbands' titles. The Duke of Montrose, whose Duchess features, is the only duke to retain the right through election to sit in the House of Lords following its reform in 1999. Following a Labour Party manifesto commitment, the House of Lords Act removed the right of most hereditary peers to sit in the Lords. Only 92 were allowed to remain pending the implementation of further reform. Of that number, 75 had to be elected from their party or group and, of the overall total, only two are dukes: Montrose and Norfolk, the latter having automatic entitlement in his role as Earl Marshal of England.

Steps to remove the power of the dukes and the rest of the ruling class had begun a century earlier. Their privileges put them above the law: they could commit crime and escape the jurisdiction of the courts and they could run up huge debts

without punishment. A handful of noblemen had control of Parliament, as many seats in the House of Commons were within their gift, especially the dukes. Five dukes were Prime Minister.*

In 1880, just before the first of the reforms was introduced, there were 431 hereditary peers in the House of Lords. Today's remaining 92 run the risk of exclusion if Labour gets back in power. Regarding it as indefensible that in the 21st century a group should have the power to oversee the making of laws simply by hereditary right, the Labour Party seeks further reforms, considerations for which include a senate that is mostly elected and partly appointed.

Inevitably, the reforms are regretted by some. The constitution of the old House of Lords allowed for the contribution of men and, more recently, women (female life peers from 1958, hereditary peers from 1963) whose backgrounds and specialist experience were invaluable in their consideration of proposed laws. They came from such fields as agriculture, the environment, diplomacy and the arts. Without that expertise, it is feared that the House of Lords will become, as one duke opined to the author, just another place for the 'exam brigade', where the views of someone with a clutch of paper qualifications and little else will be considered more valuable than those based on experience. From 2002, however, it has been possible, when a hereditary peer dies, for another to stand for election to the House of Lords in a by-election, to ensure the mandatory number of 92: some small consolation, perhaps.

So without the political power of their husbands, what remains for today's duchesses to

---

* Newcastle, Devonshire, Grafton, Portland, Wellington.

The House of Lords.

enjoy? Almost all the duchesses who feature say a common perception is that they are very rich. For some, despite the illustrious history of their title, that was never the case. For others, where there was once a fortune, it has largely been lost over the generations. Nevertheless, there are still some substantial estates in Britain owned by dukes, 11 of whom appeared in the *Sunday Times* Rich List of 2014. The duchesses of four of the wealthiest dukes feature in this book: Bedford, Northumberland, Buccleuch and Rutland.

Yet, while their wealth cannot be ignored, to place emphasis on it alone would distort the picture, for much of it lies in historic houses and art collections which are often in trust and which must be maintained. Wealth brings with it responsibility, of which the duchesses are acutely aware. The large houses that some still enjoy are among the gems of

Britain's heritage, their cripplingly expensive upkeep increasingly reliant on the enduring fascination of the world with Britain's history. The duchesses who live in such homes work phenomenally hard, while those who no longer have a stately 'pile' to maintain are fully immersed in other commitments. All have raised, or are still raising, a family.

Even where there is little money, such families are among those groups in today's Britain who are perceived as being privileged, a term which has come to be used – largely for political purposes – in a pejorative way. Although the majority of modern Britons continue to be pro-monarchy, for some the notion of aristocracy as a whole, despite its lack of political power today, is incompatible with a democratic society. Conscious of this, some dukes, wealthy or not, choose to play down their background. A couple live abroad, not using their title at all. Others now appear to consider their title meaningless. The current (12th) Duke of

Devonshire, whose family seat is the well-known Chatsworth House, has said that if required to do so, he would happily surrender his title because the aristocracy is 'dead': this from a man whose family was generally recognised to be one of the most significant in Britain until the late19th century.

The reality is that, like it or not, the aristocracy does still exist, at least for now. When a duke inherits, his wife takes a title that carries with it certain expectations and perceptions. In fact, in the 21st century, it is probably easier than ever before for the duchess to persuade us that she is not a spoilt lapdog from a bygone age. In today's world of foreign billionaires with priceless properties in London, it might be anticipated that the duchess whose husband is not exceedingly wealthy but who still has an estate to maintain, would consider that being a duchess is less of a privilege and more of a millstone. Yet none of the duchesses featured holds that view. They firmly consider that, regardless of wealth, the privilege lies in being associated with their titles, of being part of Britain's history. This applies even to those few who found the elevation to duchess unexpected or unwelcome.

The duchesses are also sensitive to the expectation to 'give back' to society, although the notion of duty, of public service, is so engrained in them that they would do so anyway. Some are aware of occasional negativity towards them or their title, saying their children avoid using them and have been bullied about them at school. But it is not easy to get to know about the duchesses as people, in order to see past the misunderstandings. Although the many charities and organisations with which they are involved are aware of their work, it is in general surprisingly hard to find anything out about Their Graces themselves without actually talking to them.

In these Internet days when one expects to be able to find information about everything on Google, when anyone who is anybody (and plenty who are nobody but wish they were somebody) has their own website, blog or Twitter account, it is unusual to be thwarted. But put the name of one of today's duchesses into the search engine and a blank is likely to be drawn. There will, however, be references to their predecessors, and there will be an abundance of ships, steam engines and even pubs named after some particularly notable holder of a role. One duke told the author with amusement that he had once been confronted by a man who proudly told him he had just bought his wife. It turned out to be a scale model of a steam locomotive named after her.

However, finding a website whose name refers directly to the wife of a current duke is rare indeed. The mere existence of today's duchesses can often be discovered only by looking up their husband, and even then the information tends to be minimal. The media do not always help. In 2009, a society magazine celebrated its tercentenary with an invitation to dinner for ten of those dukes whose titles existed when the magazine was first published. The subsequent article barely mentioned their duchesses.

Some duchesses seem to encourage this lack of information. Even those who need to attract visitors to their stately homes usually use publicity only to promote the house, appearing on the estate's website only in that context and usually pictured with the duke and their children. There were duchesses who declined to contribute to this book (although they thought it a very good idea).

The Duke and Duchess of Devonshire at Chatsworth.

A couple failed to respond to the author's request at all.

Perhaps it is easy to see why they should be nervous of publicity. The duchess of the past, despite the restrictions of her era, class and sex, had less public pressure on her than her modern counterpart. There was press interest from time to time, often depending on whether there was any gossip about her or her husband, especially in those days when dukes had power and when aristocratic marriages were often made for dynastic reasons rather than love, making affairs more commonplace. However, the duchess had little fear that a newspaper reporter would camp on her doorstep; there was no possibility of her mobile phone being hacked, no Facebook exposure or Twitter rumour-mongering, no Internet 'trolls' to make her life a misery.

But do these 21st-century hassles really affect today's non-royal duchesses? They should be able to relax a little because, being 'mere' aristocracy, they are eclipsed by an obsessive celebrity culture that reveres contestants from reality-television shows and bad-girl pop stars, who are placed above the women with titles and twinsets, even if those titles are centuries old and the clothes are by Prada (more than one duchess said that these days she is rarely invited to open events because people prefer to see a footballer's wife). It is probably safe to say that today's non-royal duchesses are not generally troubled by uninvited media interest and that is the way they like it. But this is how the misconceptions mount. Before the titles by which they are identified become no more than a quaint reminder of Britain's past, it is time to bring in this endangered species from that antechamber to see what a little scrutiny will do.

THE QUIET CALLING:
THE DUCHESS OF SOMERSET

A banquette in the far corner of the softly lit lounge of a London hotel, away from the clusters of businessmen having mid-morning meetings and travellers killing time, was a suitable place to meet the Duchess of Somerset.

London was her choice of location, as she could combine it with a charity event she was attending that evening and also meet her youngest son, at university nearby, for lunch. The seating gave her the privacy she craves, for Judith-Rose Somerset is not one to seek the spotlight. A combination of natural reticence and an awareness of the negative aspects of publicity make her reluctant to talk about herself. She prefers to focus on others and the causes with which she is involved. To her, being a duchess means discovering people in different situations: 'I haven't done one public engagement without coming back inspired.' Someone or something has always moved her. Her husband John, 19th Duke of Somerset, is also rarely in the public eye, being 'terribly private'; she thinks that, given the choice, he may have preferred not to have been a duke but nevertheless takes his title and his responsibilities very seriously.

Given their position in the aristocratic tree, their modesty is creditable. After the original dukedom held by the Beaufort family became extinct, the present dukedom was created in 1547. In terms of precedence, this more recent Duke of Somerset is the second most senior non-royal duke; as his Duchess, Judith-Rose therefore enjoys the same position. In first place is the Duke of Norfolk (created 1483) but his Catholicism makes Somerset the most senior Protestant non-royal duke. A certain glamour also surrounds the origin of the Somerset title. The family name is Seymour; the first Duke of Somerset was Edward Seymour, brother of Jane, third wife of Henry VIII, and he became Lord Protector to his sister's

Opposite: The Duchess of Somerset at Somerset House, London.

19

son, the child-king, Edward VI. The 19th Duke is Edward's descendant.

Judith-Rose is proud of her husband's history. The Seymours were an old and influential family whose seat was Wolf Hall in Wiltshire, in which county the family still owns land. Sir John Seymour, father to Jane, Edward and their siblings, had accompanied Henry VIII at the Field of the Cloth of Gold, an extravagantly splendid meeting with the French king Francis I in 1520 near Calais, aimed at improving relations between the two countries. After Jane and Henry's marriage in 1536, Edward rose in status at court and was made Earl of Hertford. When Scotland repudiated a peace treaty with England and confirmed its alliance with France, Edward, an able soldier, led the invasion of Scotland in 1544 and sacked Edinburgh; he then won a significant victory over the French at Boulogne.

Jane died after giving birth to Henry's heir in 1537 and, after Henry's death in January 1547, the Regency Council, nominated by Henry to run the government for his nine-year-old son, took control. Edward Seymour became Lord Protector and for two and a half years acted as king in all but name. He also took the title of Duke of Somerset and proceeded to make his mark. After his appeal to Scotland to join a voluntary union with England failed, he invaded Scotland again and, in 1547, enjoyed a resounding victory at the Battle of Pinkie Cleugh, the last major battle between Scotland and England. That same year, Edward began building Somerset House, his great mansion in London.

At a time of religious turmoil following Henry's break with Rome, Somerset, a Protestant, tried to consolidate the Reformation. He repealed Henry's heresy laws, which had made it treason to attack the king's leadership of the church. He imposed use of the first Book of Common Prayer, which he saw as offering a compromise between Roman Catholic and Protestant learning and abolished some Roman Catholic practices, such as the use of statues; he also allowed the marriage of clergy.

However, the changes led to uprisings in Cornwall and Devon. In other domestic matters, including protecting the rural poor against the propertied classes, Somerset was viewed by the Council as too liberal. The treasonable actions of Somerset's jealous brother, Thomas, which led to Thomas's execution in 1549, did not help Somerset's cause. On 11 October, concerned by his mismanagement of government, the Council had Somerset arrested. A term in the Tower of London followed.

In February 1550, the ambitious John Dudley, Earl of Warwick, emerged as the leader of the Council; his charm and influence over the young King saw him become Duke of Northumberland in 1551. However, Somerset was released from the Tower and restored to the Council. While imprisoned, Somerset had been impressed by the Yeoman Warders, the guards known today as Beefeaters. He vowed that if he was ever released, he would grant them any request they wanted. In those days performing their duties in plain clothes, they asked him for the right to wear the same livery as members of the King's bodyguard. On his release he obtained this right for them; they still wear that uniform today.

Unfortunately, Edward's freedom was short-lived. Accused of scheming to overthrow Dudley's regime, he was beheaded on Tower Hill in January

Yeoman Warders or 'Beefeaters' at the Tower of London.

1552. He had been much loved by the people of London, not least because his time as Regent had been free from religious persecution, and his execution provoked scenes of great lamentation. The King noted his uncle's death coolly: 'The Duke of Somerset had his head cut off upon Tower Hill between 8 and 9 o'clock in the morning.'

In the 21st century, old enmities need not spoil modern relationships; old battles are sometimes commemorated, even celebrated, by both sides. In May 2013, the 19th Duke was invited to the site of his ancestor's victory at the Battle of Pinkie to support a new book. The otherwise private Duke could not deny local newspapers and Scots battle re-enactors photographs of him brandishing a large sword over the battle memorial in a suitably triumphant pose. Judith-Rose thought the occasion looked like fun and regretted that another engagement had stopped her from attending with her husband.

In the Lord Protector's time it is unlikely that Judith-Rose and John would ever have married, for she is Catholic, like the Seymours' old enemies, the Howards: the enmity between the Dukes of

Henry VIII.

Norfolk and of Somerset is well chronicled. Behind it lay partly their religious differences, partly their respective ambitions. Both families provided wives to Henry VIII: from the Seymours came Jane, from the Howards Ann Boleyn and Catherine Howard, both nieces of Thomas Howard, 3rd Duke of Norfolk. Both families suffered executions: Ann, Catherine, Edward. Today's Duchess of Somerset acknowledges the old rivalry with a laugh: 'Oh, yes, the Howards!' In today's terms, it is 'totally irrelevant. I was at school with a lot of Howards.' School was St Mary's, Ascot, a well-known Roman Catholic girls' boarding school.

The difference between the couple's faiths was resolved, as was the religious upbringing of any future children, before they married. Not that Judith-Rose knew when she first met Lord Seymour, as he was then, of his ancestor's role in England's religious life, nor that he was heir to a dukedom. It was 1977, they were both 24 and she had just returned from living and working in Hong Kong. A group of friends invited her on holiday, 12 of them staying in a house in France. Among them was John, a friend of the boyfriend of Judith-Rose's old school friend; the two men had been at Cirencester* together.

Attempts had already been made to pair her with another young man, 'and that was over before we got to Dover!' She did not talk to John very much while they were away, when there were so many other people around. 'I'd been very busy at work, so I didn't do a lot of the outings. I think he thought I was going out with one of the other guys, which I wasn't. He was just an old friend.

---

* A major agricultural college favoured by families whose children need training in estate management.

We used to stay back at the house and read.' On the return journey she sat next to John in the car. 'He was working then as a picture restorer, having given up land agency for a while to go to London – I always joke – to find a wife. I was working at Sothebys and that was our common interest – still is, a love of the arts, decorative arts.'

He invited her to a party at Maiden Bradley in Wiltshire – where the Seymours' family seat is – but omitted to tell her it was fancy dress. She was the only one without a costume but 'he was very sweet' and she forgave him. 'And that was where it really began. We got engaged at the end of May, beginning of June.' They married in 1978.

The first time she went to John's home she was 'very scared', even though his parents were away. 'It's not a vast house, but it's a bit awe-inspiring, to say the least.' Built in the 1690s and set in wooded parkland, the beautiful Grade II listed Bradley House contains the Seymour family's memorabilia over 500 years, including items given to the first Duke in recognition of his services to the Tudor monarchy. The house was once much bigger: the present building is the west wing of a larger house, demolished and altered in 1821 for the duke of the time. Judith-Rose regrets the family's action. 'When everyone else was building enormous houses, they knocked down two wings. They had loads of houses in England and I think it wasn't their main house.' It may be a smaller house now but it can still sleep 24.

When Judith-Rose met John's parents, 'they were absolutely wonderful. My [future] father-in-law I was a little bit scared of because he called a spade a spade.' Her mother-in-law, Jane, was 'tiny, very forceful, but incredibly charming, kind and welcoming.' The 18th Duke, Percy, was a major in the British Army who had not been destined to be duke: his two older brothers had died in infancy. He lived quietly at Bradley House and rarely exercised his right to speak in the House of Lords. Jane was the daughter of a major, 'and a wonderful hostess and cook'.

Judith-Rose's upbringing had many similarities with their son's. 'We'd both had our first foreign holidays in the same place, a wonderful place in Brittany, and it was a time years ago when you could take your car on the plane – old army planes from Bournemouth. They'd done that and so had we. Our lives were very parallel. We'd both been to private schools, we had friends in common. We were brought up very similarly. He'd been brought up in a big house in the country, I'd been brought up in a big house in London. My father worked in London but we spent all our holidays in the country. So I found a very similar family. My sister and my sister-in-law are great friends.'

Her parents were quite a bit younger than her parents-in-law. Before retirement, Judith-Rose's father had been chairman of J Henry Schroder & Co., the director general of the Takeover Panel and deputy chairman of Schroeders Ltd. Her mother is 'very artistic and very knowledgeable'. Art was a major part of Judith-Rose's upbringing. 'We were brought up very much with museums and visits and talking about art. I was surrounded by pretty things.' Every year their holiday was spent by the sea, which she loved. As an adult she learned to ski so they could take their four children skiing. They still go. 'I'm hopeless! I just plod along. No one ever knows when you get back: "Oh, I've just been skiing!"'

When they married they lived mostly in London, coming down to Wiltshire at weekends.

Tactfully, she stayed in the background, not wishing to appear the pushy daughter-in-law. 'I felt they were such a wonderful couple, very difficult to emulate.' Her father-in-law's sister, Lady Susan – 'a wonderful lady' – was a strong presence in village life.

The couple also spent time at the other estate at Berry Pomeroy in Devon, near Totnes, where her parents-in-law had a smaller house. John had worked as a land agent there before moving to London. 'At weekends it was nice to get to know the farmers and everyone at Totnes, [to see] what we could do locally there. That's where my involvement started.'

On marriage, Judith-Rose became Lady Seymour. Unlike most titles, there was no courtesy title for the heir to the Somerset dukedom: John was simply Lord Seymour, rather than the usual marquess or earl. The reason for this dates back to the first duke, the source of a complicated line of descent. When Edward Seymour became Duke of Somerset, he was married to his second wife, Anne Stanhope. His first wife, Catherine Filliol, had given him two sons but Edward doubted the paternity of the elder; there was a suspicion that he was the son of Edward's father. On becoming Duke, Edward ensured that the title would pass firstly to the sons of his marriage to Anne; only on the failure of their heirs would the dukedom pass to his children by Catherine.

On his execution, all Edward's titles were forfeited. Edward's son managed to regain the title of Earl of Hertford and Edward's great-grandson, William Seymour, was made Marquess of Hertford. William also managed to restore the title of duke, becoming 2nd Duke of Somerset in 1660. However, the marquessate became extinct in 1675 and on the death of the 7th Duke in 1750, so did the other titles. It was time for the dukedom to pass to the heirs of Catherine's sons. Her elder son, whose paternity had been suspected, had conveniently died unmarried, so, in 1750, a direct descendant of Catherine's younger son became 8th Duke of Somerset. In 1793, the title of Marquess of Hertford was recreated for the 8th Duke's cousin and continues down that side of the family: the current Marquess, Henry Jocelyn Seymour, born in 1958, is the 9th.

Judith-Rose and John thought they would have a reasonable amount of time before he became Duke. In fact, they only had six years; Percy died in 1984. The new Duke and Duchess were 32. 'I think we thought [when we married] we were so young and that it was so many million years ahead.' John felt the new responsibility very keenly. Judith-Rose saw it as a challenge. 'I knew I was quite well versed in large houses – it was my training really – so I loved the idea of looking after a big house, keeping it nice, looking after its furniture, so that side of it wasn't a problem, but the responsibility I perhaps didn't understand. I understood his worry about it.' At the time, their first child, Sebastian, was aged two. 'I always remember so clearly the night John's father died. We went back home and, as I looked at my son asleep in his cot, I thought, Oh dear, what's this going to be like?'

They were happily settled in the smaller house at Maiden Bradley and Judith-Rose did not want to move into the big house. Fortunately, the Dowager Duchess, as Jane had become, did not want to move out yet, 'and we were happy to let her carry on in the way she wanted. Nothing changed, except she didn't want to do any more of her public duties so I took on her charities.' Her mother-in-law did not like making speeches, so Judith-Rose offered to do them, as long as she could read them. 'She used to learn them off by heart, which she hated, so I said I'd do them if I could read them – much to my detriment, because I can't make a speech now without reading it, which drives my husband mad, because I have to put my glasses on and he says, "Can't you remember what you're trying to say?"' She laughs.

Fortunately, Percy had been keen from an early stage that, under his supervision, John should manage the estate, so at least that aspect did not change. Her parents-in-law had also facilitated the end of a family feud whose roots lay in the 18th century and which had raised its head in 1923 after Algernon, the 15th Duke, died without any male heirs. The title of 16th Duke passed to a distant relation, Brigadier-General Sir Edward Hamilton Seymour, a descendant of the 1st and 8th dukes. However, the 7th Marquess of Hertford, George Seymour, challenged Sir Edward's claim to the dukedom. He produced evidence purporting to show that the marriage of Sir Edward's great-grandfather, Francis Compton Seymour, to Leonora, widow of a sailor called John Hudson, was invalid because Hudson had not died. If true, it would mean their son was a bastard and Sir Edward, a descendant, not entitled to inherit. The Marquess would have been the legitimate heir to the dukedom.

In March 1925, the House of Lords carefully considered the evidence. It found that John Hudson had indeed died and the marriage of Leonora to Francis was valid. Edward was the legitimate 16th Duke. When the 7th Marquess died childless in 1940, his nephew became 8th Marquess of Hertford. The legal case had caused

Bradley House, Maiden Bradley, Wiltshire.

'great animosity between the Hertfords and the Somersets until my parents-in-law decided it was quite ridiculous and phoned up [the 8th Marquess] and said, "Why don't you come and have lunch?"' They duly met up. 'So that was nice, they broke the ice. They were wonderful, [the 8th Marquess] was a marvellous man.' She refers to his son, now the 9th Marquess, and his Brazilian wife, whose family seat is Ragley Hall, Warwickshire. The two sides of the family now keep in close contact with each other; Judith-Rose's daughter Sophia was bridesmaid to a daughter of the 8th Marquess and Marchioness.

After Sebastian, two daughters and another son arrived between 1987 and 1992. 'I'd be seen going off to fêtes with my hat askew and four children and a pram and this, that and the other! That doesn't happen any more. They go for the footballer stars now. My workload has reduced considerably.' When the children were small they made their main home at Berry Pomeroy, where they built a house. Nearby stands the spectacular and atmospheric ruin of Berry Pomeroy Castle, built in the 13th and 14th centuries by the influential Pomeroy family and owned by the Seymours since 1547: 'There's only been two owners of Berry Pomeroy – the Pomeroys and us.' Now managed by English Heritage, the castle has fascinated visitors over the centuries; its reputation as one of the most haunted places in Britain no doubt assists.

Edward Seymour, the first Duke, was inspired by the Renaissance architecture he had seen abroad and decided to create a palace within the original walls, although his son was the main force behind the works. Judith-Rose says it is not clear why he chose Devon as a power base, nor that particular spot. 'The story goes that Edward had lands from Devonshire to London. Certainly not now.' After his execution, 'the family lay very low.' Edward's descendants continued to live in the castle until the 18th century, including another Edward, who was Speaker of the House of Commons and went to meet William of Orange at Torbay: 'They had the first parliament on the estate at Berry.' Edward then decided that Devonshire was too far away: 'It took eight days to reach London, and they had the lands [in Wiltshire], very much a hunting area.' Lacking the money to improve Berry Pomeroy, he sold what he could of the fabric of the castle, which had never been finished. 'He sold the great big oak timber beams from the roof – I've seen where they gouged them out – and all the lead off the roof and obviously the furniture.' Bradley House was built and Berry Pomeroy Castle fell into ruin.

When John inherited, he took up his seat in the House of Lords with gusto, in contrast to his father. He served as a crossbencher on its EU Committee and on the Agriculture and Environment sub-committees, areas where his particular interests lie. His participation gave Judith-Rose the opportunity to be involved in an historical annual ceremony, the State Opening of Parliament, when the Queen attends the House in all her regalia and delivers a speech. Full of tradition and colour, it is a unique occasion. Until the reforms of 1999 all dukes who took their seat in the House were entitled to take part in the ceremony, splendid in their scarlet robes trimmed with four rows of ermine and bars of gold oak-leaf lace, denoting their highest rank among the peers. Their duchesses had to wear long dresses; Judith-Rose recalls one year she had a lovely creamy dress. Tiaras were mandatory. 'You had to have your hair done by 8 o'clock in the morning! The performance is always the tiara, which was in the bank. There was one time I was breastfeeding and it was really fraught. My mother came to get the baby and off we went in the taxi with the tiara! It was wonderful when you got there because everyone was walking round in full evening dress and all the peers in their wonderful ermine, and the judges and everyone. Then you'd sit and wait – you all had your places and line of precedence.' She recalls that within their designated area 'the dukes sat where they wanted to', the bishops and ambassadors were 'all on the floor of the house', while the duchesses 'sat in rows, so if you've got the throne here, the duchesses will be on the left.'

Judith-Rose was never at the ceremony with the Duchess of Norfolk, which meant that as Duchess of Somerset she was the senior non-royal duchess: 'Then you had to lead the curtsey and that was the most terrifying thing!' Once everyone was seated, 'the royal dukes and duchesses would enter, so they were luckily a lead, so when the Queen came in, I'd follow one of them to see when to curtsey. No one was allowed to curtsey before me, apparently, not that I ever saw whether they did or not! It was lovely. Then we'd have lunch together.'

These days she is sometimes expected to appear in her tiara even when it is not a royal occasion. She is very involved in schools – 'I love young people and I do a lot with them' – particularly the little primary school in Devon that her youngest son, Charles, attended and who invited her in. On her first school visit, 'they were expecting me to turn up in my tiara and my dress: "She hasn't got a tiara!" There's a much more glamorous duchess now – the Duchess of Cambridge – but we're not all like her!'

Judith-Rose visited Charles's old school for the Royal Wedding in 2011, and in 2012 gave out medals for the Queen's Diamond Jubilee. 'I'm their pet duchess. I love that, it gives me great pleasure.' She sees her role as duchess as primarily being concerned with charities: 'I think people still like to have a figurehead at the top of the page.' Some of the many charities with which she is involved are local, others wider afield. She feels she has to 'put something back'.

Two charities are in Italy, to where, in 1997, she and John went to live with all the children. Their decision was due to the pending House of Lords reforms. 'My husband wanted another direction. He was very upset by [the reforms], it really changed his life, although he's stood again for it.' From 2002, it has been possible, when a hereditary peer dies, for another to be voted in by way of a by-election to ensure the mandatory number of 92. In 2011, the Duke stood for election as an independent crossbencher and came second.

John had taken over from his father 'quite young, and he'd never done a gap year, the children were the right age, we'd been doing a lot of work on our house in Devon and we just decided to do something completely different.' With the experience she and the Duke had in art, Italy was the natural choice. Rome was their first base, later Florence. They are now back in Rome, where they rent a four-bedroom flat. The children had varying degrees of schooling in Italy and all speak fluent Italian. Charles is 'very Roman', Sophia, who studied at the Orientale in Naples has a Neapolitan accent, while Henrietta's accent, having been to school and worked in Florence, is Tuscan. Of herself, Judith-Rose says, 'I cannot lose my English accent, although it veers towards Roman!' Judith-Rose particularly still spends much time in Italy, having become involved with helping to restore and maintain a monastery on Capri. Another charity, of which she is an Honorary Member, is for the victims of the 2009 earthquake at L'Aquila, in which a university residence collapsed killing 55 students.

In Italy, the attitude to titles is quite different to Britain, she thinks. 'I don't find people antagonistic in Italy. They don't have a royal family and they appreciate the tradition. They've only been a nation for 150 years; we've been one for over a thousand. They really love anything to do with our royal family and aristocrats. Here I find a lot of antagonism, and my children especially.' They were bullied at school and her youngest daughter says when people discover she has title, they change their attitude to her. 'That side I don't like. It's another reason for staying private. I don't like putting my children in that position.' While some people say they are honoured to meet her and the Duke, expecting them 'to be all dressed up', there are others who do not. 'So it's a difficult role. There's people who feel resentful that you've got something they haven't.' Some people are 'downright rude. That's hard and then you feel bad. I'm lucky in a way that I'm married to a duke. I say to the children as well, "I'm

Opposite: The Queen at the State Opening of Parliament.

The Queen's Diamond Jubilee.

proud to have married Daddy, proud to be part of his family, which is part of English history.'" Instead of being negative, she suggests, people should remember her title is historical, not personal. She is a great believer in a country retaining its history. 'It's so easy to lose everything, and I'm very keen on the monarchy. It may be an old-fashioned thing to say but it should remain.'

She believes Sebastian is looking forward to his future role. 'I think he really wants to fulfil his role very well, but he'll find it hard to work out in what sort of way and whether it will be the same as my husband or if it will change.' It is not an issue that will vex her daughters. The Duchess is not in favour of inheritance of the title by females. 'Absolutely not. With my husband's family, they lost much of their lands but they kept the title. He's the 19th Duke: it has come direct from that first Duke. I think that's important. It may sound old-fashioned.' If she had been unable to produce a boy, the title would have gone to her brother-in-law, Francis. 'I still think it important that the family name be kept whichever way it went.' Her daughters do not question the fact that their brother will inherit. 'I brought them up to know that. Everyone has to go their own path, their unique ways.'

The family's very diverse estates occupy the Duke and Duchess in different ways, both commercially and by way of land management.

'In Devon it's beautiful rolling valleys, mostly farmland, a bit of woodland, not very far from the sea. Wiltshire's completely different. It's much bigger countryside, chalk downs, wonderful woods – he's a great forester, my husband, the woods are really very special there – and farmland too. He loves both the sites.' Of the two houses, John regards Bradley House as the main home, 'because it's the family seat and all the wonderful pictures are there.' Judith-Rose brought the children up in Italy and at Berry Pomeroy, which she says exudes more of a sense of her and John as a couple.

That Bradley House today is full of interesting treasures is fortunate considering the family's comparatively recent history. The 12th Duke from 1855, Edward, lived in one of the family's other houses of the time, Stover Hall, Devon. He petitioned for and was granted the name of St Maur, which he alleged (in a period when claiming romantic but often incorrect sources of surnames was fashionable) was the origin of the Seymour name, so his eldest son became Lord St Maur. Edward was devastated when his youngest son died after being mauled by a bear in India and Lord St Maur, after fighting in India at Lucknow, then with Garibaldi for a united Italy, died of heart disease.

Dying without sons, the Duke left some of his extensive estates to his daughters and their husbands. However, he left Stover and all its contents to two children, Harold and Ruth St Maur: the illegitimate offspring of his eldest son by a mysterious, illiterate girl called Rosa Swann. The legacy was held in trust by the Duke's sons-in-law, who included Lord Thynne, who later sold some of the inheritance, including Stover Hall.

The 12th Duke's brother, Archibald, became 13th Duke and claimed his brother had plundered the estates over the years: Archibald inherited a shell at Berry Pomeroy and Maiden Bradley with just its fixtures and fittings – no contents. Archibald soon died and his brother became 14th Duke, also for a brief time. His son, Algernon, the 15th Duke, lived at Bradley House with his wife, Susan, with barely a knife and fork between them. Yet according to a contemporary writer, they lived there happily and had a delightful life. It is Duchess Susan whom Judith-Rose has chosen as a predecessor; they have much in common, including their love of travel. Before settling at Maiden Bradley, Susan travelled with Algernon through Canada and wrote a book about their experiences. She took every opportunity to become involved with Canadian life; Judith-Rose is 'impressed by her courage and sense of adventure.' Susan lived with the Canadian Indians and exhibited 'a sensibility to the culture around her'. As a young girl, Judith-Rose herself spent 15 months travelling through Canada and the USA, also 'determined to be accepted within that environment. This has been my philosophy wherever I have travelled, including Hong Kong, where I attempted to learn Cantonese instead of Mandarin so that I could communicate in the market place and make local friends.'

The Duke and Duchess spend more time at Bradley House than previously. The Duke shows small groups around the house as his parents had done, and also handles the commercial aspects. A summer programme has been launched for adults to have cultural stays there, combining English lessons with trips to local historic towns. Judith-Rose is a qualified teacher of English as a Foreign Language and had taught foreign students during the previous two summers. The Duke was not sure why she was doing it but she says she finds it 'very satisfying'. That life should be satisfying is another view Judith-Rose shares with Duchess Susan, who campaigned for charities that helped children and was 'a woman who never tired and used every minute of her life to the limit, as I like to do.'

As a duchess in the 21st century, Judith-Rose's life is rather different from that of her mother-in-law, Jane. 'I think she had a big jump too. They came directly after the war, early 1950s. Her predecessor would have seen an enormous change because before the war they would have had a lot of help; after the war they didn't. In terms of relationships with people on the estate, in our case it's much more informal.' The staff, however, still use titles. 'I remember when I first met John and went to the house for the first time, it was, "Good evening, m'lord."' Now he is Duke, they are both addressed as 'Your Grace'. With their tenants, although those of their age knew them as John and Judith-Rose before they married, afterwards some called them by their titles. However, 'the children certainly wouldn't be called by their titles.' Today's household staff at Bradley House consists of a caretaker and his wife who is housekeeper during the mornings. At Berry Pomeroy, they have a 'lovely' cook/housekeeper, who has been with the family for 26 years.

Her personal passion these days is dance. 'I danced as a little girl, doing ballet, classical. I was dying to be a dancer but then I became a bit chubby and I hadn't got a great sense of timing.' With her reed-slim figure and fine cheekbones, it is hard to imagine her any different. She tried for the Ballet Rambert but failed to get in, 'so I went off to boarding school and gave up dancing.' Years

later, when her younger daughter was studying dance for the International Baccalaureate, they needed to find a dance school in Florence. The school suggested Judith-Rose have a go too. 'I said, "You're joking, I haven't danced since I was 11!"' But she had a trial and has been with them since 2006, doing ballroom dance. The school has an international franchise, which is convenient for her. Having resolved to become more confident, in 2013 she agreed to perform in a 'showcase', which gave her 'tremendous satisfaction', and she has progressed to taking exams. She has made friends among the teachers and dancers and refers to the school as her 'second family'. In 2013, she went to Blackpool for the first time, to watch a teacher in a competition, and found the famous Winter Gardens 'mind-blowing'.

Judith-Rose Somerset is a busy woman. The first meeting with her had to be curtailed; a second meeting took place in a hotel at Paddington Station on her way back from Italy. She was booked on a train to Wiltshire, where she and the Duke had a function that evening. Unfortunately, she missed the train by a whisker but the ticket office was making it difficult for her to take the next train without having booked. Her evening appointment was threatened and she was agitated. Could she not use her title to 'pull rank'? She would not hear of it. She said her daughter once asked her to do that when she needed something urgently and she refused then, too. Eventually, she was booked on another, albeit less direct, train leaving shortly afterwards. She may be a senior member of the aristocracy but the Duchess of Somerset is entirely free of self-importance.

Opposite: Judith-Rose Somerset and Daisy.

2

THE CHARITABLE ADVENTURER:

SUSAN, DUCHESS OF SOMERSET

(1853–1936)

Judith-Rose Somerset's chosen predecessor Susan, Duchess to the 15th Duke, did not seek the spotlight either. She too was very involved with charitable causes, had a curious mind and enjoyed different experiences, leaving behind a fascinating account of her travels in 19th-century Canada. Judith-Rose admires her courage, resourcefulness and determination to make the most of life: 'I feel Duchess Susan never missed an opportunity.'

She was born Susan Margaret Richards Mackinnon in Edinburgh on 11 January 1853. Her father, Dr Charles Mackinnon, was from an old family from the Isle of Skye who had owned the parish of Strath since 1354. When Charles was born the family seat was Corry Lodge in the village of Broadford, but for generations it was Corriechatachan, which in 1773 was visited by the writers Samuel Johnson and James Boswell. In his book *A Journey to the Western Isles of Scotland*, Johnson wrote that 'Mr Mackinnon' – probably Susan's grandfather, Lachlan – treated his guests 'with very liberal hospitality, among a more numerous and elegant company than it could have been supposed easy to collect', while Boswell referred to the many good books in the Mackinnon house.

One of Susan's paternal ancestors entered Scottish folklore in 1746 for helping Bonnie Prince Charlie to hide in a cave on Skye. The Prince was so grateful that he allegedly gave Mackinnon the recipe of his personal liqueur, which the family made for their own consumption for over a century; in the 1870s, the drink went public, under the name of Drambuie. Today the family name is remembered at Broadford by the Dr Mackinnon Memorial Hospital.

Susan's mother, Henrietta Studd, was born in Calcutta where her parents had married and where, aged 17, she married Charles Mackinnon, 20 years her senior, in 1836. Like his father-in-law,

Opposite: Susan, Duchess of Somerset, in court dress in 1900.

Charles was involved in India's indigo trade. India was the main source of this most expensive and beautiful of all dyes, of particular importance to Britain because it was used for the blue uniforms of the Navy and the Army, and those of policemen and postmen. Vast amounts of European capital were invested in a very lucrative industry that, during the 19th century, employed millions of Indians and thousands of British.

Susan's father started as an indigo planter during the 1820s and later bought a factory at Chitwarrah in the Behar region, where some of the finest indigo was grown. Mackinnon and the Studds were involved in many commercial transactions, sometimes between themselves. Henrietta's only sibling, Edward, became particularly wealthy from the trade and later bought Mackinnon's old factory. Later, Edward underwent a religious conversion and renounced his wealth. Three of his sons – Susan's cousins – became renowned cricketers, one of whom also became a well-known missionary.

Although Susan was born in Scotland, some of her siblings were born in India. Her parents' first child and only son, Charles Lachlan Corry Mackinnon, was born there on 18 January 1837, but as the inscription on his grave near Dholi announced, he died on 3 November 1838. The first of Henrietta and Charles's eight daughters was born the following month; Susan was the youngest.

When Susan met Lord Algernon St Maur as he was then called (his family using what they asserted was the original form of the Seymour name), there was little expectation of his becoming Duke of Somerset. His uncle Edward had been 12th Duke since 1863, and although both Edward's

sons had since died, the heir presumptive was Edward's brother, Archibald. In September 1877, Susan, aged 24, and Algernon, 31, married at Forres on the north Scottish coast. He had already enjoyed an adventurous life; as he was not in line to inherit, he had been sent off to follow a military career. After training for the Royal Navy, he joined the British Army as an infantryman.

Algernon's regiment, also referred to as 60th Regiment of Foot and 60th Rifles, had been raised in North America in the late 1750s to help the British Army, who had suffered defeat at the hands of a force of French and Indians on the banks of the Ohio River. They were not equipped to deal with the dense forests and trackless wastes of North America, so Britain raised and specially trained a force in America, recruiting from American states and adding volunteers from British and other European regiments. When Algernon joined it was called the King's Royal Rifle Corps (KRRC).

When the Red River Rebellion broke out in Canada in 1870, the KRRC was one of the regiments called upon. Algernon, aged 24, found himself taking part in the arduous Wolseley Expedition, named after its leader, Field Marshal Garnet Wolseley. The objective was to secure Rupert's Land (now part of Manitoba, then an outpost in the wilderness) for Canadian settlement against a rebellion led by Louis Riel, a man of French extraction, who was supported by rebels from a combination of other races; they feared British dominance and suppression of Roman Catholics and their land rights. The expedition was mounted by the British Army at the request of the Canadian Government.

For Wolseley's men the only route to Fort Garry (now Winnipeg), the capital of Manitoba, which did not pass through the United States was through a network of rivers and lakes extending for six hundred miles from Lake Superior. The route was very rarely travelled by white men and no supplies were obtainable. On what was a feat of exploration as well as military ingenuity, they successfully overcame many natural obstacles before surprising and scattering Riel's rebels in a bloodless encounter. Canadian sovereignty over the Northwest Territories and Manitoba was established. Wolseley was later honoured, and on praising his men said, 'It may be confidently asserted that no force has ever had to endure more continuous labour.'

After the demanding physical challenges of the expedition it was no wonder that Algernon, a tall and athletic man, felt he could tackle anything. He stayed on in North America for a time and practised ranching. Later, he wanted to show his wife the wonders of that continent, and in 1888 they embarked on an adventurous journey across Canada. For Algernon, it was familiar territory; for Susan, it was a sometimes uncomfortable but unforgettable experience that became the subject of her book. Under the name Mrs Algernon St Maur, *Impressions of a Tenderfoot during a Journey in search of Sport in the Far West* was published in 1890, by John Murray of London. Susan said she chose the title so that readers 'may not expect great things, a "Tenderfoot" meaning in the "Far West" a person new to the country or, must it be confessed, a "Greenhorn".' However, she adapted very quickly.

Dedicated to her sisters, who had requested an account of her adventures, and illustrated by Susan, it is a fascinating description of a country then little explored, and illuminates the late-Victorian world of the upper-class traveller. However, not for Susan

and Algernon first-class hotels all the way: they adopted a more robust approach.

On 3 May 1888, Lord and Lady St Maur left England from Liverpool en route to Quebec on the *Parisien*, the 'best steamer' of the Allan Line. Their first stop was Loch Foyle, where the mail was collected and they were joined by more emigrants, who now totalled over eight hundred; the Allen Line had a contract with the Canadian Government to carry assisted passengers. On 14 May, they arrived at Quebec after some very rough weather, during which Susan discovered she was not a good sailor.

They travelled through Canada by railway, river steamer, horseback and canoe, meeting established families, Indians and immigrants. Algernon was keen to see Winnipeg again and Susan must have been proud to hear him praised. 'It is very interesting to Algernon seeing all this country again,' she wrote, 'as he was one of the officers with Lord Wolseley, who told me Algernon carried the heaviest pack during that expedition; and having both skill and experience in canoe work, he steered many of the boats down the most dangerous part of the rapids.'

The couple hunted and fished in wild lakes and rivers, often with the Indians, sometimes on their own, their achievements still praised today by Canadian sporting groups. They slept in remote ranches and basic hotels, on shingle beaches and in tents. Susan's sense of humour never failed her. After a particularly difficult camp, when she had broken a jar of jam, found the last store had failed to pack essential provisions they had bought, spent a damp night listening to 'an ominous and disturbing buzzing of insects', and 'dreamt of grizzlies', she reflected wryly:

'My advice to campers-out is to be prepared for any inconvenience, for, however complete are the arrangements, generally something is forgotten; make the best of it, feeling it is but a shifting scene in the great drama of life.'

After many adventures, she was pleased to rediscover civilisation on their homeward journey in December 1888. Before sailing from New York, she delighted in eating 'the famous American dish, terrapin', followed by a tour by Mr Tiffany himself of his famous store with its 'beautiful and costly things' displayed over five floors, and its elevator 'which mounts at twice the ordinary pace'. The book's description of their return to civilisation brings with it a reminder of Victorian class expectations that had been so irrelevant in the wilds. Susan wanted to buy some peanuts to make little Chinese dolls. However, 'to buy peanuts in the street of an American town is the quintessence of vulgarity; it would be like eating hot chestnuts at a stall in Piccadilly.' She bought some surreptitiously but the bag split and she was worried that the friend they were meeting would be 'terribly shocked at my carrying such vulgar things'.

Then there was the question of servants. Susan had taken a maid out with her. However, 'Travelling with a maid in this country is more trouble than can be imagined as, except in the big towns, no accommodation is provided, and she is consequently always in the way.' The girl was dispatched to stay with her aunt in Chicago but joined them for the return voyage. It was very rough and Susan felt 'too ill to live'. A stewardess looked after her because, 'my maid was too ill to be of the slightest use to me either going or returning. They may be willing, but as a rule, servants are not good travellers.'

After seven months away, she was ecstatic to be safely home but she had been thrilled to find 'noble rivers and far-reaching railroads … great primeval forests which the axe has not despoiled' and 'quaint, peaceful Indian villages, where sunsets seemed to linger'. As she summarised, 'We undertook our journey in search of health, sport and pleasure. We found these in different degrees but the total far exceeded our expectations.' The book sold very well.

After their return, the couple moved into Burton Hall in Leicestershire, a long way from the Seymours' other properties but where Algernon had spent much of his childhood. It belonged to his uncle Archibald but had lain empty since 1886 when Archibald had become 13th Duke and moved to the principal seat of Maiden Bradley in Wiltshire. Archibald did not want to sell Burton Hall but it was becoming neglected.

The Burton Hall estate had been bought around 1834 by the 11th Duke for Archibald, his second son. Archibald's elder brother, Edward, would inherit the title and the Seymour estates; as Edward's sons were then still alive, Archibald was not in line to inherit and needed a home. Archibald enjoyed managing the 1200-acre estate with its manor house, farms and cottages. For many years he shared Burton Hall with his youngest brother, Algernon Percy Banks St Maur, and his wife and four children, the eldest of whom was young Algernon. Algernon Percy helped Archibald, who never married or had children, to run the estate.

After Edward became 12th Duke in 1863, Archibald and his other siblings soon found intolerable the way Edward was managing the Seymour estates. When Archibald became 13th Duke in 1886, aged 76, and moved to Maiden

Bradley, he complained that Edward had left it a ruinous wreck.

Algernon and Susan must have realised that the possibility of Algernon's becoming Duke was now more likely, as only his father was next in line. Meanwhile, on moving into Burton Hall the couple carried out repairs and extended the house with which Algernon was so familiar. A keen sportsman, who, in 1913, would be made chairman of the British Olympic Association, he installed a cricket pitch in the village and bought new equipment. Susan was a great supporter and encouraged their staff's participation. They were a popular couple.

In 1891, Archibald died. His brother, Algernon Percy, became 14th Duke but died in 1894; suddenly his son Algernon was 15th Duke of Somerset. As was expected of them, the Duke and Duchess moved to Maiden Bradley; there was indeed little left of value but they lived there happily and carried out many improvements on the estate. On his death, the *Wiltshire Gazette* would describe Algernon as a landlord 'second to none'. From a distance they continued to support the village of Burton through Algernon's twin brothers, Ernest and Percy. In 1909, Algernon and Ernest built its village hall, dedicated to Percy's memory; Susan provided books and crockery and formally opened it in September.

Meanwhile, in 1905, Susan had become one of the leading organisers of the Invalid Kitchen, a charity which provided, at the nominal sum of one penny, nourishing meals for expectant and nursing mothers, sick children and convalescents, who could not otherwise afford them. The first one opened at Southwark, a poor area of London. During the Great War, the number of kitchens increased and the charity's work continued afterwards. In November 1920, for example, Susan opened a new kitchen at Windsor Street, London.

Susan was also a patron of the newly created Winter Distress League. Between the two world wars, Britain suffered great economic hardship and organisations like the League were formed to try to bring relief to those worst affected. It aimed to create worthwhile paid employment on a strictly business basis: people were to be paid the going rate in order to preserve their self respect and avoid any stigma of charity. To create opportunities for people to earn money and develop marketable skills, sponsors and funds were needed. The League also tried to offset the effects of malnourishment in children by sending them to the country for periods of up to three months; Burton Latimer, with which Susan was well acquainted, was one such destination.

Judith-Rose says that although Susan 'did not have the luck' that she has enjoyed of having children, Susan recognised the importance of young people and their part in the country's future. Susan and Algernon were very involved with Dr Barnado's Homes, which had started in 1867 and of which Algernon was made President. Their involvement included visiting homes and attending Founders Days. A programme of Saturday 26 June 1920 for a Girls' Village Home in Barkingside, Essex, announced the arrival of the Duke and Duchess of Somerset on a 'Special Through Train' from London in time for the Anniversary Gathering at 3.30 p.m. Usually, Founders Days were celebrated on Dr Barnado's birthday, 4 July, but because of the war that was the first Founders Day there since 1916. Algernon and Susan were entertained by such spectacles as 'March Past of Children and Young People trained and in training as useful Citizens of the Empire' and 'Singing by a choir of 350 Village Maidens'.

As Duke and Duchess they were involved in certain ceremonial occasions, including coronations. Although these tended to be infrequent – there had not been one since Victoria's in 1838 – Algernon and Susan were, most unusually, involved in not one but two, which fell within just nine years of each other. August 1902 saw the coronation of King Edward VII, and June 1911 that of King George V. On both occasions, Algernon had the honour of being Bearer of the Orb, a position historically held by the Dukes of Somerset, while at the first coronation Susan took her place as the most senior duchess after the Royal Family: the most senior duke, Norfolk, was unmarried at the time.

The creativity expressed in Susan's book was also found in her love of gardening; the gardens at Maiden Bradley were praised by a contemporary magazine for their originality. After Algernon's

death in October 1923, and perhaps inspired by her work for the Invalid Kitchens, Susan turned again to writing, producing a cookbook called *The Duchess Cookery Book*, published by Greyson and Greyson in 1934, consisting of recipes she had collected over the years. In the foreword, she said, 'I hope that by trying them it may improve the cuisine of many and meet with the appreciation of the ever indulgent public.' The book sold all over the world, although finding some ingredients may have proved challenging; the recipe for Deer's Head Soup begins, 'Take a scalded deer's head.'

That same year, Susan made a surprise visit to Burton and made a contribution to the hall fund. It was her last visit. On 30 January 1936, she died, aged 83, and was buried near Algernon in a wood on a hilltop near Maiden Bradley. Her involvement in many charities, including the Red Cross, brought her honours from home and abroad. 'Susan gave so much to everyone she met and worked with,' Judith-Rose says. 'Her resoluteness in many things is to be greatly admired and is an example to the whole family.'

Opposite: King George V.

3

THE ROMANTIC:
THE DUCHESS OF ST ALBANS

Romance is a recurring theme with the Duchess, Gillian Anita, who married the 14th Duke of St Albans, Murray de Vere Beauclerk, in December 2002. It is, she says, 'a very romantic title'. That note starts with the source of her husband's title; he is a direct descendant of Charles II and his mistress Nell Gwyn. The London actress had two sons by the King. The first was born in 1670 and had no title for his first six years. Eventually, after impatient remonstrations by Nell, who saw the sons of other mistresses receiving titles, the King made Charles Beauclerk the Earl of Burford and Baron Heddington. Before he was 13 he was made Duke of St Albans.

Gillian thinks that Nell Gwyn was by far the most romantic of all Charles II's mistresses. Certainly, she seems to have been less demanding than some of her rivals. Louise de Kérouaille, her French successor with whom Charles was already enchanted while Nell was giving birth, was made Duchess of Portsmouth. Another mistress, the pushy Barbara Villiers, became Duchess of Cleveland. Nell, however, did not seek a title for herself, only for her son. She was also the only mistress who did not wield or seek political influence, and family historians believe she was the only one of the King's seven or more mistresses to have remained faithful to him and actually loved him: romantic indeed.

To demonstrate Nell's humanity, which elevated her above other mistresses, Gillian says she is thought to be connected with the Chelsea Pensioners. The Royal Hospital in Chelsea was started by Charles II to provide a safe home for soldiers who were no longer fit for active service; the residents are known as Chelsea Pensioners. Story has it that Nell was the force behind Charles's decision, one version saying the impetus came when a wounded and destitute soldier hobbled up to her coach window to ask for alms.

Opposite: The Duke and Duchess of St Albans.

Certainly, Nell is known to have been kind and benevolent; her will, for instance, left an annual sum for the release of poor debtors from prison every Christmas Day, her own father having died in debtors' gaol.

Charles gifted Nell the lease (but, unlike gifts to other *amours*, not the freehold) of the Bestwood Park estate in Nottinghamshire. Once part of Sherwood Forest, it had already been for centuries a popular hunting ground for visiting monarchs and landed gentry and contained a hunting lodge dating back to Edward III. After Charles' death in 1685, Nell received the freehold of the estate from his brother and successor, James II. On her death in 1687, the estate passed to her son, the 1st Duke. When it reached the 10th Duke he demolished the medieval lodge and, in 1863, built a grand house, Bestwood Lodge, in which he and his Duchess often entertained the future Edward VII, as well as British statesmen and poets. The estate stayed in the family until 1940.

The house in which today's Duke and Duchess have lived for around 20 years is part of an elegant 18th-century terrace in London, which has probably not changed much structurally since it was built. On its walls hang old paintings, including a series of miniatures of the Duke's ancestors and a large portrait by Peregrine Heathcote of Gillian, in evening dress, painted whilst listening to Wagner: she and the Duke are passionate about opera.

According to family historians, the title came from Henry Jermyn, the Earl of St Albans, whose title Charles had created. Henry had been a very close friend of the King's mother, Henrietta Maria, and there is even a theory that he was

Opposite: Nell Gwyn.

Charles' father. Henry died just eight days before the young Charles formally became Duke, the King recreating the title in the dukedom for his son. Gillian says there is a portrait of the 1st Duke that hangs today in St Albans, Hertfordshire. Of the town, Gillian says, 'It is charming and we were entertained and given a conducted tour by a delightful Mayor a few years ago.'

Even if the title's origin had little connection with the town itself, Charles certainly had a connection with the county. Just outside St Albans is moated Salisbury Hall, where the King is known to have stayed and with which Nell is said to be associated. One of its occupants in the late 17th century, Sir Jeremy Snow, often entertained the King there, and Nell is said to have been a frequent visitor. Another Hertfordshire town with which Nell and Charles are connected is Tring. Charles granted the reversion of Tring Manor to Sir Henry Guy, groom of the bedchamber and secretary of the treasury, and his heirs. Guy was a great favourite with Charles and was employed by him in various secret services; his duties included the payment of maintenance to Nell on the King's behalf. Guy built an elegant house at Tring, where Charles and Nell are believed to have stayed. In nearby Tring Park stands an early 18th-century obelisk named after her.

A more modern connection between St Albans and the Dukes is maintained through the Royal Navy's HMS *St Albans*, a Duke class frigate launched in November 2001. The original ship was named after the 1st Duke of St Albans; the modern vessel is principally affiliated to the current Duke and is due to be relaunched in summer 2014 after a major refit. Although some of his ancestors enjoyed a successful naval career,

Murray himself does not have a naval background. Born in 1939, he works as a chartered accountant in London, and inherited the title in 1988. He has two children, Charles and Emma, from his first wife, and four grandchildren.

Gillian was married previously to Philip Roberts, but this was tragically cut short after her husband died at the age of 42 years, leaving her with three young children to raise. Gillian and Murray 'have a lot in common. We play bridge, we play tennis, we adore the opera and in particular Wagner, and regularly travel to see different productions of *The Ring*.' They first met at a dinner party at the home of Sir Evelyn Delves Broughton, her late husband's godfather, who had died in 1993. However, it transpired that Gillian's and Murray's paths had already crossed without their having been aware of it: with their previous spouses they had often visited the same places at the same time. By further coincidence, Gillian's late husband had even met Murray's father, the 13th Duke. It was, she says, as though they 'were destined to meet'.

Unlike most of the other duchesses in this book, Gillian married her husband when he was already Duke, so she did not have to experience a period of transition from a previous title to that of Duchess, with the different expectations that that can entail. Similarly, she did not need to be concerned about how a mother-in-law might view her. The Dowager Duchess of St Albans, Suzanne, was still alive when they married but she was Murray's stepmother, whom Gillian liked very much and with whose children by the 13th Duke, Murray's half-siblings, they enjoy a family relationship.

Although she was not born into the aristocracy,

Gillian knew people within those circles from her earlier life, and this naturally continued to be the case when she married the Duke. As a result, she has interesting connections with different families and generations. By way of example, Gillian has a link with Louise, the Duchess of Bedford, whose stepfather was Sir Evelyn Delves Broughton. Of others in the book, Gillian has also enjoyed a passing acquaintance with the Duchess of Northumberland, whose parents she knew, and with the Duke of Buccleuch and Queensberry who is distantly related to Murray: he too is descended from Charles II through one of his mistresses, as are the Dukes of Grafton and Richmond.

Of her own upbringing, she says: 'My mother and father were fabulous. I was educated at a convent, and home was mainly in Edinburgh.' Had she lived in England, she might well have been presented as a debutante; however, in Scotland, such a ritual was not recognised. Instead, a major event in the social calendar was the Highland Ball. Dancing featured prominently in the social lives of the young men and women of her circle, and she loved to go to dances during what was, she says, a very romantic time.

In Edinburgh, her parents' neighbours included a distinguished family, the Constable Maxwells. 'When I left school I studied Interior Design with the Constable Maxwells. Two of the daughters, Ursula and Betty, were respected artists, sculptors and designers and had a famous shop in Edinburgh, called Galloways. They were so artistic and they taught me to get the best out of even the most inexpensive of material. I just loved every second of it.' In her early twenties, she met Philip

Opposite: Charles II.

Roberts, whom she would marry. They lived in London and Gillian continued working in design with their great friend, George Spencer. She also travelled a lot with Philip to Kuwait, Cairo and other parts of the Middle East. 'But then our life together was cut short. It was some time later before I met Murray, but I feel fortunate to now enjoy a different, yet wonderful life together with him.'

Unlike today's Duke and Duchess, not all past unions in the Beauclerk family were happy, particularly in the days when wealth played a large part in choosing a spouse in aristocratic families. In 1752, for example, Jane Roberts from Glassenbury, Kent, an only surviving child and orphan whose father's death when she was 14 had left her a very wealthy heiress, ignored the warnings of her guardians and married the feckless George, 3rd Duke of St Albans. Quickly ensuring control over his new Duchess's estates, George was delighted that her fortune enabled him to pay off some of his many debtors. Unfortunately, Jane is said to have suffered from George's cruelty and lack of feeling towards her, and, in 1755, they formally separated after just two and a half years of marriage. Forced twice to flee abroad to escape debtors, he ran off to Paris with a Windsor dairymaid, had a son by her (who died), enjoyed other mistresses and was imprisoned in a debtors' gaol.

After his wild time in Europe, mostly involving women and gambling, the Duke and Duchess had a brief reconciliation in 1760. She joined him in Brussels but she was not prepared to vie for attention with his mistress, Marie Petit, by whom he had several children; he and Jane had none. Jane died in 1778. Although her Kentish estate, Glassenbury Park, could have passed to George,

and might have remained in the family today, their separation changed that.

In the absence of children, George's titles passed to his cousin. It was because of George that lovely Burford House at Windsor in Berkshire, a freehold property that had come to Nell, was lost to the family. In the 1760s George had neglected it. When he was reinstated as Lord Lieutenant in 1771, he lived once more at Burford House but, at the request of King George III, he accepted Queen Charlotte's offer to buy it in 1778. After various alterations, it became the home of their son, the Prince of Wales (later George IV) and was renamed Lower Lodge. Now part of the Windsor Castle complex, Burford House would have been a splendid family seat for the subsequent Dukes of St Albans.

Today's Duke and Duchess, however, both love living in London. 'We're both very urban and although we enjoy visiting Aldeburgh in Suffolk, by the sea, where Murray spent part of his childhood and where my daughter now lives with her family, I think I am more of a pavement girl.' Yet despite being in central London, it was difficult to locate her. The only clue to their neighbourhood was when Gillian was quoted about her opposition to a planning application, alongside writer Edna O'Brien. Her passion about things that matter is reflected in her appointment as the Patron of the Orpheus Choir in London, a role she took over from Princess Alice, Duchess of Gloucester.

While Gillian recognises that having a title can assist charitable causes, she thinks the use of titles generally is dying and that overall her title today is 'irrelevant' apart from its historical association. She does not mind if people are not aware of, or do not use, her title and she usually refers to herself simply as Gillian St Albans. She says that Murray's

Windsor Castle.

son, the Earl of Burford, does not use his title and decided his own son, born 1995, whose title is Lord Vere of Hanworth, should not use his. Some duchesses in this book have experienced hostility to their title. Gillian has not found it necessary to defend hers but says that should she find herself in such a position, she would refer to the background of the title and to the unique qualities of Nell Gwyn. Generally, she finds that if people discover she is a duchess, they respond very positively. But while titles may seem unimportant to her, Gillian likes certain standards to be maintained and generally prefers more formality than informality; she considers that these days there is a tendency to be casual. 'I had a mother who was a stickler for looking elegant, and couldn't bear it if you didn't,

and so I think to myself, I must look nice, or must try to look nice, anyway.'

Murray holds another title bestowed on his ancestor the year after he was made 1st Duke of St Albans: that of Hereditary Grand Falconer of England, which once entailed supplying the King with hawking-birds for use in all the Royal forests and parks. With the role came an income and a lavish, gold-trimmed costume; today it is a title only. However, it does give the Dukes of St Albans the honour of being the only people who share with the monarch the right to drive down Birdcage Walk, near Buckingham Palace. Although Gillian says that 'may be lovely', it bestows no practical advantage, as today it is a public right of way.

Together with the Archbishop of Canterbury and a few select others, the Duke used to receive twice a year a quantity of venison from Richmond

Park, which Charles II had spent much money improving. However, 'this was stopped by Labour when Tony Blair came to power in 1997 as an economy measure!' Because of his descent from Charles II, a Stuart monarch, Murray is the Governor General of the Royal Stuart Society, whose objectives include promoting knowledge of Stuart history, upholding rightful monarchy and opposing republicanism. Every year, the Society holds a Restoration Dinner on or around Oak Apple Day, 29 May – the date of Charles's birthday and his triumphant return to London in 1660. Until 1859, it was a public holiday in England and is still celebrated at the Royal Hospital Chelsea as Founder's Day. Murray presides at the dinner, to which Gillian accompanies him.

Gillian is reminded of the Duke's background on a daily basis by some of the fascinating objects in their house. But the bulk of many a family's heritage – property – has long gone. The Beauclerks were never fabulously wealthy. The 1st Duke, when a boy, was betrothed by Charles and Nell to the beautiful Lady Diana de Vere, the sole heiress of the 20th and last Earl of Oxford. An alternative potential match that Charles had considered had fallen through with the death of his cousin, Prince Rupert, who had been managing the negotiations. Lady Diana's ancestor, Aubrey de Vere, after whom many of the dukes were named, had come over with William the Conqueror and been ennobled. He had lived in a manor house in London, now Earls Court, where he grew vines. The family was extremely distinguished and had been very wealthy, but by the time Diana married the 1st Duke in 1694, the fortune had almost gone.

The Bestwood Park estate, which had once been Nell's, remained in the family until 1940, when the eccentric 12th Duke, known as 'Obby', sold it; it became the headquarters for Northern Command and the surrounding land and farms served many wartime purposes. Today, Bestwood Lodge is an hotel, surrounded by a country park. A family connection remains, however. The 10th Duke began mining in the area in 1872, which gave rise to the village of Bestwood. In 1952, the colliery manager started a choir, and although mining ceased in 1967, the group of singers continued and expanded. The Duke is the Patron of this acclaimed male-voice choir and, Gillian says, 'enjoys being able to support this link.'

Over the centuries, the Dukes of St Albans have owned property in many other areas, including, for a brief period in the 18th century, Hanworth Palace in Middlesex, formerly the palace of Ann Boleyn and then Catherine Parr, settled on them by Henry VIII. They also owned the Redbourne estate in Lincolnshire, which entered the family with the 8th Duke's marriage in 1791 but left it with the 11th Duke. The 9th Duke, William, enjoyed St Albans House in Brighton, a large, elegant Regency townhouse. He lived there with his wife, Harriot Coutts, née Mellon, already a resident of the then fashionable town, after their marriage in 1827, and it became the centre of fashionable society.

William and Harriot's match was an unlikely one. Harriot, Gillian's choice of predecessor, was 24 years older than the Duke, her second husband, and a determined lady of great character who unwittingly provided the satirists of her period with much material. Like Nell Gwyn, Harriot began as an actress. Although she was described by some of her contemporaries during her acting days as beautiful, in later life various

Royal Hospital Chelsea.

cartoons lampoon her (and sometimes the Duke), depicting her as growing larger and, as Gillian has noted, uglier with age. In the museum at St Albans is a hand-coloured cartoon of the Duchess dated 1829 entitled, 'Hugeous Duchess. A Piece of Court Furniture', which depicts her as a moustached man in women's clothes. A cruel caption accompanies it. It was a strong woman who could withstand such an attack.

Harriot's first husband had been the banker, Thomas Coutts, one of the wealthiest men in Britain. He was also 42 years her senior and on his death Harriot inherited a fortune. One of the properties she owned was Holly Lodge in Highgate, north London, in which Coutts had set her up in 1807. When she died in 1837, she left the 9th Duke a life interest in Holly Lodge and its contents, but on his death it passed to Coutts's granddaughter, the acclaimed Victorian philanthropist, Angela Burdett Coutts – as did most of Harriot's fortune, for Angela was like a daughter to her. Holly Lodge was sold in 1906 and subsequently demolished; a housing development from 1920 stands there now.

Although the Beauclerks did not inherit much of Harriot's fortune, a house at Aldeburgh was given to the 13th Duke, Murray's father, in about 1923, by a great-granddaughter-in-law of Thomas

Coutts by his first wife. She felt that the Beauclerks had profited too little from Harriot's estate. It was thus that Murray spent part of his childhood there, where their immediate neighbour was the composer, Benjamin Britten. A reflection of the family's time in Aldeburgh was its lifeboat from 1931 until 1959, named *Abdy Beauclerk* after a grandson of the 8th Duke who died in 1912 in a boating accident, and from whose estate the boat was provided.

Although Harriot is an outstanding and particularly intriguing duchess, there have been other Duchesses of St Albans of note. One of the most recent is Murray's stepmother, Suzanne. After a fascinating, if eccentric, childhood in France and Malaya she served in Psychological Warfare during the Second World War. She worked as a news writer in North Africa and Italy before being posted in 1945 to Austria, where her commanding officer was Colonel Charles Beauclerk, whom she later married. Suzanne became a talented writer and later an artist who exhibited at the Royal Academy.

There was also the first Duchess of St Albans, Diana, who gave the Duke 12 children and, in 1714, had the honour of being appointed Mistress of the Robes – a very important position – to Caroline, Princess of Wales. She held the post until 1717 and was the only Duchess of St Albans to do so, although later the appointment was offered again. In 1886, the Duchess Grace, an Irish heiress and second wife to the widowed 10th Duke of St Albans, was proposed as Mistress of the Robes to Queen Victoria. Mother of the 12th Duke, she was a woman of great literary and political interests, particularly on the difficult question of Ireland. For reasons emanating from the Duke's political

position under Prime Minister Gladstone, who was in favour of Home Rule in Ireland – a position adverse to that of both Grace and the Duke – she declined the appointment. The Duke explained his wife's reasoning which the Queen, while regretting that she would be unable to have the Duchess in her household, accepted with gracious understanding. Grace cultivated a wide range of political contacts, including the young Neville Chamberlain and, as a strong believer that loyalty to the Crown lay in having a united Ireland, supported the leaders of Ulster Unionism.

Today's Duchess does not need to be concerned about any political fallout, for her marriage to Murray took place three years after the House of Lords reforms of 1999, which deprived the Duke and many others of their voice in the House. There may be little power and less money left in the aristocracy now but Gillian hopes it will continue. However, she also recognises that there will be changes. On the topical question of whether women should be able to inherit non-royal titles, Gillian can see an advantage. She refers to the fact, as history has sometimes shown, that, unfortunately sons can be a disappointment, while women can be 'so responsible', and she acknowledges the pressure that the expectations of having a son and heir can put on women.

Gillian and Murray continue to live quietly, although they clearly have many friends. Gillian says she loves meeting people and being entertained. When they are not out socialising, they enjoy reading. 'We're tremendous readers. And do you know something that's really romantic? Murray has always read to me. In all the years we've been together.' Nell Gwyn would have approved.

Thomas Coutts, by Robert William Sievier.

THE ACTRESS, THE BANKER AND THE DUKE:

HARRIOT, DUCHESS OF ST ALBANS

(1777–1837)

It was the misfortune of Harriot, Duchess to the 9th Duke of St Albans, to live in an era that would become known as the golden age of satire. A contemporary cartoon that belongs to the 14th Duke and Duchess of St Albans is typical of the caricature that appeared between 1750–1830, the age of Swift, Pope and Hogarth. Harriot's extraordinary life made her ideal fodder, while the viciousness of the press towards its victims, the monarch included, makes the media of the 21st century seem positively benign.

Like Nell Gwyn, mother of the 1st Duke of St Albans, Harriot began as an actress. Unlike Nell, who won the hearts of the people, Harriot never quite managed that. They may have started life in similar circumstances but Harriot's ascension was different. It is what today's Duchess finds so fascinating.

Opposite: Harriot Beauclerk (née Mellon), the Duchess of St Albans by Sir William Beechey.

Harriot was born in 1777 to Sarah Mellon of Irish descent, who worked for a theatre manager. Harriot never knew her father, whose identity was never firmly established. One possibility is that he was an actor in a repertory company who never married Sarah. The other is that he was Matthew Mellon, a lieutenant in the Madras Infantry who met and married Sarah while he was on sick leave in Ireland but had to leave her to rejoin his regiment. He promised to take his pregnant wife out to India as soon as he could afford it but died of consumption before he could return for her. This latter scenario is the generally accepted one.

Harriot's early life was spent travelling with her mother around the country with a succession of theatre companies; they spent a lot of time in Lancashire, where Harriot made her first stage appearance. When Harriot was four Sarah married a violinist who was the leader of a theatre band; although the marriage did not improve their financial position significantly, it gave them some stability. As she matured, Harriot became an accomplished actress, and although Gillian St Albans describes her as 'monstrous-looking', she was not when she was 17: a contemporary described her as handsome. Harriot was noticed by the playwright Richard Brinsley Sheridan, who offered her a job at his Theatre Royal in Drury Lane, London. Her first performance there, in *The Rivals*, took place in 1795. A fellow actor said the brunette had a blooming complexion and coral lips, and was very tall, with a fine figure.

Harriot continued at the theatre for 20 years, during which time she attracted many admirers. One of these was Thomas Coutts, one of the richest British financiers of the time, head of the bank Thomas Coutts & Co. and friend and banker of the Royal Family. It is thought Harriot and Coutts first met in 1805 at Cheltenham, where Harriot had managed to secure the post of postmaster for her stepfather, using the contacts she was building up. Said by a contemporary to have an amiable and kind disposition, she was growing in social poise. As well as acting she was a coach in amateur theatricals, which brought her into contact with a brilliant social and intellectual set whose members included Jane Austen.

Coutts, a friend of Sheridan, had come to watch Harriot in the local theatre. His presence was not accidental: her mother had applied to him for a subscription to Harriot's benefit performance. He sent five guineas, went along and met her afterwards. He was 70, Harriot 28. He had a sick wife who had been dying for some time, his three daughters were all married into the nobility and he was lonely.

Coutts regularly visited Harriot in her home in London and fell in love with her. They continued to have ten years of friendly intimacy but it never became an affair; his wife lingered on, and although fond of Coutts, Harriot was determined to behave properly. Although she had an affectionate nature, it is not believed that love affairs played a serious part in her life. When Coutts gave her money she was open about it because she had nothing to hide. In 1807, he set her up in his attractive house, Holly Lodge in Highgate, and tried to get his daughters to be friendly to her but, conscious of Harriot's humble beginnings, and ignoring the fact that their own mother had been a servant, two of them refused, although the third, Lady Bute, tried to keep her father happy.

Eventually, in January 1815, Coutts's wife died, and two weeks later he married Harriot. By now, Coutts was 80, Harriot 37. It was a very happy match despite their age difference. She gave up acting and did her best to make him happy. Coutts spoiled her lavishly, buying expensive jewellery and all the accoutrements that the wife of a wealthy banker might expect.

Harriot openly revelled in her newfound riches and so was deemed vulgar; envy gave rise to hostility and to rumours that Coutts was becoming senile and she was exploiting him. One cruel lampoon referred to 'Harriott [sic] Pumpkin' and her marriage to 'OLD CROESUS!' and said she was 'an ostentatious Show-off under the colour of charity', who had a 'malicious disposition'. It was grossly unfair and inaccurate but the couple tried to ignore it.

When Coutts died in 1822, Harriot was said to be the richest widow in Britain. She also inherited his 50-per-cent share in the bank, which became Coutts & Co, and, as a senior partner, she took an active interest in the business. Harriot's generosity, which continued throughout her life, was directed at her three stepdaughters on whom she settled vast sums, even though two of them never accepted her, and she supported many charities in Ireland and England.

If Harriot had been lambasted for the wealth and prestige she gained from marriage to Coutts, she would find in her second marriage that she was again under attack, this time for having the temerity to join the ranks of the peerage.

Harriot's marriage to William Beauclerk, the future 9th Duke of St Albans, might not have come about had it not been for the inability of the Dukes to secure and retain any lasting wealth. From the beginning, the 1st Duke's marriage to Lady Diana de Vere had not brought any great riches into the family. By the time William's father became 8th Duke, there was not much wealth left in terms of property to carry the family into the future. Burford House at Windsor, for example, had been sold by the 3rd Duke to King George III in 1777. Hanworth Palace, once Henry VIII's, and which the 5th Duke had inherited from his mother in 1783, departed the family in an unfortunate way. In 1797, it was almost burnt down. To raise the funds to rebuild it, the 5th Duke sold a large part of the art collection that he had diligently amassed for posterity, thus some very important works left the family.

Unfortunately, his efforts were wasted. When his son Aubrey, the 6th Duke, died in August 1815, his infant son became 7th Duke. However, he had not been born when Aubrey made his will, so was not mentioned in it. The Bestwood estate in Nottinghamshire passed to the child automatically, as it was entailed, but other property that had come into the family did not. Under his will, Aubrey's wife Louisa was left Hanworth and other properties for life, with the remainder to whoever she should appoint. Unfortunately, relations were not good between Louisa and the Beauclerks, as the paternity of the baby was at first doubted; then shortly after Aubrey's death Louisa said she was pregnant again, and the family established that the unborn child could not be his.

Aubrey's eldest brother, Lord William Beauclerk, led the family in a challenge to Aubrey's will to regain Hanworth from Louisa for the infant 7th Duke but without success. Louisa then made her will, the outcome of which was that if the 7th Duke died before she did, her sister should receive everything. In February 1816, the baby, a sickly child, died, followed three hours later by Louisa. Her sister duly inherited Hanworth and other properties, and some precious Beauclerk heirlooms, including a Bible once owned by Nell Gwyn. The 7th Duke had no brothers, so, in 1816, his uncle, Lord William, became 8th Duke of St Albans.

When Lord William's son, also called William – Harriot's future husband – was born in 1801, there was no realistic expectation of either father or son becoming Duke because the 5th Duke was still alive with an heir and spares. But the inheritance moved on quickly and by the time young William was 15, his father had become 8th Duke. As his heir, William was now the Earl of Burford.

William was a child of his father's second marriage. His father's first wife, Charlotte, had died childless, leaving him her estates at Redbourne in Lincolnshire, and Bathafarn in Wales, which he sold. Redbourne had a 16-bedroom mansion, a park and 20 farms. There was also an estate about 40 miles away at Pickworth with a smaller house. He remarried in 1799 and his wife, Maria, young

Bestwood Estate.

William's mother, inherited her father's estate at Little Grimsby, Lincolnshire; although not large, it added to the Beauclerks' property. As he had no expectation then of becoming Duke, Lord William did not anticipate any entailed property coming to him.

Young William was the eldest of seven sons and six daughters. He was born at Redbourne, where his parents threw parties and balls and held theatricals, in which he enjoyed taking part. When his father became 8th Duke their financial position did not change greatly. The Duke inherited the Bestwood estate and various pictures and plates, and the office of Hereditary Grand Falconer of England, with its annual income of £600. This augmented his income from the Redbourne and Pickworth estates: without the Duke's fortuitous first marriage to Charlotte, the income of the Dukes of St Albans would barely have been that of a country squire.

When Duchess Maria died in 1822, the Duke's thoughts returned to a long-standing concern: how to increase the family fortune. He considered a third marriage to another heiress, the widowed Harriot Coutts, and he needed to get his son William, the Earl of Burford, married too. Earlier attempts by the Duke and Duchess to broker matches for Burford and their daughter, Charlotte, had failed. Their plan had been to marry Burford to Fanny Gascoigne, an heiress, and Charlotte to Lord Cranbourne, heir to the Marquess of Salisbury. Through some fault on his part, Burford lost Fanny to Lord Cranbourne, who preferred her to the needy Charlotte.

So it was that the 8th Duke of St Albans and his son both found themselves in the marriage market around the time that Harriot Coutts was starting to socialise again after the death of Thomas. Attracted by her wealth, many suitors came forward. In 1824, the Duke of St Albans attended a magnificent garden party thrown by Harriot at Holly Lodge, where other guests included the Dukes of Wellington and York. Later Harriot invited St Albans and Burford to her dinner party, to which she had invited a young heiress for Burford. Harriot was amazed when Burford – aged 23 to her 46 – paid all his attention to her. It seemed they had a shared interest in Shakespeare and before long a deep friendship had developed.

Shortly afterwards, Burford travelled with Harriot (and one of his sisters as chaperone) on her tour of Scotland. Thomas Coutts had been born in Edinburgh and was a distant cousin of Sir Walter Scott, who had visited him in London; during her tour, Harriot was to visit Scott at his home at Abbotsford. Enjoying travelling in splendour, she took a large retinue of seven carriages, 28 horses and many staff. At Edinburgh, where her father-in-law had been a Provost, she presented money to charities and a silver cup to the Provost. However, her eager expectation that she would be given the freedom of the city – a rumour she had heard – was harshly rebuffed by the Scots.

At Abbotsford, despite, upon reflection, having limited her carriages and entourage, she had an unpleasant time. Scott was charming – he wrote that he found her kind, friendly and lacking in affectation – but his female guests were not. One of them, married to an aristocrat, scorned new money. It was a taste of things to come.

While Burford could not deny that Harriot had the wealth his family were hoping for, it seems he was genuinely fond of her. In July 1825, on his father's death, he became 9th Duke of St Albans; the press now delighted in printing a mock Court Circular about their movements. Despite Harriot now being accompanied by a duke, the older aristocracy shunned her, and by association, the Duke too. The Duke of Northumberland, for example, gave them permission to view his castle at Alnwick but did not invite them to stay. Meanwhile, Scott, on another visit by them in 1825, noted in his diary that there seemed to be the beginnings of a love affair, and that Harriot conceded she might marry the Duke but did not have the intention at that point.

In fact, they married in June 1827, in the drawing room of her London house. The new Duchess was 50, the Duke 26. Her gifts to him included a cheque for £30,000 and a small country estate in Essex. Now the cartoons made Harriot fatter and uglier. A lampoon was published about the cheque, headed 'A Beau-Clerk for a Banking Concern', and went on with an imaginary conversation in which she insisted he become her banking assistant and work day and night for the business. What was overlooked, probably out of envy, was the fact that he settled the sum only of £1,000 a year on her and wished her to be as financially independent of him as possible.

Domestic life did not always run smoothly. The generally compliant Duke disliked Harriot's fits of passion which could erupt if something was not as she wanted, but he never put her down

in public: she got enough of that from the rest of the nobility. Here was someone of low birth who had, they considered, bought her way into their hallowed ranks. Although it was her money she lavishly spent, rather than the Duke's – and often on parties in which she was a very generous hostess to her guests – she was sneered at. Some of the King's brothers attended her parties, yet even the favour of the Royal Family did not help her. The Duke of Gloucester often visited the couple, yet he would not let his wife be friends with Harriot. The Duke of Wellington nicknamed her Queen Mab and refused to let her sit next to him at a breakfast.

Harriot was, however, able to cock a snook at them at the coronation of William IV in 1831, when the Duke as Hereditary Grand Falconer was invited to carry the Royal Sceptre with Cross. In the absence of some senior duchesses, Harriot stood third in place near the throne. Yet later, she was snubbed by Queen Charlotte and not invited to a ball at the Royal Pavilion in Brighton, despite being the highest in rank of all the Brighton inhabitants: she had lived there for years, moving to a larger house in 1830, which she renamed St Albans House.

At least in Brighton, where she was known, she was more able to impress the ordinary people and was not considered a showy intruder. In towns in Lincolnshire, when she and the Duke visited for the first time since marrying, crowds lined the streets; in Louth Harriot was mobbed by curious women who followed her into each shop. At Redbourne, she and the Duke put on a huge falconry display to which they invited the important county people,

Opposite: Redbourne Hall Estate.

threw a lavish champagne party and put on a firework display, all of which they repeated with even more splendour in Lincoln. Yet even there she was snubbed by the women whose untitled husbands had a firm place among the 'county set': they refused to acknowledge her rank.

Harriot could not win. Despite her good humour – which no doubt helped her when she was under attack – the nobility generally saw her as a vulgar social climber of low birth; others saw her as a flashy show off who had done nothing to deserve the position she found herself in. Yet she did not marry the Duke for money, nor did she forget her roots, enjoying talking of her life in the theatre. Her generosity to those genuinely in need was constant and was reflected in her will.

Big, bold, and larger than life, Harriot died in August 1837. Among her legacies to the Duke were an annuity for life and a life interest in Holly Lodge and its contents. The bulk of her fortune she left to Coutts' granddaughter, Angela Burdett, who was like an adopted daughter to her and under the terms of Harriot's will added the name of Coutts to her surname. At 23, Angela inherited a fortune of nearly £2 million. Like Harriot, she would use it wisely and generously and became one of the great philanthropists of the Victorian era.

Following Harriot's death, the Duke, after fathering an illegitimate daughter by a servant girl, married an Irishwoman whose dowry helped reduce the mortgage on Redbourne. They had one son who became 10th Duke on William's death in his forties, in 1849. The Beauclerks may not have been left as wealthy as they hoped by Harriot's will but her legacy would benefit countless others. Today's Duchess cannot help but admire her.

5

A MODERN TRADITIONALIST:

THE DUCHESS OF BEDFORD

Driving through the park at Woburn Abbey in Bedfordshire, on a sunny autumn morning before the gates are opened to the public, is glorious. Past the estate office and into the 3,000 acres of parkland designed by Humphry Repton 200 years earlier, rare deer lie under great canopies of trees or look up idly from nibbling grass. As the driveway sweeps round past the lake, where a heron boldly tries its luck with the fish, the house in all its majesty comes into view.

A smiling man in a Woburn-emblazoned jacket indicates a parking space in front of the Abbey and gives directions to a reception office. It is hung with portraits that the welcoming receptionist says are of the Bedford family ancestors, and then telephones Her Grace to let her know her appointment has arrived.

In the Duchess of Bedford's office the scent of fresh hyacinths picked from the Woburn Abbey

Opposite: The Duchess of Bedford with her children.

Gardens fills the air. The room with its high ceilings is decorated traditionally but with a modern twist. On the walls hang family portraits and a Gainsborough landscape. A crackling log fire provides generous heat and creates a homely ambience. The office windows offer breathtaking views towards the lake at the front of the Abbey with the bronze statue of Mrs Moss, the family's most successful brood mare. The vista seems to stretch almost as far as the eye can see, to the very edge of the Estate.

The centre table is laden with work papers and fabric samples, part of the Duchess's latest project for the Estate. In the corner of the room, in front of a huge bookcase containing leather-bound books, sit beautifully wrapped gifts. 'They are presents for the new arrivals across the Estate,' she explains. 'Whenever a child is born to any of the team working on the Estate, we like to welcome them with a present from the family.' To the side of the table stands the Duchess's wedding dress, removed from display at the Abbey for safe keeping as they prepare to close for the winter season. Dotted around the room are many personal cards and pictures of the children and members of the family mounted in silver frames; this office is clearly very much part of the Duke and Duchess's home.

Louise Bedford, petite and pretty, casually dressed in trousers and a jacket, has the calm air of a well-organised person and promises that she has allowed ample time for the meeting. Although she describes herself as first and foremost a wife and a mother to Alexandra, born in 2001, and Henry, in 2005, it quickly becomes evident that Louise is also heavily involved in the running of the Estate, along with her husband Andrew, the 15th Duke of Bedford. Louise's involvement in the Woburn Estate and various business interests extend beyond Woburn Abbey and the Gardens to include the Woburn Hotel, Golf Club, Sculpture Gallery and Safari Park. 'I like to be involved with all of the businesses and various departments, from the redecoration of the Golf Clubhouse to the refurbishment of the Hotel. I find it very exciting to hear of the birth of one of the animals in the Safari Park, which is particularly high during spring and summer months. Life here is always busy and there is never a dull moment.'

Louise is also highly committed to her charitable work, which includes her duties as a Deputy Lieutenant of Bedfordshire and the patron of various charities, just a few of which are the South Bedfordshire branch of the NSPCC, Friends of the Bedford Hospital, MK SNAP, The Bloomsbury Festival, London, and East Anglian Air Ambulance. There is also the management of their home, which involves working closely with her loyal household team on the day-to-day running of the Abbey.

Louise became part of the family when she married Andrew, then Lord Howland, now 15th Duke, in October 2000. They first lived in a cottage, one of 350 buildings on the 13,000-acre Estate. During her first year of marriage, Louise spent time getting to know some of the people who worked across the Estate, numbering over three hundred, some of whom had worked for the family for more than 30 years, as had their parents before them. 'I was overwhelmed by how welcoming everybody was.'

Andrew's grandfather, Ian, was still Duke, but in 1974 had handed over the running of the estate to his son Robin, Marquess of Tavistock, and gone to live abroad. In 1988, Robin had a massive stroke that left him with great difficulty in speaking, which he later overcame. He gave Andrew early responsibility for the overall estate, with his mother, the Marchioness, Henrietta. In 2002, Andrew, Louise and their young daughter moved into the Abbey. Sadly, in October of that year Andrew's grandfather died, and tragically just six months later Andrew's father, the 14th Duke, died unexpectedly.

Andrew and Louise were soon aware of the expectations laid upon them. 'When we first moved in, a lot of people asked, "What is your generation going to add to Woburn?"' Undoubtedly, Robin and Henrietta were a hard act to follow. 'My parents-in-law had started the Bloomsbury stud and the now world-renowned golf courses,' which was a significant expansion for the Estate. They had also put themselves and Woburn Abbey in the spotlight when they agreed to the filming of a television documentary series called *Country House*, which ran from 1999 until 2002. 'At the time, both Andrew and I felt that our priority should be to maintain a sense of

Woburn Abbey.

continuity, not least for the team who had worked for many years for Robin and Henrietta. So much had changed for everyone in such a short space of time, it was important that we allowed some time for everyone to adjust to the new circumstances. Apart from redecorating my office, I was in no hurry to make any significant change. I wanted the time to enjoy my new surroundings, spend time to understand Woburn and get to know all the people across the Estate.'

Woburn has come to evoke many images to people of all ages: an award-winning Safari Park ('a particular favourite of the children'); the Abbey itself, with its important art collection; Woburn Abbey deer park, home to nine species of deer, including the Pere David, saved from extinction by the Duke's great-great grandfather, Herbrand, who had brought them from China to Woburn in the 1880s. The Duke's father then successfully reintroduced the species to their native country, working alongside the Chinese Government, and is the only westerner to have a statue in Beijing by way of tribute. There is also Woburn Golf Club with its three tournament-hosting courses, all rated in *Golf Monthly* magazine's Top 100 courses in England and Ireland, and the Estate Hotel, recently refurbished with many individually designed bedrooms. In addition, there are the more traditional estate activities of farming and forestry. Woburn seems to have been part of the nation's consciousness for a long time. Certainly the family has owned the land at Woburn for centuries.

During one of England's most turbulent periods, John Russell served as courtier, commander, diplomat, ambassador, counsellor and confidant to four Tudor monarchs, from Henry VII to Mary, holding many powerful positions at Court. At the siege of the French port of Morlaix by the English in 1522, he lost his right eye to an arrow and was invested as a knight for his bravery. Both Henry VIII and Edward VI rewarded his skill and loyalty with confiscated monastic lands and property: at Tavistock in Devon in 1539, Woburn in Bedfordshire in 1547, Thorney in Cambridgeshire in 1550, and Covent Garden and Long Acre in London in 1552.

Following his role in defeating various rebellions and the subsequent fall of the Lord Protector Somerset, John Russell was rewarded with the title 1st Earl of Bedford by Edward VI in January 1550. Russell created one of the leading families in the realm, leaving a legacy of public office and duty that his descendants have followed. He became one of the ten richest men in England and laid the foundations of the wealth of the house of Russell, acquiring estates in London and nine counties, many of which the family retains today. Francis Russell, the 4th Earl, established Woburn Abbey as the family seat circa 1619, and it continues to be the family home to this day.

The Dukedom arose from the tragedy of William Lord Russell's execution for high treason on 21 July 1683, during another turbulent period of history. The son of the 5th Earl of Bedford, William had strong convictions and a reckless streak that eventually led to his downfall. He married the widowed heiress Rachel Vaughan, daughter of the 4th Earl of Southampton, who brought the Bloomsbury Estate and property in Hampshire to the family and tried to moderate his behaviour, cautioning him over his radical, political associations. An ardent Protestant,

William became one of the main leaders of the opposition, fearing that Charles II's policies favoured France, absolute power and that England would return to the Catholicism he abhorred.

In 1683, he was accused of being involved in a conspiracy called the Rye House Plot to seize the King and his brother James and raise an insurrection to prevent England from having a Roman Catholic king. When the plot was discovered, many of the principals either fled or went into hiding but Russell did neither and, together with the republican Algernon Sidney, he was arrested and sent to the Tower of London. At his trial, Lady Russell took notes for him which was a unique occurrence in British legal history and subsequently became the subject of a number of paintings, two of which hang at Woburn and were exhibited at the Royal Academy. Russell's defence was weak; he did not present evidence to refute the testimony of the prosecution, attempted to dismiss the evidence of plea bargainers and, although he claimed otherwise, the procedures at his trial were legal at the time. Public sentiment about his guilt was divided at the time and remains so today.

Lady Russell was distraught and bombarded the King with petitions. When she eventually gained an audience with Charles he was said to have responded that Russell, had it been in his power, would not have granted him six hours. William offered to live in exile; the 5th Earl is rumoured to have offered £50,000 for his son's life and many supporters pleaded for mercy. Charles could not concede, reputedly saying, 'All that is true, but it is as true, that if I do not take his life, he will soon have mine.'*

* Dalrymple, Memoires, 2:59-60.

Henry VII.

During the period known as the Exclusion Crisis, when the Whigs sought to exclude James from the throne, William had called for James's execution for his role in the Popish Plot, an alleged conspiracy to kill Charles and put James on the throne. James was adamant that William should die and Charles could not break with his brother, who was his heir as part of a secret agreement with France.

As a mark of respect for William being the eldest son of a peer, Charles commuted the usual traitor's sentence to a beheading in Lincoln's Inn Fields and released the body to the family for a private burial. In recognition of Lady Russell's father's loyalty, he did not claim Russell's personal estate, which would normally have been forfeited to the Crown.

William's scaffold speech was a powerful political statement. He claimed that the law had been misinterpreted, decried popery, asserted the right of resistance and cleared his conscience, admitting to participating in conspiratorial conversations. The speech was widely popular and printed a number of times. In the years that followed, the publications of William's wife, family and political friends transformed him into a martyr to the Whig cause, defending liberty and the Protestant faith. Lady Russell's grief was intense and prolonged and she became a symbol for the Whigs, although the family lived quietly until the Glorious Revolution when the balance of power was restored to them.

The letter inviting the Protestant Prince of Orange to come to England was signed by seven men including the Earl of Devonshire, whose eldest son had married Rachel and William's

Opposite: William, Lord Russell.

eldest daughter, and it was carried to Holland by Admiral Russell. William's supporters did not forget him, and the Convention that declared William and Mary King and Queen of England cited the proceedings of Lord Russell's trial as a grievance.

Within three weeks of the crown being formally offered to William and Mary, a Bill to reverse the attainder of Lord Russell had been introduced in the House of Lords by the Earl of Bedford and Lady Russell. In the Commons an amendment was made by William Lord Russell's friends to destroy all records relating to his attainder, and the Bill received the Royal assent on 16 March 1689. The reversal opened the way for the transfer of the Bedford title to William's son, and the 5th Earl of Bedford returned to government. In 1694, the Earl was elevated to 1st Duke of Bedford and Marquess of Tavistock as a mark of recognition and to redress the past.

It is probably Woburn Abbey for which the family is best known, thanks to Andrew's grandfather, Ian. On the death of his father in 1953, Ian became 13th Duke and inherited Woburn Abbey, which he decided to save despite massive death duties and neglect of the building. Through the centuries, the Russell family had produced politicians, philosophers and prime ministers, and Ian was determined to preserve the treasures in this place in which monarchs had stayed and which had been a family seat for over four hundred years.

Ian left South Africa and moved into the house. It was an enormous task to prepare it as a visitor attraction but the Duke and Duchess and their staff and friends threw themselves into it. Woburn Abbey opened to the public at Easter 1955 and was

Woburn Abbey.

an instant success. Aware of the need to maintain the momentum once the Abbey had opened, the Duke was happy to attend openings and functions and to involve celebrities, TV and film companies in order to promote the estate and to raise revenue to help cover the enormous costs involved in running the place.

In 1960, his second marriage ended in divorce and he married Nicole Milinaire. Woburn Safari Park opened in 1970, one of the first to do so. In 1974, the Duke and Duchess made the decision to leave England in order to start a new life in Monaco and New Mexico; the running of the estate was left in the capable hands of the Marquess and the Marchioness, who moved into the house.

By the time Louise became Duchess of Bedford in 2003, there had been significant change for the family and the Estate. The transition must have been hard for Louise but she was very fortunate to have her mother-in-law living nearby to ease the process. 'For everyone concerned things had changed quite quickly, and I was very thankful that Henrietta was there to guide us through what was a new beginning for Andrew and me. She understood first-hand the magnitude of the position that I was to hold and the responsibilities that came with it. After all, Henrietta and Robin were a key driving force behind establishing the Woburn known by so many today. To this day, I am grateful for her kindness and the knowledge she passed down to me, as there was much for me to learn and appreciate about the Estate at the time.'

Louise is keen for her children Alexandra and Henry to understand that they are all very lucky and privileged to live at Woburn. 'Obviously, there is a certain amount of formality that comes with living in the Abbey. Without the fantastic help of the household team, we would not be able to live here and I would not be able to get involved and help with the charities as I do, or help Andrew run the Estate.'

Indeed, historic houses like Woburn Abbey, with around 120 rooms, need a team of passionate people to keep it properly maintained. 'Every person on the Estate has a unique role and I like to think of us all as one big team. The Estate could not run without them and everyone plays a vital part in passing down their knowledge and understanding of the house and estate.' As for the Head Butler, 'I suppose to some it may appear old-fashioned but he manages the household team and is invaluable. I could not lead my busy life without him. We have visiting dignitaries and I host fundraising events and dinners throughout the year at the Abbey, which take a considerable amount of organisation.' As an employer, Louise appreciates that she has 'a fair amount of responsibility for other people's lives. We all lead very busy lives and I am conscious that everyone on the Estate needs to have a healthy work-life balance. It is always important to be considerate of the needs of others.'

Louise thinks her upbringing and young adult life helped to prepare her for Woburn. 'I'm a great believer in fate and we are all here for a reason.' The eldest of three girls, Louise grew up in their London house and in their West Sussex estate with her parents. She attended an 'old-fashioned' prep school in London. 'I had an idyllic and very happy childhood, full of wonderful family holidays abroad and in England, with two loving parents who were very passionate about family life. I also had a wonderful nanny, who came to live with us when I was very young and was with us for nearly 20 years. Nanny Margaret was a Princess Christian nanny and, in our busy family life, she was a solid rock, as our routine never changed. I have very fond memories of Nanny Margaret in her uniform and we are still very close friends today.'

When Louise was 11, her parents divorced and Nanny Margaret was invaluable in continuing their routine. 'Wherever we went, Nanny went, so we couldn't say, "Daddy lets us stay up until midnight."' Her father remarried and she has a half-sister; her mother, Rona, married Sir Evelyn Delves Broughton. Louise gained three stepsisters from her mother's second marriage and all of them are good friends. Sir Evelyn had an estate, Doddington Park in Cheshire, where Louise, by now at Benenden, an independent boarding school in Kent, would spend many hours on her pony in the holidays, as well as in West Sussex with her father.

After school, Louise spent a year in Florence at the Dante Alighieri School where she studied Italian, while staying with an Italian family along with some other English girls. This was followed by a year at St James's secretarial college in London. 'Then I got a real travel lust.' She lived in Kenya in Africa for a year, staying with friends. In her office a poster-size photograph shows a laughing Louise with a monkey on her back, an experience she obviously remembers fondly. Although she had intended to be away only for a few months, she helped at a safari company and continued travelling. 'I learnt a lot about myself during my time travelling, as well as many other life skills.'

Louise as a child.

On returning home, Louise landed what must have been a dream job as an assistant to a producer in an advertising agency. Although building the business was hard work and very busy, the agency understood Louise's passion for travel and she was able to combine travel and work. Her next venture was to drive with a friend in a Ford Pinto from New York to San Francisco. 'The trip was great fun and we had a few adventures along the way!' Louise's other excursions took her around Australia, Thailand and back to Africa where she and a group of friends drove a Landrover from Nairobi down to Botswana and then took many train journeys, in between hitchhiking back to Nairobi. 'I love meeting people and different cultures. I think everyone has a story to tell.' Spending time alone, sometimes in difficult situations, 'is a good way to understand what you can cope with and I guess you learn to be comfortable in your own skin.'

Back in the UK, the advertising agency Louise worked for amalgamated with a larger business and Louise and six of her colleagues went on to establish a new advertising firm. Louise's career in advertising was to continue for more than ten years. She also worked for a wine merchant, spent a season at a wildlife park and worked as an assistant to a wardrobe mistress at the Royal Opera House.

Louise does not believe that becoming a Duchess has changed her personality or her enthusiasm for life. Although her priorities had to change with the new responsibilities that came with the title, she still feels like the same young woman who travelled, sometimes alone, around the continents of Africa and Asia. Louise is, however, conscious of the perception of her title from others. 'Due to the popularity of programmes such as *Downton Abbey*, it seems that some people think of duchesses as being quite grand old ladies. People start calling you Your Grace, which makes me feel much older.' When people meet Louise they are surprised she is young, although at 51 she does not think she is.

Louise credits her strong work ethic and positive attitude to her parents. 'My mother has been a wonderful mother, always very supportive and is a seriously switched-on lady.' Rona was one of the first women on the Council of Lloyds and still sits on various boards, while Louise's father Donald, inspired by his own father, was a very successful property developer during the 1960s, an exciting era for the industry. Louise enjoys nothing more than spending time with her family and friends when time allows and feels fortunate to have such wonderful family around her. 'I love times like Christmas and the school holidays, when all our families get together.'

When Louise met Andrew, a Harvard graduate, he was an auctioneer and director at Tattersalls, the bloodstock agents. Andrew asked her out to lunch and 'he really made me laugh.' She was about to go into hospital for a short spell and Andrew was 'fantastic' because he himself had

spent six months in hospital in America when he was 15. Andrew was on tour with the singer Neil Diamond, a family friend, and was a passenger when the car hit a tree; he broke his hip and had to have a replacement. 'Andrew has always been there for me and is always incredibly caring.'

Andrew and Louise were together for about 18 months before getting engaged. 'I was always quite independent and had never been in a rush to get married, but then you always meet people when you least expect it, don't you?' The wedding was at St Margaret's, Westminster, with six hundred guests; their going-away car was an early Rolls-Royce belonging to Mary, the 11th Duchess, whom Louise has selected as her chosen predecessor. The reception was at Claridge's Hotel out of respect for her late father: he had his own table there, where he and Louise would dine every month. It is of great sadness to Louise that, due to her father's sudden illness and untimely death, he and Andrew never met.

Alexandra, Louise and Andrew's first child, was born in 2001, 'which was wonderful, I must say, although I think it's not ideal to be pregnant in your first year of marriage' – she laughs – 'because ,however wonderful marriage is, if you haven't lived together before, and we hadn't, it's all a little bit trial and error. I suffered from quite bad morning sickness, so I wasn't at my best and there was a lot going on. *Country House* was being filmed, so it was a very busy year!'

Louise had not felt any pressure from Andrew to have a boy; being older parents, they considered themselves lucky that they had a strong, healthy daughter. When she was pregnant for the second time she resisted the temptation to find out the sex, thinking, 'If it's another girl, it's meant to be.' Had

Louise not had a son, the title would have passed to Andrew's younger brother. However, Henry arrived in 2005. 'Henry loves Woburn and he's always asking about the history and the workings of the Abbey and the Estate. He spends many hours helping the gardeners and maintenance teams, learning hands-on how the Estate operates on a day to day basis.'

Nevertheless, Louise thinks it is important to bring Henry up so that he feels that there is no pressure on him. Louise feels fortunate that she was allowed to follow opportunities when she was young and wants the same for her children. 'When you're born into a family like ours you do have certain responsibilities. However, I think it is very important that Henry is able to make his own life choices and that when he comes back to Woburn he has really experienced life, which means Andrew and I could be very old, still living here!' she laughs. 'The Abbey is Alexandra's and Henry's home and, aged 12, if Alexandra could choose the house to live in, she would live in a very modern house, which would be "much cooler, Mummy!" However, I know Alexandra appreciates that the Abbey will always be part of her life and they get on very well. I'm sure she'll have her say!'

On the matter of girls inheriting, Louise says that Andrew was an interviewee on the subject for a Sunday magazine in February 2013. He said it was 'ridiculous' for girls to feel failures and that both his children will be 'kicked out into the real world' first, but if Henry wanted it, 'he gets first crack.' Louise says, 'I think Alexandra would be just as capable as Henry of taking it on. They're both quite together, they are both growing here

Opposite: Louise on her wedding day.

up here and they both love it.' However, Henry already spends a lot of time with the team on the estate and is gaining an understanding of the work involved. Also, 'I think it is quite hard for the name. If a daughter inherits and she marries, then each time the surname will change.' That would be a shame, she says, 'because you always associate Woburn with the Bedfords. But it's a rapidly changing world. I think as long as there is someone who loves the Abbey and cares for it, it would not worry me.'

Louise does not want to particularly draw the children's attention to their titles at this age. People on the estate call the children by their first names, but Louise says that this will probably change when they are older, maybe 21. Both children also attended the local village school, 'and that was great because they have made local friends, who often visit and know Woburn Abbey simply as Alexandra and Henry's home.'

As for her own title, she still feels like Louise Crammond, as Andrew sometimes fondly calls her. Regardless of title, 'We're all the same, and I think the main thing in life is to be happy in your own skin.' She does not think the title is essential for Woburn.

The allocation of Louise's time is dictated by the specific needs of the Estate as they arise and by projects she is working on. Weekends can also be busy if there is an event on, and there are regular meetings with the heads of the various business departments across the Estate. Happily, Louise has resolved the question of what part of her legacy will be to Woburn. Having grown up with a kitchen garden she wanted to have a go herself and undertook a short gardening course in London. She soon realised, however, that 28 acres was not something to tackle on her own, and the garden redevelopment project began with the help of the Estate Gardens Manager, Martin Towsey, and his team of gardeners, drawing inspiration from the original plans in Repton's red book for Woburn Abbey, still kept in the library at the Abbey.

It has been a very exciting time since the project commenced. 'The gardens have achieved Royal Horticultural Society "Partner Garden" status and won awards, including the Hudson's Heritage Award for new commission in 2012 and The Georgian Group Architectural Award for Restoration of a Garden in 2013,' says a justifiably proud Louise. 'The gardens have continuously evolved over the past ten years and still do so. We have detailed five-year plans that we work towards – we are now in our third one – and every year at the annual Woburn Abbey Garden show, I open a new feature or unveil our latest project to the public. We encourage our visitors to watch us grow and indeed, every year the gardens do grow. They are now an attraction in their own right and many of our visitors return year on year to see what new developments have taken place.'

Conscious that they must 'keep Woburn going and moving forward for the next generation,' her next project is the state rooms in the Abbey. A great deal of research on the decorative history of the house and the collection has been taking place for over a year and a number of exciting discoveries have been made. 'We're currently discussing our long-term plans for the Abbey, which will transform the experience for all our visitors.'

In the meantime, the 2014 exhibition 'Peeling Back the Years', which the Duchess is co-curating, will tell the story of the discovery of one of the earliest Chinese wallpapers imported into Europe, which was hung in the 4th Duke's private bedroom in 1752. Visitors will learn how to unravel and read the history of a room and discover the changing designs of Chinoiserie through the many Chinese wallpapers and silks at Woburn. A trail of artworks in the collection will show how the fashion for Chinoiserie influenced the collecting taste of the Dukes of Bedford in terms of both interior and exterior design.

All this has to fit around her charity work and her duties as a Deputy Lieutenant. 'If you're in a position to help people, I think you should do it. It is part of the role.' As one of 27 Deputy Lieutenants, her role is to support the Lord Lieutenant of Bedfordshire as the Queen's representative in the county, a post held by three previous Dukes of Bedford. There are also charities in London that she supports when she can, and her work with their local church. Every year, Louise organises the Estate Christmas Carol service at the church, an event attended by the many staff and local parishioners of Woburn. 'The service is quite magical, the church is candlelit and the atmosphere very festive. The local village school children perform a Christmas medley, and the children and I hand out mulled wine and mince pies to everyone at the end of the evening.'

Louise is also patron of Friends of the Bedford Hospital, which was started by the Mary, the 11th Duchess. A qualified nurse and radiographer, Mary opened a cottage hospital in Woburn which, together with a temporary hospital at the Abbey, became a military hospital during the Great War. In her sixties, Mary took up flying, unexpectedly a relief from the tinnitus she suffered. Dubbed 'The Flying Duchess', she achieved worldwide fame until her mysterious death. In 1929, Mary and her co-pilot broke the record for flying to India and back in eight days and, in 1930, they broke the record for flying to the Cape of South Africa and back in 20 days. In March 1937, Mary took a flight to increase her solo flying to two hundred hours. She may have decided to fly over the flooded Cambridgeshire fens but no one is sure of what went wrong during her last flight. The weather took a turn for the worse and by teatime she had not returned. Mary was never to return to Woburn. Four wing struts were found washed up along the East Anglian coast. Today's Duchess of Bedford admires Mary's courage and achievements and shares her love of travel and the outdoors, especially of fly-fishing.

As for the future of the aristocracy, she realises its members today are less interesting to the media than celebrities but believes the aristocracy does have a future. 'The aristocracy has helped shaped our landscape and our rich history. Having an aristocracy makes England unique in many ways. Like everyone, its members have had to change with the times but I am hopeful they will still have their place in the world in the future.'

To be given a tour of much of the house by the Duchess herself, overtaking the curious groups of visitors, is a privilege. Louise says the dining room, with its 21 'views of Venice' painted by Canaletto, is particularly glorious when candlelit, which they like to do for formal evening events.

Every year, Louise and Andrew leave work behind and go away together for a few days. When Louise has the chance she likes to go salmon fishing, her passion from a young age as a result of many holidays in Scotland, and one that she shares with the Duchess Mary. In Scotland, where she and Andrew have a lodge and spend family holidays with their children, she likes to sit on the riverbank relaxing. 'I just switch off. I introduced my passion for fishing to Andrew and now we both fish together. Andrew also enjoys playing golf, a particular passion of his father's. Henry is learning to play too. But I haven't yet learnt!' It's not surprising, given the many work and family commitments Louise has to juggle.

Theirs seems a strong relationship. 'I think love, friendship and commitment carry you through most situations. We are a team, we have each other and very supportive families and friends. Woburn is a wonderful place to live and we are very much enjoying our part in enabling future generations to enjoy its rich history and beautiful surroundings.' With the help of the Duchess's drive and her positive outlook, no doubt they will.

Louise with her husband Andrew.

6

REACHING FOR THE SKY:

MARY, DUCHESS OF BEDFORD

(1865–1937)

In August 2013, Louise Bedford watched with pride and a little trepidation as her eight-year-old son Henry, the future Duke, soared in the skies above Woburn Abbey in a vintage de Havilland Tiger Moth plane. The 1930s bi-plane, used by the RAF for training purposes, was taking part in the 28th International Moth Rally at Woburn, and young Henry had just become the fifth generation of his family to fly in a de Havilland aircraft. He naturally flew as a passenger but 85 years earlier his great-great-great grandmother was the first member of the family not only to go up in such a plane but to actually fly it.

Mary, Duchess to Herbrand, the 11th Duke of Bedford, is often known as The Flying Duchess, but aviation did not feature in her life until she was 60. In four years she progressed from no flying experience at all to breaking records. It was a remarkable feat but it was a hobby she

Opposite: Mary, Duchess of Bedford.

took up after an extraordinary life looking after the sick and the wounded. Her dedication was especially surprising given her privileged position as a member of one of Britain's richest families, and the fact that she was not from a medical background.

Born Mary du Caurroy Tribe in Hampshire in 1865, she was one of five children. Her father, Walter Tribe, was a clergyman in the Church of England. When Mary was two he accepted a post as a chaplain in India, to where he and his wife Sophie moved, leaving Mary and her sister, Zoë, to live with an aunt and uncle in Sussex. The girls were reunited with their family in 1873.

Mary's education took place at Cheltenham Ladies' College, an acclaimed girls' boarding school, and in Zurich, where she studied languages and other skills young ladies were expected to have. By 1881, her father's ministry in Lahore was established and Mary, then 16, joined her parents there. It was a lifestyle she quickly adapted to and loved; hers was not a conventional family and they enjoyed an open-air lifestyle. However, not long after her arrival Mary caught typhoid, to which she attributed the deafness that afflicted her later in life.

Her father's life involved travelling among the people within his ministry. After Mary had recovered her health, Walter was transferred to Dharmsala in the Punjab and she loved to accompany him on his tours. Today's Duchess shares with Mary the thrill of discovering unknown regions, including India. Father and daughter travelled over the Rohtang Pass in the Himalayas, an ancient trade route notorious for its unpredictable snowstorms, into Lahaul. The journey was made more arduous by the fact that they had just one pony between them and would ride and walk in turns.

In 1886, Walter was appointed Archdeacon of Lahore and they moved to Simla, by then the summer capital of British India. At a dinner given by the Viceroy, Lord Dufferin, Mary met Lord Herbrand Russell, aged 27, Dufferin's aide-de-camp. After a short separation, during which Herbrand sent Mary a series of love letters, they married in January 1888 at Barrackpore, India. Although his father was 9th Duke of Bedford, Herbrand did not expect to inherit because his older brother was the heir. Like many second sons, Herbrand had gone through university, then into the British Army, serving as a Lieutenant with the Grenadier Guards.

After a lengthy honeymoon, later that summer they went to Cairnsmore in Galloway, which became their Scottish home and where their only child, Hastings, was born in December. It has been said that Mary went into labour while they were out walking and gave birth in a shepherd's hut, with two farmhands to assist. That may not have been true but it is known to have been a traumatic birth; today it is thought she probably suffered post-natal depression. She never wrote or talked about her experience but the fact that they had no more children suggests it was not something she wanted to repeat.

Sadly, in 1891, Herbrand's father killed himself; he was declared temporarily insane while suffering from pneumonia. Herbrand's brother, George, became 10th Duke but, in 1893, he too died, a diabetic, aged only 40. Suddenly, Herbrand was 11th Duke of Bedford, a position neither he nor his new Duchess had imagined. Although they had residences in Belgrave Square, London, they spent little time in town. Mary preferred Woburn and continued to enjoy the outdoor life. In an entry in *Every Woman's Encyclopaedia*, dated between 1910 and 1912, her skills in shooting and fishing were extolled: her shooting record for a day was said to be two hundred pheasants, and she once landed 18 salmon weighing two hundred pounds – much to the envy of today's Duchess.

Mary's privileged life did not blind her from social injustices, and as well as supporting young people in troubled circumstances, she was a member of the Women's Social and Political Union, from which came the suffragettes. Although she publicly distanced herself from their militant activities, Mary visited some suffragettes who were in prison and was a supporter of its group, the Women's Tax Resistance League. This advocated the non-payment of taxes by women until they secured the vote, and here Mary was more vocal. She loved skating and often visited the Prince's Skating Rink in Knightsbridge. In April 1913, the suffragettes' newspaper, *The Vote*, under the heading 'Distraint on a Duchess', reported that a silver cup was taken from her as payment of taxes due in respect of the Rink. The report said Mary had instructed the WTRL to point out that the distraint was out of order because, as a married woman, she was not liable to taxation, and that the tax assessment and demand note should have been served on the Duke. However, Mary had allowed the authorities to proceed in this irregular way, 'because she wished to use their mistake as an opportunity of making her protest against the treatment of Woman Suffrage by the present Government in the practical way of refusing to pay taxes until women are enfranchised.'

On the home front, the Duchess's life was not much troubled by domestic matters. Young Hastings, with whom she had little close contact, was given to a series of nannies and tutors and did not see another child until he was sent to Eton in 1901, aged 13. Mary and the Duke had over two hundred staff for Woburn and their London houses, including eight chauffeurs, most of whom the Duke, at least, never saw. There was little to interest Mary in the daily affairs of running a household. Travel was far more thrilling, and, after being introduced to yachting in 1896, she bought a steam yacht called *Sapphire*, sailing to the northern coast of Norway and along the West Coast of Scotland. A family friend, Miss Flora Green, wrote of Mary that 'no one place could hold her for very long. She had the wanderlust too strongly rooted in her being.'

Mary had a scientific interest in nature, especially birds. In the remote Fair Isles, she spent happy days birdwatching, sometimes with the appropriately named Dr William Eagle Clarke, a noted ornithologist, who dedicated his major work of 1912 to her in recognition of her abilities as a field naturalist. She had already become one of the first women to be admitted to the Linnean Society, a group of eminent naturalists.

Flora Green wrote that Mary had 'a very tender and understanding heart for all creatures. [...] It was always good to see her skill in nursing a sick animal back to health.' This interest, together with a fascination with medicine that had started when she eavesdropped on Red Cross lectures at school, led to her opening the small Cottage Hospital in a house in Woburn Village in 1898. She undertook a series of medical lectures at the London Hospital and in 1903, with the help of the Duke's money, replaced the old Cottage Hospital with a new model one, medical and surgical, which she designed herself. The pretty site she chose reflected her appreciation of the effects of nature on the damaged body and mind. In a later era she could have become a nurse or even doctor, but in the early 20th century it was not considered a fitting profession for someone in her position.

The Duke was Colonel of the Bedfordshire Regiment, and, in September 1914, after the Great War began, he paid for the creation of a training depot for soldiers on his land at nearby Ampthill. That same month the Cottage Hospital, still under Mary's supervision, admitted the first soldiers from Bedford. At Woburn Abbey itself, Mary converted the indoor riding school and tennis court into a second and much larger hospital to hold 80 beds, an operating theatre, X-ray room and other facilities. Four smaller rooms were later added for another 20 beds. A long verandah in

Military Hospital, Woburn Abbey.

the Abbey garden was used as an open-air ward, which greatly benefitted patients suffering from septic wounds. The Abbey Hospital soon began taking wounded men direct from the Front.

Mary served her apprenticeship on the wards, starting at 5.45am, but after a few months she began training in theatre work. The first resident surgeon she employed at the Abbey Hospital was Mr Bryden Glendining, regarded as brilliant in his field. By 1917 – by which time she was 52 – she was surgeon's assistant. But her learning did not stop there. Having had training in the rudiments of radiography, she received weekly instruction from Professor Russ from London who, impressed by her speed in learning, asked if she would like to learn more about radiotherapy, the treatment of diseases by X-ray and radiation. Mary did not hesitate and achieved a high degree of efficiency.

Working with professional nurses under the instruction of her matron, Mary never forgot she was an amateur and was grateful that, over 50 and deaf, she was gainfully employed in war work. Staff and patients called her Sister Mary, and although she could seem aloof, probably partly as a result of her deafness, she was greatly concerned with her nurses' welfare. They were accommodated in the Abbey and Mary converted a house, Battlesden, on the Woburn estate, with its terraced gardens and pools, into a free holiday home for war-weary nurses.

The patients also enjoyed entertainment. A cinema was installed, entertainers hired and concerts given. Patients could take the air in the 40 acres of the Abbey gardens. In fact, fresh air and ventilation were things Mary was obsessive about, due to her love of the outdoors and the knowledge of its benefits.

At the end of the war in 1918, the Army Council asked Mary to continue her work for the wounded for another two years. It calculated that during the war, 2,453 soldiers had passed through her hospitals. Afterwards the wards were used for treating army pensioners and Mary continued working. Along with other voluntary nurses, she received the Order of the Red Cross, 2nd class: the 1st class was reserved for professional nurses. In 1920, the Abbey Hospital was closed and the Cottage Hospital, by then called Woburn Surgical Hospital, became a civilian unit for surgical cases only. Mary continued there as surgeon's assistant and radiologist, as did Mr Glendining until his death in 1927.

The hospitals had always been funded by the Duke, although he had other interests. Apart from his regimental involvement, he shared with Mary a passion for the conservation and welfare of animals; in particular he is credited with saving various endangered species and establishing some at Woburn. For 37 years, he was President of the Zoological Society, of which Mary was a Fellow. Then in 1926, Mary developed another interest, from which the Duke was unable to dissuade her: flying.

Attracted to the romance and freedom of flying, Mary was also aware that her deafness was getting worse and she dreaded the idea of a dependent old age. The hospital had settled into the routine of a civilian hospital and she could take occasional leave without it being disruptive. On 17 June 1926, aged 60, she took her first flight, from Croydon to Woburn, accompanied by her instructor. She was not a natural and for the first two years did not make as much progress as expected. Although she had excellent eyesight, her deafness disadvantaged her in learning, as the only contact between instructor and pupil was a telephone system consisting of tubes and headphones, and wind noise was always present.

However, with her usual determination, she persevered. After several short flights to Europe, in 1928 she took the first of her historic flights, travelling to India with a pilot, Captain Barnard. Other long-distance flights with him followed, sharing the flying, and they achieved records for flights to India and South Africa. Her journeys

abroad in those early days of aviation sometimes involved her and her co-pilot in highly dangerous situations, including being shot at as they flew over a desert area; the men attested to Mary's remarkable physical and mental strength and endurance.

Eventually she could fly solo. In September 1930 Mary took on a personal pilot and had an aerodrome installed at Woburn, building a hangar in which to house her planes. In June 1931, aged nearly 66, she was granted a licence and by late 1932 had flown 45 hours solo. The media reported Mary's escapades with admiration, calling her The Flying Duchess, a title she was not keen on.

In early 1937, Mary was saddened to discover the Duke would not continue to fund the hospital. At the end of that decade he would reopen it as a private nursing home, calling it Marylands, but the Duchess would never know that. On 22 March 1937, aged 71, she took off from Woburn in her de Havilland Gipsy Moth to clock up the balance of flying time necessary to renew her licence: she needed less than one hour. The weather was suitable and her pilot suggested a course towards Cambridge. By 4.30 p.m., she had not returned and a snowstorm had set in.

The Duke asked the Chief Constable of Bedfordshire to alert the police in neighbouring counties that her plane was missing. In spite of efforts by the police and Royal Air Force, nothing was seen of the plane until 2 April, when a strut was washed ashore at Great Yarmouth and identified by Mary's pilot. The three remaining struts were eventually washed ashore on the coast and similarly identified. Mary's body was never found.

Opposite: Duchess Mary in nurse's uniform.

'The Flying Duchess'.

There was speculation that it was suicide as a result of depression, although those who knew her said there were many things that could have gone wrong. The general feeling was that she had flown out over the sea by mistake, ran out of fuel and gone down. No satisfactory conclusion was ever reached.

Mary received several honours, including Dame Commander of the British Empire. It is ironic that this woman of many talents should devote so much of her life to the welfare of others, yet be almost a stranger to her own son. But as Louise Bedford will have told young Henry, his great-great-great grandmother's achievements, particularly in an era where women were still restricted by sex and class, were truly remarkable.

GOOD MANNERS, BETTER FORTUNES:

THE DUCHESS OF RUTLAND

For over five hundred years, the home of the Manners family has been Belvoir Castle – pronounced 'Beaver' and meaning 'beautiful view' – perched on a hilltop overlooking the Vale of Belvoir in Leicestershire. However, the family had land in the area long before they had the castle. The first title, the Earl of Rutland, was created by Henry VIII in 1525 for Thomas Manners, great-grandson of Richard Plantagenet of York. Although Thomas lived to a reasonable age, his next four successors all died in their thirties, which was early even for their times. In the Manners family, inheritance of titles has tended to take place either earlier than anticipated or in an unexpected way.

The 6th Earl, Francis, lived until 54, dying in 1632, but his two sons died in infancy. Their deaths have passed into folklore, for they were said to have been caused by a curse put on Francis and his Countess by Joan Flower, the

Opposite: The Duchess of Rutland.

foul-mouthed mother of two daughters, Margaret and Philippa, who had been dismissed from their positions as servants at Belvoir Castle. The Earl and Countess also became extremely ill. The sisters were accused of being instruments of their mother's craft and after Joan died dramatically in Lincoln gaol, convincing the jury that she was guilty of witchcraft, they confessed. They were executed around 1618. At Bottesford Church, the monument to the dead children bears testimony to their deaths by 'sorcerye'. In the absence of a male heir, the title passed to Francis' brother.

Even some of the Dukes did not escape the supposed curse. The dukedom was created in 1703 for John, the 9th Earl. His son, the 2nd Duke, died in his forties and the 4th Duke at 33. In 1894, Robert, Lord Haddon, the son and heir to the

Introducing the Duchess of Rutland

8th Duke and his wife, Violet, died at the age of nine. His brother John became the heir. So afraid was Violet that she would lose John to the Great War, that she used her connections to prevent him going. He became 9th Duke but always bore the shame, especially as many of Belvoir's estate workers were killed. Fortunately, his grandson David, the current and 11th Duke, was not thrust prematurely or dramatically into the title. He inherited when he was 39 on the death of his father, aged 79, on 2 January 1999.

Becoming duke is an emotional time. Grief at losing a father, together with assuming a new role, can be a difficult combination to deal with. For the new Duke of Rutland, the situation was particularly challenging because not only was he now head of the family with responsibility for a 15,000-acre estate, he also faced death duties of almost £10 million. Urgent repairs needed to be done, too, which were also estimated to cost in the millions. Fortunately, Emma, his Duchess, two months pregnant at the time with their fourth child, had acquired much practical experience in her life, which proved to be invaluable in turning around the ailing estate. Not for her wafting dreamily around the grounds draped in diamonds as earlier duchesses may have had the luxury of doing. Instead, she was more likely to find herself unblocking a gutter in the middle of the night with a mackintosh over her nightdress.

Emma had had an interestingly varied career. As Emma Watkins she trained to be an opera singer and an actress but dropped out of drama school. There was a period as a land agent, another as tour guide, and another buying and selling farms. She also set up her own successful interior design business in Herefordshire,

obtaining commissions from all over the country before moving up to Leicestershire. She married David, then the Marquis of Granby, in 1992, when she was 30 and he 33. Before moving into the castle in 2001, they lived in a six-bedroom house on the estate, during which time they ran a garden-furniture and conservatory business in a converted barn behind their house, and she had a stand at the Chelsea show.

The prospect of looking after the Belvoir Estate might have deterred someone less devoted to the countryside than the Duchess. A farmer's daughter from Wales, Emma is passionate and knowledgeable about the countryside. 'I love farming. We had a Hereford herd of cattle here, we've just bought a thousand sheep again. I love everything about the countryside. I never know what to do when I'm in London other than spend money!'

The Estate comprises 16,000 acres, of which 12,000 acres are for crops, 1,654 are woodland and the rest is permanent grassland. There was once far more but, like many estates, it was necessary to sell off thousands of acres to meet tax demands after the Great War. The Estate is divided into two categories: 'in hand' where all the farming and other businesses are managed by Belvoir, and 'let' where the farming and other enterprises are rented by tenants.

The current castle, completed in the early 19th century, is the fourth on the site; earlier buildings had suffered complete or partial destruction during the Wars of the Roses, the Civil War and a major fire in 1816. After years of hard work to renovate and repair the castle, the Duchess's sense

Opposite: Belvoir Castle and the Vale of Belvoir.

of style is today reflected in the family sitting room, a beautiful hexagonal space with windows at the corners giving a wide view across the valley. On bold-patterned wallpaper hang portraits of children and favourite pets. The castle has long been known for its Chinese wallpaper: when the Brighton Pavilion was redecorated, the designers came to Belvoir to copy its wallpapers. It is something in which Emma has a particular interest, having launched her own design of wallpapers and materials. There are elegant but comfortable sofas, bright cushions, interesting ornaments.

Elsewhere in the castle are exquisitely decorated rooms whose names reflect their history: the Wellington Room, which frequently hosted the great Duke; the King's Room, used by members of the Royal family, notably George IV, Queen Victoria and Edward VII. There is the Elizabeth Saloon, named after the 5th Duchess, Emma's chosen predecessor, who was responsible for the building of the present castle, and the Tapestry Room, whose walls are adorned by pieces made at the famous Mortlake factory established by Charles II; the room was used in the film *The Young Victoria* as Queen Victoria's bedroom at Buckingham Palace. In total, there are over 100 rooms, which contain paintings by Gainsborough, Reynolds and Holbein, and outstanding collections of furniture, silks and sculpture.

Emma had a realistic idea of how she might run things at Belvoir once David inherited in 1999. The Duke and Duchess threw their energies into the ailing estate and Emma became chief executive of Belvoir Estates, with David as chairman. The beauty of the place today and its sound condition is a testament to the blood, sweat and tears Emma has put into it since becoming Duchess. Later that same year she was delighted to give birth to their first son, Charles, the Marquis of Granby, heir to the dukedom: a brother for his three sisters. In 2003 she had their last child, another son: now they had 'the heir and a spare'.

Yet having five children did not deflect from Emma's role in the running of the estate. When the recession hit in 2008, she noticed they were losing 70 per cent of the income from their shoots, which she had co-hosted in the past; corporate clients could no longer afford the luxury. Something drastic had to be done. On her parents' farm she had run the beating line with her spaniel while other girls 'were baking cakes', so she had a little knowledge of what a shoot was about. It was not enough. She set about visiting shoots around the country and learning from those and from her head keeper, and studying the role shooting plays in conserving the countryside. The experience enabled Emma to make changes that in just five years would make Belvoir one of the best shoots in the country. Now she travels around the world selling Belvoir to Americans, Russians and Chinese and hosts shooting parties to groups from all over the world. Maintenance of the fabric of the castle alone costs around £100,000 a year, which can be met from a good shooting season. Belvoir has also twice hosted the annual CLA Game Fair.

The castle is a spectacular place to entertain and be entertained. For the Duke's 50th birthday in May 2009, the same year that the family celebrated five hundred years of being at Belvoir, the Duchess somehow found time to organise a fabulous party with a Twenties theme for five hundred guests, of whom 320 could be seated for dinner in Belvoir's grand dining rooms.

Sadly, however, Emma discovered David was having an affair. In early 2012, the couple decided to separate but to carry on living in the castle in separate wings so that David could have easy contact with the children, and for the practical purpose of running the estate. Emma and the children remained in the Nursery Wing while David moved to the Shepherds' Tower. They still have meals together when the children are around and he is very much involved with their lives.

Emma had met David Granby, as he was then, in 1990 at a dinner party in London after the annual show, Decorex, for the top professionals in interior design. They were introduced through a mutual friend, Christopher Cole, whose family firm Cole & Son is famous for its wallpaper, which it supplies to the Queen. David's card said 'Marquis of Granby', which made Emma think he might own a pub of that name. Until then she had not known any Lords, nor even any Honourables. David made it clear that evening that he was very impressed by her: 'I think David would admit he was looking for a girl who understood his world.' Her love and knowledge of the countryside must have reassured him, and clearly her skills helped enormously in getting Belvoir onto its feet.

'I think the interior decorating has been useful as he's never had to employ anyone to come and do the decorating,' she says. Knowing how to source materials and being practical generally also helped because 'Belvoir's a big place to get your head around.' Even her training in opera and drama has assisted in the frequent transition, when the house is open to the public, from public face of Duchess to private person: 'There's always a private door – you go through the door and become a duchess and you've got to be able to

swing into that part and swing back again, and keep your feet on the ground.'

That Emma Rutland has adapted to such major changes in her life is typical of her determination, illustrated by how she dealt with the transition from farmer's daughter to Duchess. Applying her artistic and practical skills to the ailing castle may have come naturally to her but joining the aristocracy was not something she found easy. Her background was a 'very simple' one. From a family of Quaker origins, she was the eldest of three children and helped her mother run the family bed-and-breakfast business, while her two brothers helped their father with farm duties. On marriage she became Marchioness of Granby, to be addressed as 'Lady'. She was 'traumatised' about becoming titled. 'I remember asking my mother-in-law how I should behave, what I should do, and she said "Just be yourself. It grows with you. People will either like you or not, so just do it your way."'

Her mother-in-law is 'the most wonderful woman'. Born Frances Sweeny in 1937, the Dowager Duchess has not had the most settled life herself. Her mother was the beautiful socialite Margaret Whigham, whose first husband was Charles Sweeny, an American amateur golfer. When Frances was 14, her parents divorced and her mother took as her second husband the 11th Duke of Argyll, making her his third wife and Duchess. Margaret's many extramarital affairs and the disclosure of some explicit photographs led to their very public divorce, finalised in 1963. The scandal inevitably but unfairly tarnished both the Argylls and the Rutlands. Frances and her mother became estranged after falling out.

Happily for Emma, her parents-in-law greeted

Margaret, 11th Duchess of Argyll, with her daughter, Frances, Duchess of Rutland.

her with open arms. 'Very, very supportive, hugely warm. I've never experienced anything but friendliness from the Manners family on any level. They've been totally embracing. I got so many things wrong. I wrote to them the first time I'd been to stay, and I'm quite dyslexic, and I wrote "Dear Duk and Dutchess". She was determined to learn and was not afraid to seek help from others. 'I bought a book of etiquette, Debrett's. I asked my mother-in-law about how people sat around the table.' It was 'a real learning curve'. Although she was not yet Duchess, Emma wrote for help to the Duchess of Devonshire. At that time it was Deborah, known as 'Debo', who had enjoyed a privileged upbringing as one of the famous Mitford sisters. After marrying the Duke of Devonshire, she was lauded for having changed the fortunes of one of Britain's major stately homes, Chatsworth in Derbyshire. 'She wrote back and said, "Come and see me and I'll tell you whatever I can." I found her an amazingly inspiring woman.' The key point that came out of that lunch was to let the estate – looking ahead to when it would be theirs to run – evolve and grow and to develop it gradually. 'She was a great help to me.'

Despite the knowledge Emma had gained during seven years as Marchioness, becoming Duchess in 1999 was 'a real shock'. Her mother-in-law handed her a huge black box of keys and wished her good luck. 'There's been no training, no book to read, no ground rules on how one should do it and you can't force it. It's something that needs to evolve and grow within you. It's quite scary being a duchess when you've been a Welsh farmer's daughter and you think, "How do you do it?" You always imagine duchesses to be a bit crusty and live in a tower and be screaming at staff, which is what a lot of the people here will say I most probably have done and do do, but we have a very tight team and we all roll up our sleeves and get on now.'

A vivid memory she has of that transitional period is of a film being made in the Castle called *The Haunting*, starring Welsh actress Catherine Zeta Jones and Liam Neeson. Emma had a house party staying who wanted to meet the stars: 'I was just this new duchess, so off we went and asked the producer if he would mind getting the stars to come and meet the duchess.' Neeson, she thinks, 'looked out of the window and thought, "I think I'll pass on that" – me with all my motley crew of friends.' Her fellow countrywoman was more accommodating. 'Dear Catherine came out of her caravan with all her curlers in and said in an American accent, "Oh, gee, it's so cool to meet you," and I said [assuming a Welsh accent], "Oh, Catherine, I'm a Welsh girl, and I'm a duchess. I haven't lost my Welsh accent, so what's happened to yours?" She said, "Oh, I've got it when I want it."'

Emma thinks the reason that exchange stayed in her mind was that 'the key thing in life is to retain your roots and the foundation of who you are, and it doesn't matter really where you go, but to remain very grounded about where you're from.' She is under no illusions about her position in relation to the land. 'I do feel this is all a wonderful privilege to be trying to get the estate

right and the land right and hand it as a parcel to my community and to my son and to society in a stable way for the next generation. But I don't own any of it.'

Emma sees the role of duchess as primarily being in relation to one's local community. As Duchess of Rutland she thinks that for people in their surrounding area, Belvoir represents 'in a changing world where there are many vulnerabilities, a great sense of stability.' It provides 'a great sense of life carrying on, continuation, lineage and line, a sense of stabilising the world we live in, in your local community'. For that reason she feels strongly that she and the Duke have a social responsibility with Belvoir: it is important 'to hand it over in a better state. We're just custodians so I don't in any way feel any of it belongs to me. I just have a job to do, to make it work and then to hand it over, protecting it and embracing it and stabilising our little community'. She thinks that outside their community, 'it means absolutely nothing to be a duchess', except in America, because 'Americans love duchesses.'

The responsibility she feels towards the community also meant taking actions that, although they were for the long-term good of the estate and locality, did not seem that way initially. Although that community provides the people for the team on which Emma relies for running Belvoir, she had to make huge changes when she became CEO that made her unpopular. 'I've made hundreds of people redundant but I had to, to get a grip of it. It's business.' The precarious position of the estate when David inherited it was 'a bit like the *Titanic* going towards the iceberg.' The result was a smaller but 'very strong team with great advisers.' Her core team is made up of 12 full-time staff for the estate and the castle. Every Monday morning at 7 a.m. she has a round-table meeting with her core team, during which they go through the next two weeks' plans. In addition, she uses contractors for specific tasks and has meetings every two months with her advisory board of experts.

She and the Duke have a small household staff for themselves and the children: one part-time cleaner who also can cook (and having been a chalet girl for a season, Emma is no stranger to cooking); a full-time helper who has developed from nannying the children when they were small to looking after the family generally, including helping with the horses; and a full-time couple. For business purposes, Emma also has a personal assistant.

As Patron of several hospices she uses the castle whenever she can for charity work. 'We raise hundreds of thousands of pounds every year on the estate and the castle, so that's where the castle comes into its own. People know they can come here and approach me and ask, "Would you mind...?" as long as costs are covered. The doors are open but it is a business and that's one of the biggest culture changes I've made in this community, which is it has to be efficient. We can't be a charity, and – I'm sure all the estates get this – I think there was some of the hangover from previous generations when the estate and the duke and duchess were the social security when there was no social security.'

The Belvoir Estate owns more than 320 residential properties. Emma acknowledges that the changes were difficult for local people, because 'the rents are proper commercial rents on the properties but the properties are the main income

to keep everything going. You have to make clear business decisions.'

Those decisions include developing their existing businesses and starting new ones but, following the advice of Deborah Devonshire, letting the estate evolve rather than doing some-thing overnight. 'We've had no immense gardens made or adventure playground built. You have to have a very long vision of the estates, getting them right and turning them round, and it's not a quick fix.' An example of Emma's long-term vision was the five-year plan she launched in 2004 to transform the gardens, beginning with those created in the early 19th century by Duchess Elizabeth, wife to the 5th Duke of Rutland. Intense planting had continued until the Great War, when the garden had descended into overgrown chaos; little had been done since then. Further plans included the construction of an ornamental pond and the restoration of the original Yew Maze and Victorian vegetable garden.

Always in Emma's mind is the importance of visitors to Belvoir. 'I love people being here and sharing our home: that partnership with people is absolutely one of my key things. We live here and we share our heritage with people, that's how we work.' They have set up the Belvoir Trust, a cricket charity, which brings in about three thousand children from Leicestershire and the surrounding counties of Lincolnshire and Nottinghamshire who have never been into the countryside. 'I think the general public are almost more interested now in the hinterland of the castle than the castle itself, how [an estate] actually works.'

The Duchess's charitable interests have benefits that extend wider than the locality. The Belvoir Trust has developed a relationship with a charity in Rwanda called Cricket Without Boundaries, a cricket-development and AIDS-awareness charity dedicated to educating and developing local communities around the world through the spread and growth of cricket. In 2013, Emma spent two weeks in Rwanda, helping to coach children in schools and orphanages, training new coaches and delivering HIV/AIDS messages.

The issue for any employer must be how to create a pleasant working environment without encouraging too much familiarity, which might undermine respect. Most employers, of course, do not have a title. Staff are clearly not shy about putting their head around the living-room door to ask the Duchess a question, although it is always prefaced with 'Your Grace'. What is the attitude of people outside the community when they find out she is a duchess? 'I think it's up to you. I find myself over-compensating to try and make people feel comfortable.' She is aware of the importance of a title to charities because it helps them, 'so that's what I've grown to understand, to respect it and never take it for granted. There is no place for arrogance when one has a title. I think you have to earn respect, it doesn't go hand in hand; there's humility with it, a total respect of what's gone before. It's a great honour. I think I'm very lucky: I have a wonderful life and five wonderful children and I have to really respect this role and do my best to make it all work.'

Those children naturally have titles too. Coming from her background into the world of the aristocracy, and raising children in the opulence of Belvoir, made her aware of the importance of keeping them grounded for the future – not easy when their father frequently appears in the *Sunday Times* Rich List of the wealthiest people in Britain. The girls, the Ladies Violet (born in 1993), Alice (1995) and Eliza (1997), were brought up to think of themselves simply as Violet, Alice and Eliza Manners, although Emma now wonders if she underplayed their position, that one 'can sometimes get it wrong'. Once her two eldest daughters were out in the world, they found that 'to certain society, titles are very attractive', and that they may be pursued for that reason. 'I think they're quite shrewd but they've got to work that one out for themselves. I've had to learn that, and it's something my husband has known from day one. He has a great ability for judging individuals and seeing if they're genuine or not. I think it's something you develop.'

Being titled and attractive, the older girls provide the society magazines with good copy and do not give any indication of being embarrassed by having a title. Their younger brother, Charles, however, has yet to become accustomed to his situation. At his school the pupils were asked to Google their homes. 'Charles was horrified when they Googled his. He ran out of the room. I have to teach him, "Don't be embarrassed about your heritage, that's where you live."' He had not long been at the school after attending prep school. 'I think when you go to a new school you just want to be Mr Average but it wasn't until he went to prep school at nine that he knew he was a marquis: he's Charles Granby to us.'

After three girls, Emma must have been relieved to have a son and heir at last, yet she says, 'I never questioned that I wouldn't.' But she was aware of the expectations. 'I remember some lady, at one of those hunting balls in Leicestershire, coming over to me after Eliza was born, this wonderful little treasure, commiserating with me as though there'd been a death, saying, "I'm so sorry to hear your news. I'll have to give you some tips on how to produce a boy," and I remember thinking, "Wow!" I just didn't get it because I'd never questioned that I wouldn't. I didn't come into this family and think, "I'm not going to produce a boy." I never questioned that I wouldn't make it successful. That is my outlook on life.'

She acknowledges it is something over which women have no control, and it was not easy for her. 'I had ten pregnancies for five children. I wanted seven children. So, yes, the gods are with me. I'm lucky enough to have had any children, and I do have five wonderful children but God willing, I was going to crack on and have a go. That's just the way I am.'

If, despite her optimism, she had not had a boy, the next in line would have been the Duke's youngest brother, Edward, who lives in another family property, the medieval Haddon Hall in Derbyshire. David had another younger brother, Robert, born in 1961, but he died before his third birthday. A cousin, Peverel Manners, who runs the very successful Belvoir Fruit Farms that produces fruit cordials, was another possible heir, so 'there was always a continuation.'

With her positive approach to childbearing, Emma was unlikely to have an issue with male primogeniture, the inheritance of titles by the male line. She is clear on her position. 'This estate is entailed, and I'm a farmer's daughter from Wales and there was not a moment in my life growing up on that farm when I imagined that a stick or blade would ever be mine, because that's how farms continue: the boys farm, they need a livelihood. If you ask my oldest daughter her views, she'd be horrified at the thought of the responsibility and

taking this on. It's a huge weight for a young girl to carry.' It is important, Emma says, to 'know the rules within your own family, and they are there at present, set in stone, so that's how it is.' Her daughters 'just don't want to go there. But we're lucky enough to have two sons.' Charles knows what is expected of him. 'I tell him, "There's no way you're coming back until you've cut your teeth somewhere else and proved to me you can do this job." So, they know the rules, and so did I on my Welsh farm. It's no big deal.'

It seems that the Manners family is set to continue the male line at Belvoir for at least the foreseeable future. As to the future of the aristocracy generally, she views it in a similar way to the Royal Family. 'It all depends on how the individuals who have the privilege of being whoever they are manage that, and how we see that in society. I think you've only got to see the new roles that the Royal Family are taking on, they're doing an amazing job and I think outside the UK it's really valued; here in the UK it's always challenged. There are a lot of challenges from the past.

'There's a perception about titles and aristocracy that maybe has been earned over time or maybe not – there are good examples and bad,' she explains. 'Sadly, the press always goes for the bad and gives the system a bad name.' To find out how you, as a titled person, are doing in your particular role, 'you have to ask your surrounding area whether you're getting it right or not.' She thinks the aristocracy is 'a great asset to tourism and as ambassadors of heritage to a foreign market,' and that Britain's heritage is one of its unique selling points. Emma has further contributed to the understanding of that heritage by writing books about Belvoir and its history, and about shooting. She has also used

Haddon Hall.

her background in interior design to put together a range of fine furniture.

In preserving the heritage of Belvoir, she has some inspirational predecessors. Her mother-in-law, Frances, was 'passionate about pictures' and has restored them all. 'When you study the duchesses as I did when I was writing my book about the family over one thousand years, you realise that it's a wonderful tapestry of what that private inheritance has – the layers of interest that each woman brings to the home.' The contribution of earlier duchesses gives Belvoir 'a rich and exciting feel'. It marks the difference, she says, between private heritage and National Trust, 'where many of these homes have been frozen in time, which I know has saved the heritage but it's sad not seeing homes evolving, because they become empty shells.'

With those views it is not surprising that her choice of predecessor is the 5th Duchess, Elizabeth, who inspired the building of the current castle and the landscaping of the grounds. She came from Castle Howard, the great stately home in Yorkshire, and had 11 children, of whom seven survived. 'She instigated James Wyatt to build this castle, she died young and I sometimes feel I'm finishing off the job that she started,' says Emma. With her talent and determination, the Duchess of Rutland is bound to succeed.

The Drawing Room in Belvoir Castle…

8

REGENCY SUPERSTAR:
ELIZABETH, DUCHESS OF RUTLAND
(1780–1825)

In the Mausoleum at Belvoir Castle is the beautiful tomb of Elizabeth, Duchess to the 5th Duke of Rutland. Aged 45, she was in the prime of her life and work when she died in November 1825. She was the mother of 11 children, four of whom died before her and are represented in the elaborate sculpture above her tomb, holding a crown of glory over their beloved mother as she ascends to the clouds. Light shines on them through windows stained with ruby, topaz, amethyst and emerald.

For today's Duchess of Rutland, it is a fitting tribute to her heroine, whose work she is honoured to feel she is continuing. So much at Belvoir today is a testament to Elizabeth's extraordinary vision and skill. Not only was she responsible for the building of the present castle and the landscaping of the gardens, she made improvements to every aspect of the estate.

Opposite: Elizabeth, Duchess of Rutland.

Without Elizabeth, it is hard to envisage how the Belvoir estate might have evolved.

She was born Elizabeth Howard in 1780, a daughter of the 5th Earl of Carlisle. Her mother, Isabella Byron, was a great-aunt of Byron the poet, whose guardian the Earl was appointed in 1798. Elizabeth was brought up in Castle Howard, the Yorkshire seat of the Howards, so was accustomed to vast houses. The building of Castle Howard had started in 1699, and was still unfinished nearly a century later when Elizabeth was born. The Earl ensured its eventual completion and filled it with his collection of paintings; Elizabeth's experience of seeing her father planning and organising the work on the house must have influenced her in her later life.

When she met her future husband, John Manners, 5th Duke of Rutland, she looked forward to seeing his family seat in Leicestershire, which would be her new home. The first occasion was shortly before their marriage in 1799, when she

Castle Howard.

was 19 and he approaching 21, and she was said to be horrified. The building was the third on the site, rebuilt after the Civil War. A squat, mid-17th century mansion, it was almost in ruins. There was little furniture and only the pictures seemed worth saving. Even the servants were disagreeable, and were either drunk or absent. How Elizabeth's heart must have cried out for the splendour and organisation of Castle Howard.

John was born in the Manners' London house in 1778 but had spent little time at Belvoir because of his father's commitments. His father was Charles Manners, then the Marquis of Granby, who became 4th Duke in 1779 and enjoyed a distinguished political career. Among other honours, George III made him Lord Steward of the Royal Household and Lord Lieutenant of Ireland, where he threw

many banquets at Dublin Castle. When not in Ireland, the Duke and Duchess preferred living at their house at Cheveley Park, a large estate near Newmarket in Cambridgeshire, which had come into the Manners family through Charles' mother, a daughter of the 6th Duke of Somerset. The result was that very little of their time or money was spent on Belvoir.

Incidentally, Charles's father should have become 4th Duke, but died when he was still Marquis of Granby. A great soldier who became Commander-in-Chief of the British Army, his name is commemorated in many British pubs.

As it turned out, there would be little chance for Charles and his Duchess to make any improvements to Belvoir for John as their heir, because just eight years after becoming Duke, Charles died in Dublin of liver disease. In 1787, at the age of nine, John became 5th Duke of Rutland.

His father did not leave much money for his widow, so Belvoir was again neglected. But young Elizabeth Howard was prepared to overlook this, because she and John fell deeply in love, writing to each other daily. She may also have gained some idea of John's love of the good life before they married. To celebrate his coming of age earlier in 1799, he had a two-week-long party, which included dinner for four thousand guests.

From the beginning, John's life was a busy combination of public duties and hectic socialising. In that significant year which saw his coming-of-age and their marriage, he was made Lord Lieutenant of Leicestershire as his predecessors had been, which included a role as Colonel of the Leicestershire militia. When he was not occupied with his public duties he spent October to April hunting and shooting. Even the first Christmas after they married, when Elizabeth was pregnant with their first child, John went to London and left the petite and pretty Elizabeth on her own to host a house party at Belvoir. He spent the rest of the winter hunting from his lodge in Lincolnshire.

However, she knew he was happy for her to refurbish the castle as she saw fit and he actively encouraged her. From the archives it seems that she drew up plans in 1799 for a new castle. She discovered that in 1780 the 4th Duke had commissioned plans from the great architect, Capability Brown, but nothing had been done. Helpful as the plans were, Elizabeth did not consider they went far enough. She wanted a comfortable new fairytale castle in the Regency fashion, which looked to medievalism: what was called the Gothic style. With sound judgment, in 1801 she engaged James Wyatt, the most

prominent architect in the country, who had been appointed Surveyor-General. His many distinguished clients included the Prince Regent at Windsor Castle. Elizabeth wanted to retain and embellish the original building, rather than razing it to the ground.

From the beginning of the project, the Duke instructed his friend and private chaplain, Rev. Sir John Thoroton, rector of nearby Bottesford Church and a gifted amateur architect, to supervise the project. Together with Elizabeth's extraordinary skills and passion, the result was one of the finest Regency manor houses in the country. She also turned her attention to the gardens. She saw the entire Vale of Belvoir as her garden and was merely framing the views with her valley gardens. In Belvoir Woods, away from the castle, is a woodland footpath lined with azaleas and rhododendrons. At the end of it, through an old iron gate, lies Elizabeth's garden, a sloping, horseshoe-shaped enclosure protected by trees. The Duchess's Garden is also known as The Spring Garden after its natural water spring. Many of today's grand old trees, including some massive oaks, date from that period, while some of the yews descend from those grown for ships' timber during the Battle of Trafalgar in 1805. Her passion for spring flowers is still found there in the descendants of her plantings. Amid this natural amphitheatre stands one of her creations, a 'root and branch' summer pavilion, made from tree roots and branches, with wattle and daub walls. It is a magical place.

Despite being so busy, Elizabeth also managed to organise the hectic social calendar that John so enjoyed, including shooting parties, and had 11 children. Sadly, she was able to enjoy four of them for only a short time: Caroline died at the age of four; George five weeks; another George ten months, and Adolphus three months.

When a fire broke out in the castle in 1816, Elizabeth rebuilt and repaired it with the help of the Rev. Thoroton and James Wyatt's sons – Wyatt had been killed in a carriage accident in 1813 – and by 1825, the work was almost complete. She was also deeply involved with the farm on the estate, which at the time had around 700 acres, and she was acknowledged for improvements in the breeding of cattle. But Elizabeth's skills were not confined to Belvoir. In 1817, she completed designs for an entrance to Hyde Park Corner and for a proposed quay on the south bank of the Thames. Her most ambitious project was plans for a new royal palace.

A contemporary view sheds light on Elizabeth's character. She was a friend of Mrs Arbuthnot, mistress of the Duke of Wellington, who frequently visited Belvoir. She said Elizabeth had 'extraordinary genius' as well as 'vanity and folly'. According to her, the 'fine ladies' of London did not like her because she was 'far above them'. Perhaps as a result she had few female friends but she was a constant friend to those she had. However, if women did not like her very much, she had no such problem with men, to whom she was very attractive. Although she and the Duke clearly enjoyed at least a degree of intimacy from the number of children they had, he left her alone for long periods. An early admirer of Elizabeth was Beau Brummell, the society dandy. Later, she developed a close and, today's Duchess considers, probably scandalous relationship with His Royal Highness Prince Frederick, Duke of York and Albany, second son of George III.

Frederick had been married in 1791 to his cousin Princess Frederica Charlotte, daughter of the King of Prussia, but it was not a happy marriage and the couple soon separated. If Elizabeth and Frederick were indeed lovers, she could not have hoped for one of much higher status, for when his elder brother, the Prince Regent, became George IV in 1820, Frederick became heir to the throne. His father, George III, had decided he should have a military career. He commanded several major campaigns, although his success in the field was mixed: it is he who became, somewhat unfairly, the subject of the rhyme, 'The Grand Old Duke of York'. Nevertheless, as Commander-in-Chief of the Army, he was responsible for a massive programme of reform and was in charge of preparations against Napoleon's planned invasion of Britain in 1803.

Where Elizabeth and Frederick first met is not certain but he certainly shared with her husband a passion for horse racing. John turned his estate at Cheveley Park into a thoroughbred centre of note, breeding four Classic winners; in the 21st century it is still regarded as one of the most successful stud farms in Europe. Of the racehorses owned by Prince Frederick, two won the Derby. Even if Elizabeth did not have the time or inclination to attend any races, she is likely to have organised and hosted lavish after-race parties, where she would have had the opportunity to become familiar with the Prince.

Parties were something the Duke of Rutland particularly enjoyed, especially for his birthday. On Friday, 18 November 1825, Elizabeth was inspecting progress on the work in the grand

Opposite: Prince Frederick.

drawing room, which was supposed to be ready for the Duke's 47th birthday the following month. She also took her usual exercise and wrote some letters. That evening she had an attack of the symptoms of the disease from which she had been suffering for a year, which caused inflammation of the chest, although the next day she seemed a little better. But at 2 a.m. on the Sunday morning the family's surgeon, who slept in the castle, was summoned and found her condition serious. Other doctors were called, one coming from London, but it was clear nothing more could be done. She remained conscious and aware of what was to come. On 23 November, she died, the Duke at her side. The King and Prince Frederick were among the first to be told the sad news.

Her friend Mrs Arbuthnot wrote that Elizabeth would be 'a most dismal loss' to her husband, for 'she managed all his affairs for him; he did nothing himself and his estates, his houses, his family, everything was under her rule.'

Her funeral was described in *The Gentleman's Magazine* in December 1825. It began with an elaborate procession from Belvoir Castle that included at least 34 horses and her favourite pony, and her duchess's coronet carried on a crimson velvet cushion. She was taken to the family vault at Bottesford Church but later moved to the mausoleum. Indeed her death was the impetus for its building; the foundation stone was laid in March 1826 by Prince Frederick. Coincidentally, in June 1825, just a few months before her death, Elizabeth had laid the foundation stone of York House (Lancaster House today) near St James's Palace in London, the house that Frederick had commissioned one of Wyatt's sons, on Elizabeth's

advice, to build for him. Sadly, neither of them would see York House completed.

Tributes to Elizabeth's life continued. In January 1829, an article in *Bell's World of Fashion* recounted celebrations at Belvoir Castle for the Duke of Rutland's birthday in December 1828, three years after his wife's death. The glittering occasion, where guests included the Duke of Wellington, was the first entertainment Rutland had given since Elizabeth's death. The focus of the party was the opening of the grand drawing room whose progress the Duchess had been monitoring a few days before she died. At one end stood a full-length white marble statue of 'the late amiable and greatly regretted Duchess', while on the ceiling, in separate sections, were richly painted portraits. In the central section were the Duke and Elizabeth; other sections contained paintings of members of his family and the now deceased Prince Frederick, 'who was much in the habit of honouring the Castle with his presence and its excellent possessor with his highest confidence and his purest friendship.' His death in 1827, of dropsy and cardio-vascular disease, occurred in the Duke of Rutland's London house.

Whatever the reality of the relationship between Elizabeth and Frederick, and despite her husband's absences, John loved her to the end. At Cheveley, he planted a tree-lined avenue in her memory, called Duchess Drive. At Belvoir Castle, as Emma Rutland points out, although few rooms today are laid out exactly as Elizabeth would have known them, the overall effect is a powerful evocation of the Regency period. Even without her glorious memorial in the mausoleum, her legacy is all around.

Opposite: An artist's impression of Beau Brummel meeting Lady Elizabeth Howard.

9

OF MUSIC AND MANSIONS, OF BALLADS AND BARDS:

THE DUCHESS OF BUCCLEUCH

Her mother was a journalist and a founder of the prestigious Women of the Year lunch, a left-wing feminist who married an aristocrat and Conservative peer while remaining a political radical. Her husband, Richard Montagu Douglas Scott, is a direct descendant of King Charles II. She took a degree in sociology at the left-wing London School of Economics (LSE) and became a respected journalist who, in her position now as a duchess and the chatelaine of three stately homes, eschews the more traditional expectations of the role.

There are interesting contradictions in the life of 'Duchess Bizza' as Elizabeth Buccleuch likes to be known. Her initial hesitation about being included in the book probably stemmed from a fear of portrayal as a froth of a title, an heir-breeding prop to an ancient family. That would have been a travesty. There are many factors that elevate

Opposite: The Duchess of Buccleuch.

Elizabeth Buccleuch, although there is one which differentiates her and the Duke from everyone in the country and which cannot sensibly be ignored: their status as landowners. The property arm of the family, Buccleuch Estates Limited, of which the current Duke is chairman, owns around 240,000 acres in England and Scotland. It makes the family the biggest landowners in Britain, comfortably ahead of the country's other major landowners, who include Prince Charles and his Duchy of Cornwall, and the Duke of Westminster.*

But whatever one might choose to infer from that fact, the reality is that both the Duke and Duchess studiously avoid any hint of grandeur and 'don't really "do" titles'. Before the author met the Duchess, she met the Duke, who stood in for his wife when she had to cancel an appointment. The easiest place to meet was at a coffee bar near

*In terms of land value, however, no one comes near to the Duke of Westminster, who may 'only' own 165,000 acres of rural land but they are said to be worth several billion pounds.

their London house. 'Do call me Richard,' said the 10th Duke of Buccleuch and 12th Duke of Queensberry KBE, President of the National Trust for Scotland, former President of the Royal Geographical Society, trustee and director of numerous companies and public bodies, as he removed his scarf and joined the queue to buy the coffees. Born in 1954, this former Page of Honour to the Queen Mother inherited myriad titles upon his father's death in 2007, but thinks that 'titles are not really important, and shouldn't be.' It is ironic, then, that he should have not one but two dukedoms, as well as a multiple surname which derives from families into which his ancestors married and from which come the extensive estates and the four remaining stately homes: Boughton House in Northamptonshire; Drumlanrig Castle, Dumfriesshire; Bowhill in Selkirk; Dalkeith Palace, Edinburgh.

Richard recognised that once he became Duke there was less time for his wife's previous professional life. For some duchesses this could prove difficult, he said, when they have had a life of their own and seem expected to restrict themselves to opening flower shows and the like. But Elizabeth was determined to find an acceptable alternative to such traditional expectation.

Born Lady Elizabeth Marion Frances Kerr (pronounced 'Carr') in 1954, the Duchess of Buccleuch is petite with thick dark hair, a trim figure in jeans, shirt and colourful scarf. She was the fifth of six children born to Peter Kerr, 12th Marquess of Lothian, a politician and man of letters, and Antonella (known as 'Tony') Newland, the daughter of Major-General Sir Foster Newland, director of the Middle East Medical Services. Although Elizabeth's 'very eccentric'

mother was proud of the Kerr family, an ancient Borders clan, 'she absolutely didn't give a damn about being grand', despite becoming Marchioness on marriage. When Elizabeth pursued the journalistic career she was determined to follow after the LSE, she found that her mother's words of advice were true: 'You've been born with a silver spoon in your mouth but all it means is you have to try doubly hard to succeed.'

No one was going to employ Elizabeth Kerr as a writer because of her privileged background, nor would she have wanted that. When she left university, it was the mid-1970s, not the 1950s when certain journals had sought the titled to give their publication 'class'. Yet the expected route for young aristocratic women like Elizabeth was still to go to finishing school, after which they were deemed sufficiently polished to enter into Society and find a husband. It was Elizabeth's own decision to pursue the career she was 'desperate' to do. Although her mother later became a journalist, she had married at 21 and devoted herself to motherhood. Tony Lothian was, says Elizabeth, a complex person who had led a 'very paradoxical life where she always wanted to be her own woman'. She was an impressive act to follow. When Elizabeth was one year old, Tony started the Women of the Year Lunch celebrating women's achievements; she later founded a literary award (which Elizabeth now administers) and received an OBE for charitable works.

One valuable lesson she taught her daughter was that a woman could achieve anything she wanted to do. Ideally Elizabeth would have liked to be more of an investigative journalist, but she landed a job on *Kaleidoscope,* a prestigious arts

Boughton House, Northamptonshire.

programme on BBC Radio 4 that had started in 1973. 'I had to work very hard to get my NUJ card and I had to prove myself by making programmes people listened to. I couldn't have gone into the BBC as a privileged person.' The experience was 'wonderful'. The programme would run until 1998, although she did not work there for its lifetime. She met Richard, then the Earl of Dalkeith, who was also working for the BBC, in its World Service. Sharing a passion for the arts, they were a good match and fell in love, marrying in 1981. Despite her left-wing politics, Tony Lothian must have been pleased for her daughter: 'She had a desire for her children to marry well.' They certainly did that, although not consciously setting out to follow their mother's wishes: two of Tony's daughters married earls and another a clan chief; her sons married dukes' daughters.

Elizabeth and Richard moved to Scotland and lived in Nithsdale, Dumfriesshire, the area where the Buccleuch family had lived for centuries. They were near Richard's parents, of whom Elizabeth was extremely fond and grateful that the Duke did not expect them to live in one of the estate's great houses. The Duke, known as Johnnie, ran the houses with his wife Jane, despite a severe disability. He had entered Parliament in 1960 as Conservative MP for Edinburgh North when still Earl of Dalkeith but, in 1971, a serious riding accident paralysed him from the chest down. Eventually, with much help from Jane, he returned to the Commons in a wheelchair. On the death of his father the 8th Duke in 1973, Johnnie took his place in the House of Lords and, among other causes, campaigned successfully for the rights of the disabled.

Meanwhile, Elizabeth and Richard initially 'lived quite a simple life'. Richard became a district councillor for the Conservative party and Elizabeth went to work for a local radio programme; she thought it was very important to be involved with their community. She had three of their four children and 'did the usual things countesses do – opening flower shows and getting involved with charities. I chose my charities carefully because I wanted to be able to make a difference to them, so I didn't take on every one of them.' They then took a decision which she says was 'probably slightly controversial': to send the children to private schools in London because there were no suitable schools in Dumfriesshire. They kept their house and still spent time there.

In 1992, she had their last child and second daughter, Amabel, and then took up the offer of various public appointments. It was a fascinating and extremely busy time that she loved. She was

chairman of the Scottish Ballet for ten years at a time of great transition, and not only presided over many new additions to the company's repertoire but also took them touring worldwide, from China and Japan to Canada and America. She became a trustee of the Museums of Scotland and was head of fundraising to build the prestigious National Museum of Scotland in Edinburgh.

Elizabeth was then appointed a trustee of the British Museum, becoming a friend of Neil MacGregor, its much-lauded director, and chairing the Friends of the British Museum. She was aware that her title made her visible to those and many other charitable bodies with which she was involved but found it ironic that she was nominated for the British Museum by a Labour government. Richard too held high-profile appointments, including vice-chairman of the Independent Television Commission (ITC) and a Millennium Commissioner. The children by then older, Elizabeth continued to be deeply involved with her commitments. 'And then Richard's father died. And since then it has become – slightly more complicated.'

Of course she knew it would happen one day but when it did, in 2007, the effect on her was unexpected. Not only was she 'desperately sad' but she was also apprehensive about following in the footsteps of her mother-in-law, Jane, who was 'the epitome of a kind and innovative duchess and a very hard act to follow'. Elizabeth had been happy as Countess and appreciated that it had enabled her to do many things she enjoyed. It was different now. 'It was probably the most traumatic moment, not only for me and Richard but for my children. Now I was top of the tree and I remember just before Richard's father died, talking to my eldest son – he's a chartered surveyor – and he said, "Mum, I'm not sure I want to be an earl." And I said to him, "I'm not sure I want to be a duchess but we're going to have to cope with it." And I think what I've tried to do in the past few years since becoming a duchess is to form it in the way that feels best for me.'

It was not easy. For the first time she had to consider 'what sort of duchess' she was going to be. 'One of the most interesting things was I had a pretty sure sense that I wasn't going to change terribly. What was difficult was that, because I was a duchess, people's expectations of me changed. I knew I had to make these houses relevant and I knew I had to nurture my children, especially my sons, into a role they were incredibly nervous about. They've all been brought up in this century. They're very ungrand – you won't see them in *Tatler* or whatever.'

The children were aged between 15 and 25. The eldest two were in the course of sorting out their lives, Louisa as an artist and Walter a chartered surveyor, 'and suddenly they were understandably uncertain about how this might change their lives.' Elizabeth tried to reassure them that they could go on with their own lives, as she would with hers. 'I was writing this book about my mother and doing various other things. The last thing I wanted to be was a "duchessy" duchess and that's why I came up with the idea that the most important thing for me was looking at the duchesses who preceded me, most of whom were fairly dotty: if not dotty, totally original.'

Not only did she have a new identity to become accustomed to, she had three major houses and their important collections to think about. She felt strongly that the houses needed a reason for existing, not just opening for the public, and she decided that each of them should have a theme in order to achieve this. It was something that previous duchesses had not done. She wanted to 'bring these houses alive'. The knowledge she had acquired in her work with museums would be invaluable.

Elizabeth leaves the wider estate matters to her husband, 'because Richard does that very well', and focuses on the houses. She knew her strength lay in communicating with people. Elizabeth visits the houses around once a month, talking to their staff and to their visitors and, vitally, helping each house to develop its own theme. It is a huge task because of their number – most duchesses with a stately home only have one to worry about – and their historical importance. Of the four ducal lines that descend from Charles II, Buccleuch has been the most successful in accumulating and maintaining wealth. The first duke, the one from whom Richard descends, was the Duke of Monmouth, the title given to James, the illegitimate son of Charles and his early mistress, Lucy Walter. It was rumoured at the time that Charles had actually married Lucy, which gossip continued for centuries and if true would make James his legitimate heir.

The handsome James was married off in 1663 to the pretty, rich, 12-year-old Anne Scott, heiress to the house of Buccleuch and Countess of Buccleuch in her own right. The Scotts of Buccleuch were an ancient and wealthy family of chieftains. Before their marriage, Charles saw to it that James would take Anne's surname and continue with it, thereby ensuring a right to the Scott family fortunes. He bestowed various titles on James from which Anne would also

benefit, including the Duke of Monmouth, and in celebration of their marriage created the first Dukedom of Buccleuch. James and Anne became the Duke and Duchess of Buccleuch and Earl and Countess of Dalkeith.

However, following his father's death, James led the Monmouth Rebellion in 1685. Declaring himself the legitimate king, Monmouth attempted to capitalise on his position as the son of Charles II and his Protestantism in an attempt to depose his Catholic uncle, James II. The uprising was unsuccessful; Monmouth recanted too late and was beheaded. There would not be another Duke of Monmouth; the King would re-grant to Anne the Scottish peerages but her husband's English titles were forfeited. In the 18th century some titles were restored to James' grandson, the 2nd Duke of Buccleuch, but Monmouth was not among them.

The estates the family owned expanded through fortuitous marriages. The 2nd Duke of Buccleuch took as his first wife Jane Douglas, sister of the 3rd Duke of Queensberry, bringing that line into the family. Then Henry, 3rd Duke of Buccleuch, brought in more Scottish estates, which he inherited from his mother, heiress to the Duke of Argyll. From Henry's cousin, the 4th Duke of Queensberry, he inherited estates in Dumfriesshire, including Drumlanrig Castle, and also the Queensberry title, becoming the 5th Duke. In 1767, Henry married a daughter of the Duke of Montagu, Elizabeth, enjoying as a result various Montagu lands, including Montagu House in London and Boughton House. The triple inheritance is reflected in the family surname, Montagu Douglas Scott. It is Elizabeth Montagu

Opposite: The Duke of Monmouth.

who is the present Duchess's inspiration and chosen predecessor.

Although the family is still very wealthy, much of the land is upland, which Elizabeth says 'isn't worth anything'. On the other hand, the huge art collection is priceless 'but is all owned in trust and we couldn't sell it even if we wanted to.' There were, once, more houses. Until 1917, for example, they still used Montagu House in London, since demolished. Dalkeith Palace, near Edinburgh, built for Anne, the Duke of Monmouth's widow, is still owned by the Buccleuchs but has not been lived in by them since 1920. It is now a European study centre for the University of Wisconsin, USA.

When the purpose of these houses changed, their treasures were moved to Bowhill, 30 miles southeast of Dalkeith, in the Buccleuch family since 1745. Until the Great War, it was a huge but simple retreat for country pleasures, holding paintings largely of favourite hounds and horses. Now Bowhill shares with Drumlanrig and Boughton one of the most important private art collections in the country. It is also important emotionally to the family because of its association with Richard's kinsman, Sir Walter Scott, a great friend and neighbour of the 4th Duke, Charles, and his wife, Harriet. Elizabeth says Bowhill's theme has to be literary. 'It's a wonderful house but one of the most important things about it was that Walter Scott was a kinsman, and Richard and I sponsor, and I'm a judge, on the Walter Scott Prize for historical fiction. My vision is that Bowhill will become a sort of literary centre.' The previous evening she had returned to London from judging the shortlist for the Walter Scott Prize, which she and the Duke founded in 2009.

Drumlanrig Castle.

The house Elizabeth visits the most is Boughton in Northamptonshire, the only one of the family's estates in England. In 1945, the American diarist, Chips Channon, wrote of the house that 'its richness, its beauty and possessions are stupefying.' At that time the chatelaine was Richard's grandmother, duchess to the 8th Duke, known as Molly. They had only been living there since 1935, as the house had been closed from about 1850. Channon wrote that the Duchess often had difficulty in choosing which of her five tiaras to wear. Elizabeth says she adored Molly, whose maternal grandfather was the Duke of St Albans – another line descended from Charles II – but thinks 'she was aware of her position.' Nevertheless, Molly was the epitome of the duchess as matriarch and knew everyone in the community. That sense of community, whose continuity could be ensured by a well-run estate – the old retainership, where families would be assured of work and looked after from one generation to the next – has changed. Now,

Richard said, his gamekeeper's children are going to Cambridge, 'which is as it should be.'

For Boughton, Elizabeth decided that the theme should be a musical one after discovering a music archive there, which has turned out to be 'fairly unique', and which for the past two years she has been cataloguing with friends. They have been putting on concerts there, maintaining the musical tradition: 'The Montagus knew Handel and Corelli.' But in the 21st century the houses need to pay their way on a more immediate and practical level. Boughton, Elizabeth says with a note of regret, has become part of the wedding circuit, as have many stately homes. Coincidentally, on the musical theme, she is pleased that it was chosen as one of the sets for the 2012 film of *Les Miserables*, in which one of her daughters played a part as an extra; and they were both happy to be involved with the popular television programme, *The X Factor*, which filmed a special there.

Drumlanrig Castle, once a Douglas property, has been described as one of the most romantic houses in Scotland. The dramatic theft in 2003 of one of Leonardo da Vinci's paintings, *Madonna of the Yarnwinder*, in which Richard and his father were held to ransom for its return, resulted in extra interest in the house after its recovery in 2007. Elizabeth says, 'Drumlanrig is slightly more difficult because it doesn't have a natural theme to it.' It seems to attract visitors without one.

Having responsibility for three great houses does not faze her. 'I was lucky that I was the daughter of the Marquess of Lothian, so I grew up from a very early age knowing that with this privilege came responsibility, so I never really worried about it.' She was brought up in one of the Kerr family houses, Monteviot House in the Borders, where her father's family had owned land since the 16th century.

The reactions of visitors to the Buccleuch houses are important to her. 'I think because I'm a radio journalist, interviewer by nature, I'm actually curious about why people want to come and see us and if they want to know more.' She and the children like to listen to visitors talking and try to help with queries if the guides cannot. 'The peculiar thing is that people have no idea who we are. They know who Richard is because he's there in all the photos but they haven't got a clue who the rest of us are. But I've been very lucky that I've been able to bring my children up in that way and because they're not remotely in the public eye, for which I totally give them credit.'

Walter has been ambivalent about his titles. From his birth in 1984, he was Lord Eskdaill, a title dating from the early 17th century. When Richard became Duke, Walter technically became Earl of Dalkeith but he chose to remain Eskdaill for about four years before he was ready to change. As a chartered surveyor and heir to the dukedom, his future as a major landowner is one for which he is being well prepared. Elizabeth is 'pretty sure Walter will want to inherit but he's also said he wants to divide responsibility – with his younger brother!' Charlie works for Christie's, the art business. Walter has said to him, 'You know about art, so you can do that bit!' Generally, though, Walter does not dwell much on his future title: 'I honestly don't think it's crossed his mind.'

On the question of girls inheriting, Elizabeth says, amused, that it is the last thing Louisa would want to do even if she could. She thinks the rules will change. 'It will require an Act of Parliament but I think it is possible. I think it will happen.' She refers to certain Scottish families where titles have passed through the female line. In anticipation of the royal birth in 2013, the rules of succession to the throne were changed to allow a daughter to inherit, 'so I think it all depends on how things turn out. I think if we have a lot of queens it would be hard for the aristocracy to hold out against it.' As the royal baby turned out to be a future king, that view will not be tested yet.

For all her education and achievements, Elizabeth Buccleuch was subject to the same pressure as every other woman over the centuries who has married a title; she was expected to produce an heir. She must have felt it keenly when their first child was a girl. 'I'll tell you something that will horrify everybody. When I was about to have my beloved Louisa, which was when I was quite young, my father-in-law had organised a bonfire and fireworks, and when I had her they were all cancelled.' She laughs. 'Then 22 months later I had Walter and he had a bonfire, fireworks, whatever, and she's never forgiven him!'

Being 'quite left wing', she was not happy about the reaction to her daughter. She thinks at least part of the reason for the keenness on the male heir was financial. When Walter was born, she was annoyed that the first congratulatory telegram was from the financial advisers who were working out the tax situation. 'When I had Charlie, someone sent a telegram saying, "Well done on the heir and spare," and I thought, "Rubbish", I really did, that was too absurd.' She does not think she would have felt a failure if she had not had a boy, 'but I would very much have missed having a son, let alone two, and also having two daughters has been a blessing in my life.'

Elizabeth thinks that by the time Walter

has children, times will have changed further, including on the religious side. For if there were any expectations of her from Richard's family when they married, it was to do with religion. She was raised by committed Roman Catholic parents and attended a convent boarding school, Woldingham, adhering to the faith as she grew up. Richard, however, is an Anglican Protestant, as the Buccleuchs have been for centuries: 'That was a complication.' It was resolved before they married, after much thought and discussion with others. These included her mother-in-law, an Anglican like Richard's father, and the late Cardinal Hume, the Archbishop of Westminster and highest prelate in the Roman Catholic Church of England and Wales. It was decided that any sons would be raised Anglican and any daughters Catholic, 'which was pretty dramatic, except that our daughters decided fairly early on that they wanted to make up their own minds.'

The most important things for Elizabeth in her role as duchess are those that identify her in her own right, above all as a writer, at times as 'a museum curator'. But she would not wish her view to be taken as diminishing the role of duchess, which she considers to be important. 'It's ancient. I certainly don't think in the 21st century it has to be what the public perception of a duchess is. I think the whole public perception of duchesses has changed.' There are, nevertheless, some expectations. As Duchess of Buccleuch, the staff that she and Richard employ 'expect kindness and understanding, and there is this peculiar change between deference and equality.' The estate business and houses have some three hundred staff altogether. For the houses they usually have a general manager, about six cleaning ladies and, depending on which house, tearoom staff which are normally franchised out. 'I don't think we're excessive. Each house, depending on its business, has to have a general manager, archivist possibly, gardeners, whatever, but quite honestly we can't afford a huge, huge staff. We don't have footmen or butlers or anything like that.'

Elizabeth says her mother-in-law, Jane, who married the 9th Duke in 1953, was a duchess in an era when duchesses were considered 'important'. She had been a model for the Queen's designer, Norman Hartnell, although, Elizabeth says, she hated being called a model. 'She loved her houses, she adored her children and I think all she wanted for all of us was that we would respect the name of Buccleuch – I think that's very important.' Jane was also aware of the importance of the clan above the label of a title, 'a specifically Scottish thing. If you're the Duke of Buccleuch you're head of the Clan Scott. My father was head of the Clan Kerr and my brother [former politician Michael Ancram, now Marquess of Lothian] is now.' There is also a sense of old Scottish families being entwined. Her brother-in-law, Donald Cameron of Lochiel, is a cousin of the Duke of Montrose, himself head of the Clan Graham. There is a 'huge equality' about clanship; Walter Scott had emphasised the importance of the clan in his letters to his friend the Duke of Buccleuch, reminding him that his most important position was that of Chief of Clan Scott.

Elizabeth and Richard are sometimes aware of strong feeling about the family's wealth, particularly 'a resentment that Richard is extremely wealthy', although she says it 'only comes through the left-wing press'. As a young woman, Elizabeth was not spoilt financially. 'I remember asking my father when I was about 20, why I was living on an overdraft.' She laughs. 'I think I had £50 as my overdraft limit. He said, "Because it's good for you." He never had that much money, so any money I earned was mine but, until I married Richard, I grew up on a £50 overdraft limit and from my father, I think into my forties, I got £400 a month.' She says her children are all well off compared with her and she tries to remind them of that. They all earn their own living now, although each has 'a bedrock of money they can use'. However, the children are also aware that they have a few friends who are far more wealthy than they.

She is patron or president of many charities and tries to be fair in her commitment to them. 'If I work very hard for them and raise money for them, I'll give them probably what they might charge for a ticket for a dinner in London.' As Duchess, the duties she carried out as Countess have diminished and she laughingly agrees that the public these days tend to want to see a footballer's wife. 'And so does my husband! He had Cheryl Cole come to do *The X Factor*. The entire estate came out to see her!'

Times have certainly changed in many ways. Certain previous Duchesses of Buccleuch, as was undoubtedly the case with other titles, saw themselves as required to maintain a certain image in what were, after all, less egalitarian times. Richard's great-great grandmother could be pompous, according to another duchess. Louisa Jane, Duchess to the 6th Duke, had a role within Queen Victoria's household and was herself a daughter of the 1st Duke of Abercorn and a granddaughter of the 6th Duke of Bedford.

In 1897, aged 61, she was a guest at the christening of the Duchess of Marlborough's son, to whom the Prince of Wales was a godfather. The Duchess of Marlborough wrote in her memoir that, 'As Mistress of the Robes to Queen Victoria, [Louisa Jane] was very much aware of the dignity of her rank and position,' and proceeded to describe with amusement Louisa Jane's horror when she was seated next to Marlborough's housekeeper.* Louisa Jane, who later became Mistress of the Robes to Queen Alexandra, died in 1912, and was surely one of the last of her kind. Elizabeth herself admires the Royal Family, especially the Queen: 'She's an amazing woman.'

More recent members of Richard's family were rather more approachable than Duchess Louisa Jane. Long before their marriage, Elizabeth knew Richard's aunt, a daughter of Molly, who by marriage had become the Duchess of Northumberland. Until her death in 2012, she was the mother-in-law of Jane Northumberland, the current Duchess. Elizabeth Northumberland was a very popular duchess and she had an 'immense' influence on the young Elizabeth Kerr. 'She was probably the most amusing, vaguely eccentric, totally honest, totally unaffected woman I've ever met. I adored her and all my children adored her.' Elizabeth Kerr was the same age as Elizabeth Northumberland's eldest son, Harry; she grew up with him and they went skiing together. In 1988, he became 11th Duke of Northumberland, his mother becoming the Dowager Duchess, but, tragically, he died in 1995, propelling his younger brother, Ralph, into the title.

When she became the Duchess of Buccleuch,

Elizabeth did not know what she would call herself. 'I didn't want to be Her Grace, so I pondered about "Duchess Elizabeth" for about three days and then everyone started talking about Duchess Elizabeth and I realised it was about her [Elizabeth Northumberland].' Eventually, she decided on 'Duchess Bizza', which is her nickname and, because Queensberry is in her title, 'I'm now "BBQ", which I love!' The most important thing to her is that the name of Buccleuch lives up to the values that she thinks it has always embodied: mostly public service but also culturally.

Having a title in the 21st century is not always easy in practical terms, as other duchesses have found. When filling in a form online and being asked to complete the box marked 'title', often the choices are limited. Elizabeth often has to be 'Mrs Buccleuch'. She tells of when she was chairman of the Scottish Ballet. 'We were going on tour in Japan and the only thing we could fit in for me was "The". So I arrived in Tokyo airport as "The" and nothing else! I managed to survive like that all the way through!'

Considering her passion for creating themes for the houses, Elizabeth's chosen predecessor is perhaps unsurprising. It is her namesake, Elizabeth, née Montagu, who started the musical archive in the late 18th century. Married to the 3rd Duke, 'she was a collector and was much loved.' No doubt in the future the same will be said about Duchess Bizza.

*From *The Glitter & the Gold* by Conseulo Vanderbilt Balsan.

Opposite: Richard and Elizabeth.

THE MONTAGU HEIRESS:
ELIZABETH, DUCHESS OF BUCCLEUCH
(1743–1827)

Elizabeth, wife of Henry, 3rd Duke of Buccleuch, is a source of delight to today's Duchess. From her family come the Montagu estates, including Boughton, and a long tradition of the musical arts. Elizabeth's love of music and of dance continued the patronage and passion of earlier Montagus and led to her compilation of a magnificent collection of music and ballet scores that was recently rediscovered at Boughton. Duchess 'Bizza' is collating and archiving this precious collection, unique in private hands, and hosting concerts to share it with music lovers: no wonder Elizabeth is her chosen predecessor.

Although she was Elizabeth Montagu when she married Henry, Montagu was not her surname at birth in May 1743. Her father was George Brudenell, 4th Earl of Cardigan, a courtier who served as Chief Justice to George II. The Montagu surname would come later from her mother's family. Lady

Mary Montagu was a daughter of John, 2nd Duke of Montagu, and Lady Mary Churchill, a daughter of the Duke of Marlborough. Elizabeth had an older brother, John, Marquess of Monthermer.

In July 1749, when Elizabeth was six, her grandfather, the 2nd Duke of Montagu, died suddenly of a violent fever. He had no surviving male heirs, bringing his titles to an end. The Montagu estates passed to his wife, but she died two years later and the estates passed to her daughter, Elizabeth's mother Mary. They included Boughton, which had been in the Montagu family since 1528 and was not far from Deene Park, the seat of the Brudenells. Mary also inherited Montagu House, a large property in Whitehall with an extensive river front, where her father had enjoyed holding musical soirées. It was the second house of that name; the Duke had commissioned it in 1731, while he was living in another, older Montagu House in Bloomsbury, later acquired by the British Museum.

Opposite: Lady Elizabeth Montagu by Thomas Gainsborough.

As his wife Mary had inherited the Montagu estates, George Brudenell assumed that name for himself and his children. By 1752, the Montagu family were living in Montagu House and enjoying all the culture that London could offer. That year the King made George a Knight of the Garter and appointed him Constable and Governor of Windsor Castle, a post he held until his death. In 1766, the titles that had become extinct on his father-in-law's death were revived, thus George became 1st Duke of Montagu (of the second creation). Celebrating his new status, the Duke commissioned the building of Montagu Villa, later renamed Buccleuch House, on the riverfront at Richmond, and laid out gardens behind it on Richmond Hill, which were greatly admired.

Any fond hope the Duke may have had of passing on the Montagu title was extinguished in 1770 when John, his son and heir, died aged 35. John had always suffered from poor health but still travelled extensively through France and Italy, collecting many of the paintings and items of furniture that can be seen at Boughton and Bowhill today. Created Baron Montagu in his own right, John died unmarried with no male heirs. His mother Mary died in 1775, and in 1776 his father the Duke was created Baron Montagu of Boughton in the County of Northampton. When he died in 1790, the Montagu dukedom became extinct and the Barony passed to Elizabeth's youngest son. To Elizabeth passed all the Montagu estates.

It was the gain of the Buccleuchs, for since May 1767 Elizabeth had been the Duchess of Buccleuch. Her marriage to Henry Scott took place at Montagu House when she was almost 24 and he not quite 21: a special licence was required to enable them to marry a few months before Henry was due to come into his inheritance. Henry was a clever and cultured young man who had received the best education available to one in his privileged position. He had been Duke since the tender age of four; his father, the Earl of Dalkeith, had died of smallpox in 1750 and his grandfather, the 2nd Duke of Buccleuch, died the following year.

Fortunately for young Henry, his mother Caroline, eldest daughter of the 2nd Duke of Argyll, remarried well. The brilliant Charles Townshend was Chancellor of the Exchequer and ensured that Henry and his younger siblings received a sound education. After Henry had finished at Eton, Townshend secured a tutor for him and his brother, Campbell: Adam Smith, the celebrated moral philosopher and later political economist, whose book *Wealth Of Nations* is regarded as one of the most influential books ever written, providing the intellectual foundation of free trade and economic expansion.

Smith resigned his position at the University of Glasgow, to tutor the boys and, in 1764, began a tour of Europe with them. In October 1766, while they were in Paris, Campbell died, still in his teens, which precipitated Henry and Smith's return to Britain. They remained close friends until Smith's death in 1790; his teachings would be invaluable to the Duke.

After their wedding in May 1767, Henry took his new bride to the Buccleuchs' main seat, Dalkeith Palace outside Edinburgh, which he had never seen before. He was intending to celebrate his coming of age there in September, but celebrations were delayed because a few days beforehand his stepfather Charles Townshend died suddenly. Contrary to Townshend's intentions for him,

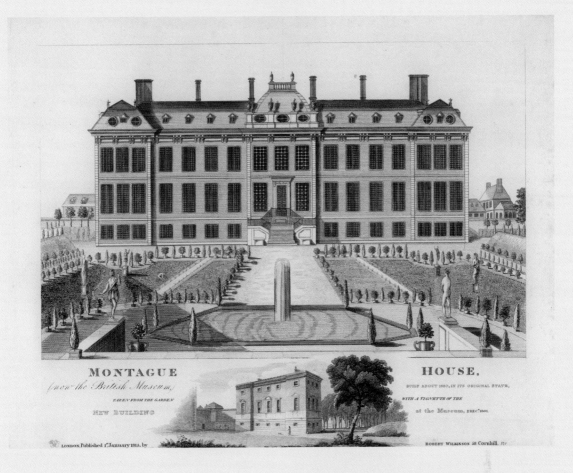

MONTAGUE HOUSE,

The first Montagu House in Bloomsbury, which became the home of the British Museum.

Henry decided not to enter politics but to devote himself to helping Scotland.

The Duke and his new Duchess were welcomed by their tenants, whom they are said sometimes to have visited in disguise. Elizabeth was described by a contemporary as being 'extremely beautiful' with 'black eyes of an impressive lustre, and her mouth, when she spoke, uncommonly graceful'. Slightly built, she was a little taller than average, 'active and elegant'. She was also said to be shy and took some time to be at ease in company. Perhaps

it was this demeanour that led the future King of France, who met her at Dalkeith Palace, to remark that of all the crowned heads of Europe he had met, the 'formal and dignified bearing' of the Duchess of Buccleuch left him feeling 'embarrassed'. However, at Court she would become a favourite; in 1776, for example, George III sent her a pair of chaise horses when he heard one of hers was lame.

Not long after the couple's arrival in Scotland it seems that the country looked to Henry, pupil of Adam Smith and a friend of the Solicitor-General of Scotland, for leadership. The young Duke had returned to his Scottish estate, which had become neglected since his grandfather's death, and threw himself into trying to improve Scotland's economy. He led public campaigns and founded a new bank to provide crucial credit for economic development; in 1777, he was appointed Governor of the Royal Bank of Scotland. When France, as a supporter of American independence, declared war on Britain in 1778, Henry raised a regiment of 'fencibles', or volunteers, for home defence. He became the first President of the Royal Society of Edinburgh, and, in 1793, when war broke out with the French Republic, he advised on the creation of a Scottish militia. On his death his friend and kinsman, Sir Walter Scott, wrote that 'the Duke's mind was moulded upon the kindliest and most single-hearted model.'

Elizabeth's close involvement in many charities ensured that theirs was a busy life, but there was room for music. Elizabeth's musical influences had begun early. Her Montagu grandfather was the Master General of the Ordnance to King George II, meaning he was responsible for military music. In February 1749, the King decided to celebrate the end of the War of Austrian Succession, in which Britain had been involved, by holding a spectacular firework display. George Frideric Handel, composer of *Zadok the Priest* for the King's coronation, was commissioned to provide music. The Duke of Montagu already knew Handel but unfortunately on this occasion the views of king and composer were at odds, and it was up to Montagu to resolve the situation.

Handel had originally intended to include 16 trumpets and 16 French horns in his composition but decided to reduce the number to 12 of each and add some violins. Montagu was dismayed because at first the King had not wanted any music at all, but when Montagu told him the number and type of instruments Handel was proposing, he had been satisfied; nevertheless, the King said he hoped there would 'be no fidles [sic]'. In March 1749, irritated by Handel's proposed changes, Montagu wrote to the Comptroller of His Majesty's Fireworks, Charles Frederick, telling him of the problem and saying that the King 'will be very much displeased'. Thanks to Montagu and others, whom Handel regarded as mere amateurs, a compromise was reached which seems to have omitted any strings. However, before the performance other problems followed which, as letters show, nearly ended in Montagu telling Handel to take his composition elsewhere.

No doubt young Elizabeth was taken to see the performance in Green Park, where an enormous wooden structure was constructed for the fireworks display, which took place after the music had finished. She may have been distracted by the pavilion catching fire, but hopefully she missed the wrath of its French designer, who was so upset by the fire that he drew his sword on the Comptroller, Charles Frederick, and was taken into custody.

Elizabeth's grandfather was also a significant figure in London's theatre world. Today's Theatre Royal Haymarket began life in 1720 as the Little Theatre in the Hay, built by a young carpenter, John Porter. Unlike theatres such as Drury Lane, however, it did not have the necessary Royal Patent to operate and was constantly being closed down. Porter's luck changed when the Duke of Montagu came back from France with a troupe of French actors and a play, *La Fille a la Mode*. The Duke found neither of the Patent Theatres keen on presenting a piece in a foreign language, so he turned to the Little Theatre, providing them with their first professional production. The play premiered on 29 December 1720. It was not a major hit but, now established as a professional playhouse, the theatre's reputation grew steadily. The Duke was also a friend and patron of the French dancer Antony L'Abbé, the foremost choreographer of his day.

With such a background, no wonder Elizabeth grew to love dance and opera. Living in Montagu House, with its music room and its harpsichord, she was in easy reach of the theatres and often attended premieres of French ballets and English and Italian operas. London in the 18th century was an exciting time for opera, and Handel's music really established its popularity; he was sent abroad by the Royal Academy of Music to attract the best available singers to London. Elizabeth bought the scores of many productions she had enjoyed and these now form part of Boughton's music archive, along with catalogues of performances enjoyed by earlier Montagus.

Whatever Elizabeth watched, and in whichever theatre, there was little of the respectful silence expected today. She would have had to tolerate the noisy chaos of the 18th-century theatre, where the audience was as visible as the performers and walked about socialising and playing card games, while young men cruised the aisles in the pit to flirt. Only when the aria began would the audience stop talking and listen to the great showpiece that everyone recognised, after which their socialising would resume. During a performance in 1763 at the Covent Garden Theatre, there was even a riot after management announced it was stopping the cheap seats concession; this allowed people to come in for half-price near the end to see the short after-pieces that followed the main event. The riot destroyed the interior of the theatre and forced the reinstatement of the concession. Elizabeth may well have seen that particular opera, *Artaxerxes* by Thomas Arne – a complicated story centred around the assassination of Xerxes, King of Persia – when it premiered at Covent Garden on 2 February 1762.

After their marriage, living at Dalkeith Palace, the Duke and Duchess of Buccleuch enjoyed musical entertainment. They liked to sponsor musical anthologies, and music was dedicated to and written specially for them, including a jig and a reel called 'Dalkeith House'. Talented musicians, such as Nathaniel Gow, could rely on their support. A young man from a musical family, Gow had been one of the King's trumpeters for Scotland and became a successful violinist, playing the lead in fashionable bands at society events. He named a piece for Elizabeth, 'The Duchess of Buccleuch's Favourite', and also wrote 'The Duchess of Buccleuch's Strathspey' for her. Gow named a march after the Duke, and a flamboyant reel called 'The Duke of Buccleuch and his Fencibles' was published in 1788.

The inheritance by Elizabeth of the Montagu estates and collections meant an injection of wealth into the then land-rich, cash-poor Buccleuch holdings. When added to the estates inherited by Henry during their marriage, and those already in the Buccleuch family, it meant they had a substantial choice of residences. Adderbury House in Oxfordshire, which had belonged to the father of his mother Caroline, came to Henry by 1768, when he commissioned changes to it. On Caroline's death in 1794, Henry inherited Caroline Park House, a mansion in Edinburgh, which he leased out. In 1810,

Henry inherited Drumlanrig Castle through his grandmother, Lady Jane Douglas, daughter of the 2nd Duke of Queensberry, whereupon he augmented the family surname to Montagu Douglas Scott. However, he would spend little time there. Only Montagu House and Buccleuch House, as Montagu Villa in Richmond was now called, were used by the Duke or Duchess if they were in London, and Dalkeith Palace remained their principal home. Even magnificent Boughton, known as the English Versailles because of the French influence via the 1st Duke of Montagu, 'slept' for nearly two centuries.

Henry died at Dalkeith in 1812, aged 65, but the musical tradition in the family continued. Elizabeth, now the Dowager Duchess, continued to live in Scotland for a short time. She and Henry had had seven children but lost their firstborn son, George, in infancy; their next son, Charles, became 4th Duke but died in his forties in 1819. His wife, Harriet, had already died prematurely, so their six young children were orphaned. The eldest son, Walter, Elizabeth's grandson, became 5th Duke of Buccleuch, aged 13.

Neither Elizabeth nor Walter could have dreamed that three years later, in August 1822, just after he had finished at Eton, Walter would be called upon to receive King George IV as a guest at Dalkeith Palace. The King's visit to Scotland was the first time a reigning monarch had visited the country since 1650. It was a momentous occasion, for which the King was to stay at Dalkeith Palace en route to Edinburgh – the usual royal residence, Holyrood, was not deemed to be in suitable condition. It was a huge responsibility for the 16-year-old Duke and Elizabeth may well have returned to Scotland to give support and advice to her grandson.

Dalkeith Palace.

Sir Walter Scott, whose novel *Waverley* had romanticised the Highlands and impressed the King when he was still Prince Regent, was charged with arranging the visit and providing entertainment for the King. Scott put on pageants into which he incorporated tartan; it was as a result of this that the tartan kilt became part of Scotland's identity, the King being happy to sport one despite being very portly and wearing flesh-coloured hose to soften the glaring impact of his bare knees. At Dalkeith Palace the King

treated his young host with kind and paternal attention, which no doubt was of relief to Walter who, among other duties, had to give the King's musical requests to the band: the Buccleuchs' protégé, Nathaniel Gow, had been summoned to play with a select group of musicians, to the delight of the King who was already acquainted with Gow's talent.

As the Duke approached his 21st birthday in November 1827, his grandmother was living in Richmond. Elizabeth was said to be an early riser and a great walker, which had kept her in good health. However, just four days before Walter's coming-of-age she died, aged 83; his birthday celebrations were postponed, just as his grandfather's had been. Sir Walter Scott wrote that Elizabeth 'was a woman of unbounded beneficence to, and even beyond, the extent of her princely fortune. She had a masculine courage and great firmness in enduring affliction, which pressed on her with continued and successive blows in her later years.' Having augmented the Buccleuch estates, Elizabeth's further legacy was her contribution to the knowledge of the musical arts in Britain: a legacy that is, for today's Duchess, exciting and inspirational.

TO CAPTURE THE CASTLE:
THE DUCHESS OF ARGYLL

On a misty Scottish morning the great grey green fortress of Inveraray Castle by Loch Fyne looks forbidding yet fascinating. On the shores of Scotland's longest sea loch there remains even now a sense of the isolation that this castle, seat of the Dukes of Argyll, and its little town once experienced. The thrill of the unknown and the chill of suspense that emanate from the castle walls are a potent combination.

But from inside those walls, and drowning out the echoes of the past, comes the joyful sound of children's voices. For this exquisitely furnished castle is also a comfortable family home, thanks to Eleanor Argyll. Dressed casually in jeans and trainers, hair caught back and with no time for makeup, she takes stock of the day ahead, hoping her three young children will carry on playing so that she can get on undisturbed. On a chilly spring morning she looks like any other busy young mother who needs to get on with running the family business.

However, this mother is the Duchess of Argyll, wife of Torquhil Ian Campbell, the 13th Duke, head of one of Scotland's oldest and once most powerful families, and she is preparing to open one of Scotland's biggest tourist attractions for the summer season. She is at pains to show that, while she recognises she is in a very privileged position, she is not so very different in some ways from other young mothers: small children, family home to run, a budget to keep to.

Most families, of course, do not own a beautiful stately home, but maintaining it comes with its own problems: 'Those houses don't come with the funds they used to!' The family seat demands

Opposite: The Duke and Duchess of Argyll with their children.

 Introducing the Duchess of Argyll

constant revenue and is not something they could easily sell – not that they would wish to. One of the earliest of the Duke's recorded ancestors was brother-in-law of, and companion to, Robert the Bruce, and the family was rewarded with lands at Loch Awe and Ardscotnish. From at least the early 14th century, the original castle of the Campbell chiefs, Innischonnell, stood in safe isolation on a small island in the middle of Loch Awe: the ruined high walls are still visible in winter.

In the late 15th century, Innischonnell was abandoned and the first Earl of Argyll founded the burgh of Inveraray, building himself a fortified tower house and beginning the long process of opening up that part of the west coast of Scotland. Around 1720, his descendant, the 2nd Duke of Argyll, living in less violent times, decided the fortified tower was no longer appropriate, so he built, like many of his contemporaries, a mansion house in the style of a castle. As home to the Dukes of Argyll, the Chiefs of Clan Campbell, the castle is also the symbolic home of the Clan, its members worldwide.

Almost all of Eleanor's time is taken up with Inveraray. She sees the main role of a duchess in the 21st century as looking after the stately home – if there is one. 'For many duchesses, sadly over the years money's got tighter and tighter,' she says. 'Not everyone has a great big pile to try and finance.' The castle has been part of her life ever since she married Torquhil in 2002, when she was 29. Unusually, he was already Duke, having inherited in 2001 at the age of 33. His father Ian, the 12th Duke, had died suddenly at the age of 63, thrusting on his son the responsibility of his many titles much sooner than expected. When they married, they were the youngest non-royal duke and duchess.

Torquhil met Eleanor through his younger sister, Louise, when Eleanor went to stay with her one weekend; the girls had been debutantes together. It was not a whirlwind romance. 'It took us forever to get engaged, 11 years. We went out off and on for years and years.' Having a 70,000-acre estate to maintain may be daunting but Eleanor must be better equipped than many to do so. She was not raised in a house the size of Inveraray but 'perhaps in a more normal-size house'. That description may be relative, for she was born into the Cadbury family of chocolate fame. Her father, Peter, is a banker, previously chairman of Close Brothers Corporate Finance. She acknowledges she was very lucky to have the upbringing she did. Her parents travelled a lot and she spent time in London, Gloucestershire and Cape Town, where her mother had grown up. School was Kensington Prep School in London, then Downe House School in Berkshire, an independent girls' school where she was a boarder; it was the same school that Kate Middleton, now the Duchess of Cambridge, would attend as a day pupil a few years later.

Eleanor read English Literature at Durham University, which she loved, then worked in book publishing, followed by public relations (PR). This combination of creativity and marketing equipped her very well for promoting Inveraray Castle, for which it is constantly necessary to devise innovative ways to widen its appeal and keep the money flowing in. Her view of her position is pragmatic: 'It's not going to be like that film where you marry and walk around the shrubbery all day. You have to do a job. I used to PR other things and now I PR the castle.'

Opposite: Inveraray Castle.

One lucrative and interesting way of promoting it, she found, was to allow a Christmas special of a very popular television series, *Downton Abbey*, to be filmed there. Apart from the income she knew there would be a spin-off of public interest in the filming, which would add to the castle's appeal. Filming in one's home would, for many people, be an intrusive experience, but Eleanor found it 'brilliant. I think our lives are quite goldfish-bowly anyway. You'll do anything to keep that place going.' She has no problem sharing the place with strangers. 'I think we're very lucky because it's an amazing house, and it's too big to actually live in. The rooms are fantastic, they're all original, hand-painted from the 1700s; they're exquisite. So to have to share it with other people is rather nice. We have our own apartment and children are so adaptable.' It is a wonderful life for the children. 'It's in the middle of the countryside, so they can just get on their bikes and off they go. They can build camps in the garden. We've got a river at the end of the garden so they can throw stones and go fishing.' The castle is also famously said to be haunted; people's experiences over the centuries have led to documentaries being made there.

Yet despite the need for publicity, Eleanor does not usually give interviews about herself, confining promotion to their business enterprises. 'I'm not really interested in people knowing about me. I don't think I'm a particularly exciting person to know about. I'm not a self-publicist. I've got three small children, I've got a castle to run and I've got plenty of things going on. I'm not the sort of person who needs to be seen at the school gates in a magazine.' For the benefit of promoting the castle she has done a few pieces about the family for the magazine and newspapers. 'But I don't want to walk down the street and get recognised: it would be hideous!' A photograph of her face on the cover of a well-known, if rather tawdry, celebrity magazine on her bookshelf, turns out to be a joke birthday card.

Eleanor embraces the social fluidity that was not found in earlier generations, when certain groups tended to marry only their own kind. 'I think we've all changed. I think in the old days the aristocracy only married the aristocracy, and my family were Quakers and you only married into that group. My father's a Cadbury, whose ancestors were Birmingham industrialists, my grandmother was a Milward – they made knitting needles and sewing machine needles – so the industrial families often married each other. You sort of stuck in your own bit whereas we're more fluid now, aren't we? My children are at school with such a complete range of people, which is brilliant.'

That social fluidity is very recent in this case. Torquil's marriage to Eleanor is the first for several generations where a Duke of Argyll has not married another member of the aristocracy, at least as their first wife. Toquhil's mother Iona, now Dowager Duchess, is the daughter of a Scottish Baronet, Sir Ivar Iain Colquhoun of Luss; until his death in 2008, he was Chief of the Clan Colquhoun. The first duchess to Torquil's grandfather, the 11th Duke (although she was not the 12th Duke's mother), was the Hon. Janet Gladys Aitken, daughter of the 1st Baron Beaverbrook. The 10th Duke, Niall, did not marry, but they were all outdone by the 9th Duke, John (known as Ian), who, in 1871, married royalty: Princess Louise, a daughter of Queen Victoria.

Opposite: George Cadbury, third son of John Cadbury who founded the Cadbury cocoa and chocolate company.

It is she who Eleanor has chosen as her favourite predecessor.

Eleanor Argyll's background has its own significance in Britain's history since the Industrial Revolution. The Cadbury family were Quakers who believed that all human beings should be treated equally and should live in peace. Their tea, coffee and chocolate business was started in Birmingham in 1824 by John Cadbury, who was involved in the Temperance Society, to provide an alternative to alcohol, which John believed was a cause of poverty. The award of a Royal Warrant in 1854 as manufacturers of chocolate and cocoa to Queen Victoria saw the business expand under John's sons, Richard and George. They bought land outside Birmingham in what was then countryside to build a factory. The area became known as Bournville, and George built a village to provide homes, education and leisure for his workers in a healthy environment as an alternative to the city life of Birmingham. Successive generations of the Cadbury family continue the good work.

With the family's historic emphasis on temperance, it is ironic that Eleanor should have married a man who acts as an ambassador for Pernod Ricard Distillers, promoting Scotch whiskies around the world. The company's premier whisky is Royal Salute, launched in 1953 to mark the coronation of Queen Elizabeth II; one of the Duke's hereditary titles is Master of the Royal Household of Scotland, so he was a fitting choice of ambassador. However, not only does the Duke's profile help to boost one of Scotland's oldest industries, it also serves a charitable function. The brand sponsors various charity events, and, since 2010, has partnered an annual polo match with Sentebale, a charity set up by Prince Harry and Prince Seeiso of Lesotho to help children there. The Duke has attended the matches at the Greenwich Polo Club in New York – the experienced Prince Harry is a player – and presented the Sentebale Royal Salute Polo Cup Trophy to the winners.*

The Duke does not play polo but nevertheless has the unusual distinction of having been captain of the Elephant Polo Team. The sport started around 1982 and is played largely in Nepal and Thailand. One of the whiskies the Duke promotes sponsors the Scottish chapter of the sport. Eleanor enjoyed the involvement they had in the game, which is not taken too seriously. 'It's brilliant, hilarious. It's just lots of different teams and playing on elephants that are well looked after and used to being handled by humans.'

Eleanor is also involved with charities, something she sees as part of her role as duchess and because she has what she calls a 'privileged life'; she hopes to spend more time with them when the children are older. She raises money for Scottish charities by means of a lunch in London called Women of Achievement. The beneficiaries in 2013 were two Scottish girls from the Prince's Trust who were helped to get started in business. She also helps raise the profile of tourism in Argyll and the Isles, which 'has amazing things but it all needs bringing together. And I'm lucky because I've got one of the key things people come to Argyll for.' She works with local food and drink producers, musicians and craftsmen, and set up a festival in Inveraray which takes place

*Coincidentally, Sentebale means 'forget me not' in Sethoso, the language of Lesotho, and the Campbell family motto is *Ne Obliviscaris* – 'Do not Forget'.

each September. Called The Best of the West, it celebrates the best of the west of Scotland's food, drink and music.

Part of her role as Duchess of Argyll is to support the Duke in his role as Chief of Clan Campbell, which is extremely important 'because historically that's why we are where we are. It's one of the biggest clans there is.' She says there is even more interest in Clan Campbell abroad than in Scotland; its societies in Australia, America and New Zealand are huge, the members passionate about their heritage. She refers to 2009, when Scotland held its first Homecoming Year to celebrate the 250th anniversary of the birth of its poet, Robert Burns. Around 35,000 people of Scottish descent from overseas came to Edinburgh to celebrate their heritage.

Before the children arrived, Eleanor and the Duke frequently visited clan societies abroad. When the children are older they intend to resume those activities but in the meantime they send out Clan Campbell newsletters. When members from overseas visit the castle, she and the Duke are always 'thrilled to see them'. He personally greets them and spends time with them.

Indeed, it is thanks largely to the loyalty of the Clan Campbell members that Inveraray Castle is still in a condition to make it worth visiting. On 5 November 1975 – Guy Fawkes Night – the townspeople were enjoying the traditional bonfire in Inverarary when 'they turned round and there was a better bonfire going on in the castle'. Fire was ripping through from the top storey, destroying pictures and furniture. It was a terrifying sight. Vast torrents of water from the fire fighters cascaded through the state rooms, causing great damage. However, 'the people from the town were

amazing' and helped in every way they could. Torquhil was just seven years old, Louise, three.

The insurance money was not enough to restore the castle properly and their father could have taken the money and given up on the place. But he was mindful of his role as Mac Cailein Mór – the Gaelic title of Clan Chief of the Campbells. The castle had survived another fire a century earlier and they were not going to let this one defeat them. Eleanor praises her parents-in-law. The house was not fit for habitation, so the family moved into in a cottage on the estate before moving into the castle's basement. The Duke and Duchess flew around the world visiting Campbell clan members and asking them for money to keep their heritage going. Fortunately enough money was raised to be able to restore the castle sufficiently for it to reopen to visitors three years later.

Eleanor clearly has a great deal of affection for the Dowager Duchess, Iona. 'My mother-in-law's brilliant. She's completely different from me. She's much more practical. She makes curtains, she can make headboards, she makes Charlotte beautiful little Campbell tunics – I'm hopeless with that sort of thing. She's a fantastic cook and gardener. I'm very lucky. I can go to her and say, "Help! We've got a clan gathering coming up and Charlotte needs a bigger dress!" and overnight, something amazing will appear.'

Iona and Ian also gave Torquhil a more settled childhood than Ian himself had had. In 1934, Ian's father, Ian Douglas Campbell, the 11th Duke, had divorced his first wife, Janet, after seven years of marriage. His second wife from 1935 was Louise Clews, an American; she gave birth to Ian in 1937. In 1940, while fighting in the war with the Highland Division, Ian was captured by the Nazis and held

The 11th Duke and Duchess of Argyll.

prisoner for five years. He became Duke in 1949 on the death of his childless cousin, Niall, and with Louise and their children moved into Inveraray.

In 1951, the Duke and Louise divorced and he remarried that same year. Fourteen-year-old Ian's stepmother was the beautiful, previously married socialite, Margaret Sweeny, who became the next Duchess of Argyll. However, in 1959, the Duke began divorce proceedings on the grounds of her frequent adultery. The extremely public, sex-ridden divorce case lasted until 1963; the family would continue to be associated with it long afterwards. The year the divorce was finalised the Duke married for a fourth time, his wife outliving him.

Of his post-war relationships, Eleanor is

sanguine: 'I think if you marry a man who's been in a prisoner of war camp you're taking on a hell of a package anyway, because who knows what went on there. You're going to have a damaged person on your hands in whatever way.' Even so, the Duchess Margaret seems to have done the title few favours, but Eleanor sheds a rare, positive perspective on the woman who brought such terrible publicity on the family. Margaret is credited with greatly improving the castle. The previous Duke, Niall, an academic man, 'had tendencies to madness so he chose not to have children. He could see "the wee folk".' He did nothing to the castle, which fell into neglect.

It was Margaret who, with enthusiasm, the help of an architect and, most importantly, money, assisted her husband in a major programme of repair and renovation on his becoming Duke. The castle opened to the public for the first time in 1953. The Western Highlanders had a lot of time for her. 'Margaret is really respected in some ways because she was really fantastic to the town and the castle. She was amazing because she came with money and put it into a place that didn't have much money.' However, Margaret's emotional legacy cannot be ignored. 'But the way she behaved with the family of course was terribly upsetting for everybody because nobody wants a scandal, and it was a pretty exciting scandal. And it was absolutely everywhere. She tried to say my father-in-law was illegitimate and she forged letters. She behaved really badly when it came to the family but on the other hand she provided jobs in the town that needed jobs, so...'

There are those who believe the current incumbents should be making more of Margaret's contribution. It is an issue about which Eleanor makes no apologies. 'We get hugely criticised for not spending hours publicising her but I don't think it would be right. I don't have any problems with people asking questions but I don't think it would be right for me to say, "Here's our celebrated ancestor" because she behaved appallingly when it came to the family, whatever her reasons were. Her marriage was obviously deeply unhappy but there's always two sides, aren't there? But I can't put up great posters praising her because it would be disrespectful to Torquhil's father, who obviously had a terrible time with her.'

In 1969, the Duke left Inveraray and moved back to France with his fourth wife. While Ian and Iona were still Marquess and Marchioness of Lorne, the Duke asked them to uproot from London and move into the castle with baby Torquhil. They were settled there by the time Ian became 12th Duke in 1973.

It cannot have been easy for Iona being faced with responsibility for the castle when she was just 24. Do people compare Eleanor with the Dowager Duchess? Eleanor does not think so. 'I think everyone's just getting on with what they're doing. And we're so different. She did the children's party and now I do the children's party.' Every Christmas, Eleanor invites 80 children to tea: if she did not, she would be 'in trouble!' However, 'it's a very small community, so everyone's doing their best. They know Iona does beautiful church flowers whereas I do terrible church flowers! I'll do something else in other ways.' But she is not expected to stand on ceremony. 'That's the thing about the West Highlanders. They're brilliant, they're quite different from Londoners. People all have a job to do. I walk down to Londis [the supermarket] and have a chat and walk back home again. Everyone's just getting on with their business.'

Some people have certain expectations of what a duchess will be like. 'I think people expect that I should be terribly grand. So when I turn up probably in my trainers I'm in now, they're a bit surprised. I think they assume you should be terribly snooty or grand or whatever but no one can get on in the world like that these days. It doesn't work.'

Although Eleanor may present her role as duchess as non-glamorous, there is, not surprisingly, a more glamorous side. She is, for example, sometimes required to act as lady-in-waiting to Prince Andrew, the Duke of York, which she says is 'a huge honour – and various members of my husband's family have been lucky enough to have such a role.' Eleanor's attendances on the Prince include visiting charities and attending dinners, which she enjoys very much. On one occasion during the week of the Church of Scotland's General Assembly, she spent ten days at a stretch visiting different charities with the Duke. One charity she found particularly interesting, in Glasgow, tries to sort out the Protestant/Catholic problem by working with schoolchildren and sending them to Belfast where the city is making good progress with tackling such issues. She feels that it is beneficial to 'teach them from this age that there's actually not much difference between all of us.' In a busy week they also attended the reopening of Glasgow's renowned Hunterian Museum, Scotland's oldest museum, after a major refurbishment.

Eleanor also attended Prince Andrew at the General Assembly itself; he had been chosen by the Queen to be her Lord High Commissioner at the annual ceremony at which a new Moderator is appointed. Eleanor and Torquhil are usually involved anyway because of his hereditary role as Master of the Royal Household in Scotland.

Eleanor considers herself and the Duke very lucky to be invited to interesting events. That year it included visiting Iona, the island famous for its ancient abbey, for a celebration of St Columba. The Dukes of Argyll owned the island from the 17th century until 1979 when they sold it to the Fraser Foundation, which presented the island to the nation. In the Duke's role in promoting Scottish whisky, he and Eleanor also usually attend the Keepers of the Quaich,* a celebratory dinner for the whisky industry to thank everyone for their part.

In her role as a mother, Eleanor must equip her children for dealing with the titles they have inherited and prepare Archie for his future role as Duke, at the same time trying to keep them grounded. 'Archie's the Marquess of Lorne and he knows he's called Archie Lorne and he knows his siblings are called Campbell. I think he probably knows he's got a title and I don't think it crosses his mind. And we're – I hope – down to earth and wouldn't flag him up as being special to anyone else, so he's at a school where I shouldn't think the other children would know what's going on.' Nevertheless, she does not draw Archie's attention to his title and does not put it on envelopes. 'When he's a bit older, of course, he's going to have to take it on board.'

That time may come sooner rather than later.

*A Quaich is a ceremonial shallow drinking cup with two handles.

When Torquhil was a just little older than Archie and himself Marquess of Lorne, he was Page of Honour to the Queen for two years. In the longer term, 'He knows that one day he's going to be a duke and he knows that one day he's going to inherit but he's also got to get a job and work jolly hard, because that place needs a job! You can't just have an estate, you need a job to pour the funds in.'

Eleanor managed to produce 'the heir and a spare', then a daughter. But the idea that women (other than members of the Royal Family) should inherit titles is one on which she is not keen. She says it is necessary to have a son because 'that's how the system works at the moment.' At the same time, she does not think that anyone has looked into the issue properly. She believes it is important, as far as possible, to keep the title with the house, 'otherwise you're just throwing history away. Maybe I'm just saying that because I had the boys first. But I do think it's great that the Duke of Argyll is still living in Inveraray Castle – that's what it's all about, isn't it? Dukes are a dying breed, so you've got to just hope you have your sons.'

In this case, it was particularly important that she have a boy. The family historian told Eleanor early on that there were no male relations left and made it clear what she had to do if she could. 'If we'd had no boys, the title was going to die out.' When asked whether, as an alternative to the title dying out, she would have been happy for Charlotte to take the title – after all, it would still be Argyll blood – despite a change of surname on marriage, she admits it would not be terrible, 'but it would still be sad.'

Naturally, they have lots of staff to run the tourist aspect of the castle but Eleanor is in charge of the tearoom and the shop, for which she does the buying. On the domestic front, they have a 'fantastic' nanny who travels between London and Scotland with them, and a caretaker and a housekeeper who look after the castle. 'They're brilliant. They'll do the cleaning everywhere and change the light bulbs and whatever it is but they're very much for the public side as well. I'm also perfectly capable of making a bed or doing the ironing.' There is less money these days for staff, she says, and with all the gadgets available for housework, it is not necessary. Thanks to the internet she does not even have to be at the castle in order to communicate; she can just as easily work from her London home, or anywhere else she and the Duke have to be.

The Internet may have opened channels of communication but the Duchess has also experienced its negative side. Ironically, it was Eleanor's lack of grandeur and her 'hands-on' approach that provoked a barrage of unpleasantness in response to a newspaper article she was asked to write. She says it was an 'insignificant' piece, in which she happened to say why they did not have any staff but it provoked an online response. 'I said something like, "I make the children's beds" and they were saying, "So she should, stuck-up bitch." You think, "For goodness, sake, read the whole article!" The experience made her even more sympathetic to the unprovoked anonymous attacks some people endure: 'But, hell's teeth, I'm lucky if that's all I'm getting, when there's poor people whose children get murdered and they have that awful stuff written about them, saying they deserve it. You think, "Oh, God, how can people write that!"' She does not know if it is because of

Isle of Tiree.

her title but she believes there is ignorance about people's wealth; they see figures in newspapers and assume that it is all money available to spend. 'But it's not money to spend, is it? It's because there's a castle that needs a lot of help. It would be a tragedy if it wasn't part of our history.'

Progress has happened rapidly even since she was a child, and traditions that were alive when she was in her teens may not exist by the time Lady Charlotte reaches adulthood. One of those traditions is 'coming out' as a debutante. Eleanor went through the process, which is how she met Torquhil's sister, Louise. Until 1958,

girls from certain families were presented to the monarch as a sign of their acceptance in Society; it was also an acceptable way of announcing one's eligibility for marriage. Even when Queen Elizabeth stopped the tradition of presentation to Court, a form of the ritual continued. Eleanor was not very keen when she first received a letter inviting her to take part. She thinks she received it because her mother and grandmother had both been presented at Court. As they had 'come out', and as she had friends who were doing it at the same time, she agreed.

The letter was sent by a man called Peter Townend, who was behind the society 'bible', *Burke's Peerage*. Sadly, he has since died but Eleanor says, 'He was hilarious, a walking encyclopaedia of British Society. He knew absolutely everything, I don't know why he made it his job to know but he was very good at it. He'd remember literally through the ages who was married to who. And then everyone has parties. It's just to meet people, I think. I was lucky, I knew lots of people. I lived in London but if you'd grown up in the West Highlands, for example, it was a nice way to meet people.' The path to marriage was no longer part of it. 'Now we all wanted to go and work but it was a nice way of making friends, an easy crowd of people.'

She does not know whether she would want Charlotte to take part or whether the process will still be going on by then. 'Maybe nowadays it's full of a different crowd who'd want to buy their way into it, I don't know.' Could the daughter of a Russian oligarch not have taken part when she did? 'No, not at all. You did it because your mother and grandmother had done it.' Eleanor sees her mother a lot and describes her parents as 'brilliant grandparents'. If she and the Duke have to fulfil a duty at a weekend, her 'darling mum' will have the children.

There are other parts of the Argyll estates that she also manages, including Tiree. The last island in the Inner Hebrides after Mull and Coll, Tiree is accessible by ferry. With stunning white beaches and blue sea, it is particularly famous for its windsurfing and shooting. 'If you're into snipe shooting, it's the golden ticket.' Eleanor also rents out two cottages for holidays that she took on and modernised. She shows photographs and describes the island as 'Paradise. There's diving for mussels and happy children on the beach. You can sit up there and watch them pottering

and know they're all right. It's very natural.' With corncrakes and basking sharks, it certainly sounds idyllic.

Eleanor's choice of predecessor, Princess Louise, Duchess to the 9th Duke, sounds as if she shared some of her characteristics, although she would probably be too modest to agree. Louise was 'very feisty. Queen Victoria didn't want all her children to marry cousins because they realised that the haemophilia was such a problem, so they broke away from marrying all royalty. That was considered a big scandal at the time. She [Louise] set up the Girls' Public Day School Trust, and I'm a GPDST girl, which was an amazing institution.' Eleanor talks also of Louise's campaigning for women's rights and her talents as a sculptress; her sculpture of Victoria at Kensington Palace still adorns the grounds.

Louise brought a public spirit to her role, in the same way as Eleanor has as Duchess. Inevitably, time has changed the role in some ways. With Inveraray Castle being open to the public today, Eleanor says the modern role is an unpaid but interesting job. 'You definitely take it on knowing you've got a hell of a lot to do. As my husband said, you've got to hand the Castle on in a better state than you got it because otherwise why are you bothering? You could sell it on to some oligarch. Not that they'd live in the West Highlands, I don't think. People come to Britain mainly for our heritage, so you might as well make the best of it.' Eleanor Argyll seems to be doing just that.

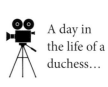
A day in the life of a duchess…

12

A ROYAL DUCHESS:

PRINCESS LOUISE, DUCHESS OF ARGYLL
(1848–1939)

In the Victorian Room at Inveraray Castle stands an exquisite maplewood writing desk that belonged to Princess Louise. It was a gift from her mother, Queen Victoria, on the occasion of her marriage in 1871, aged 23, to John Campbell, the Marquess of Lorne, son of the 8th Duke of Argyll. When Lorne became 9th Duke, Louise would be one of the rare examples of a royal princess who was also a duchess. There were some who considered the match beneath her.

Not Victoria, however. The Queen was delighted to have such an occasion to give her clever and independent-minded daughter a present, for finding a suitable husband had not been easy. Born in 1848, the sixth of Victoria and Albert's nine children, Louise was very intelligent with a lively mind. Early on she exhibited great talent in dancing and drawing, and despite the fact

Opposite: Princess Louise, Duchess of Argyll.

that Victoria had said she would turn out to be 'something peculiar' because of the unrest in Europe at the time, she acknowledged her daughter's talent, which was soon recognised by others. It is the expression of that talent and Louise's commitment as a feminist, still resonating in the 21st century, that endear her to Eleanor, Duchess of Argyll.

Louise's childhood was largely happy but strictly regimented. Her education took place at whichever of their homes the Royal Family was resident in at the time: Buckingham Palace, Windsor Castle, Balmoral. The curriculum for her and the younger children was a broad academic one devised by Prince Albert, although when they were on holiday at Osborne House on the Isle of Wight it included, unusually, such practical skills as cooking, farming, carpentry and gardening. As Louise matured it was not enough for her. She felt strongly about the education of girls and suffrage, and was not inclined to toe the royal line, which caused friction with her mother.

Louise felt particularly frustrated when, after her father died on 14 December 1861, Victoria insisted on a prolonged period of mourning for her beloved Albert. Louise's social life after 'coming out' as a debutante in 1865 was subject to limitations simply because she was royal, and it was restricted further by Victoria's attitude to mourning. It was a trying time for the spirited young princess.

Fortunately, her creativity was given an outlet. Although her rank prevented her from pursuing a career in art, she was permitted to have lessons from the acclaimed sculptress, Mary Thornycroft, and then in 1868 was enrolled at the National Art Training School in Kensington. Her studies were interrupted, however, because from 1866 she had been working as her mother's secretary and companion, a tradition and obligation as the eldest unmarried daughter. Louise dutifully served her mother for several years at a difficult period: Victoria's increased seclusion was starting to attract public criticism.

Meanwhile, passionate and spirited Louise fell in love with a tutor appointed for her younger brother, Leopold, in 1866. The clever, attractive Reverend Robinson Duckworth was naturally not considered a suitable proposition, and Victoria dismissed him in 1870, although she liked him well enough to secure his appointment to a parish. It is alleged that an affair with another tutor followed. Clearly the question of Louise's marriage needed to be addressed.

Tall and slim, with brown hair and blue eyes, Louise was said to be the most beautiful of Victoria's children. Many suitors were suggested from the European royal families, although the number of eligible princes was limited: they had to be Protestant and healthy, with an independent position and fortune. Her sister Victoria was married to Frederick III of Germany and suggested Prince Albrecht of Prussia, but the Queen was reluctant as Louise would have to live abroad. Princess Alexandra, Louise's sister-in-law, proposed her brother, the Crown Prince of Denmark, but Victoria was opposed to another Danish wedding. Others were suggested but vetoed.

Louise, however, wanted to choose her own husband. Victoria started considering noblemen rather than royalty, and unusually allowed Louise into Society so she could view possible husbands. Lorne, a gentle and educated man, was already known to Victoria. From 1868, he was the Liberal MP for Argyllshire, which he would remain for ten years. His father, George Campbell, Duke of Argyll, was a Cabinet Minister and brilliant orator whom Louise had admired since childhood; his mother, Elizabeth, was Victoria's Mistress of the Robes and her close friend, as Lorne's grandmother had been. Lorne and Louise were very attracted to each other but the match initially caused an outcry among the family and courtiers. Lorne may have been heir to a dukedom but he was still one of the Queen's subjects, and no member of the Royal Family had married a subject since 1515, when Henry VIII's sister, Mary, married the Duke of Suffolk.

However, Louise would be bringing fresh blood into the family at a time when the monarchy was unpopular with the nobility. Victoria gave her approval, supported by her Prime Minister,

Opposite: Princess Louise and Queen Victoria.

Gladstone. They were married on 21 March 1871 at Windsor Castle, whereupon Louise became Her Royal Highness the Marchioness of Lorne. Breaking with tradition, she wore a veil that she had designed herself.

Their life together started well enough. Determined to improve opportunities for women in those restricted times, in 1872, Louise became the first president of the newly formed National Union for Improving the Education of Girls of all Classes above the Elementary, which was actively supported by Lorne. That year she also helped set up, and sponsored, the Girls' Public Day School Company (today the Girls' Day School Trust) for parents who could not afford their daughters' education. Sadly, in 1873, Louise, who had suffered poor health since childhood, was told that the reason she had not yet been able to conceive (the doctors assumed the problem was hers and not Lorne's) was the meningitis she had suffered at 16. Louise took water cures as advised but, to their deep disappointment, their marriage remained childless.

Louise's energies instead went into public service, and, in 1875, she founded The Ladies' Work Society. This helped gentlewomen who found themselves in financial hardship in an era when there was little choice of a working profession. Taking on paid work, even in more acceptable positions such as governess, meant a serious loss of social standing. Her Society enabled women to improve their needlework skills and work from home on orders received by the Society for embroidery and clothes. Such were the excellent standards that their work formed part of major exhibitions in Britain and abroad.

In 1878, her mother's Prime Minister, Disraeli,

chose Lorne as Canada's fourth Governor General, the youngest to have held the post. Louise endured homesickness at the beginning and they both experienced some initial hostility; the Canadians seemed to resent the imposition of royalty on the country's un-royal society. However, *The Canadian* newspaper wrote at the time that the appointment was well received and welcomed Louise, expressing the love Canada felt for Victoria, which extended 'with fervour towards the fair young daughter who, during her residence among us, has been, and will be, the first lady in the land.'

The couple's popularity grew. Louise encouraged accessibility at Government House, and when they travelled she referred to herself as 'Mrs Campbell', to avoid the formal ritual that accompanied her official persona. But, in February 1880, during their first winter in Canada, they were involved in a serious sleigh accident, in which Louise suffered severe concussion and was lucky to escape a broken skull. She would suffer from headaches and depression for the rest of her life.

Louise was sent back to Britain to recuperate, Lorne visiting her when he could, returning to Canada in 1882 when the couple went on a tour of the United States and up to British Columbia. Meanwhile, a threat had been made on Louise's life by the Irish Fenians, who sought independence from Britain. She would be safer on British soil and so decided to winter in Bermuda. Their route to Charleston, from where she would sail, took them through the dangerous bandit and Indian country of the Wild West: not the usual kind of journey for a princess.

Opposite: The 9th Duke and Duchess of Argyll.

John returned to Ottawa in February 1883, to open Parliament, and Louise joined him later. Although her stay in Bermuda, in whose life she played an active part, did much for the island's reputation, it did little for the couple. Conscious of threats to their safety and rumours of their failing marriage, Lorne requested he be relieved of his position as Governor General. He did not, however, discuss it first with Louise, who objected to leaving. They returned to Britain that October.

Despite being apart for some time, they had made an impression in Canada. They encouraged the establishment of the Royal Canadian Academy of Arts, the Royal Society of Canada, and its National Gallery. Louise served as Patroness of the Ladies' Educational Association and other good causes. The province of Alberta – one of Louise's middle names – was named after her, as were Lake Louise and Mount Alberta.

On returning to Britain in 1883, Louise became extensively involved with the art world, exhibiting for example at the Royal Academy, the Society of Painters in Watercolour and the Grosvenor Gallery. She had avant-garde tastes and commissioned Edward Godwin, a progressive architect/designer, to design her studio at Kensington Palace. In 1893, she completed the marble sculpture of her mother that still stands in Kensington Gardens, and was one of the female sculptors considered by the Royal Society of British Sculptors for inclusion in the Franco-British Exhibition of 1908. Passionate about increasing educational opportunities, she promoted the Recreative Evening Schools' Association for children in the East End of London, the forerunner of evening classes later held throughout Britain.

But Louise and Lorne were not getting any closer. Lorne could be stubborn and domineering with her, and the lack of children did not help. By 1884, Louise had fallen out of love with him, although, while passion may have dissipated on both sides, there was still respect and affection. There was talk of her lovers, particularly the acclaimed sculptor and medallist, Sir Joseph Edgar Boehm, a favourite of Queen Victoria from whom he received many commissions. Certainly, Louise completed part of her training in his studio and they were good friends, but the fact that she was there when he died in December 1890 fuelled speculation that they were lovers. In nervous anticipation of gossip, Boehm's executors burned his personal papers and accounts within a few days of his death. They did, however, present to the Victoria and Albert Museum in 1892 Boehm's plaster cast of Louise's left hand, the purpose of which is unknown.

Lorne and Louise's political views were also diverging. In 1896, he won the South Manchester seat as a Liberal but he and his father were forced out of the Party by Gladstone's Home Rule Bill, which they opposed. Louise was disappointed when at the next election Lorne stood for the Liberal Unionists.

Rumour also linked Louise romantically with the young architect, Edward Lutyens. Her friend Gertrude Jekyll had introduced him, and when Louise needed a designer in Scotland, she commissioned Lutyens. In 1896, Louise and Lorne had taken as their main Scottish residence Lorne's childhood home of Rosneath Castle. Situated on one of his family's estates on the Gare Loch since 1489, it was in danger of being sold off to pay his father's debts. The Duke's problems had started in 1876 when his wife, Elizabeth, suffered a stroke. The following year a terrible fire broke out in Inveraray Castle, necessitating expensive restoration and improvements. After Elizabeth's death in 1878, George remarried, was again widowed and took a third wife in 1895. Unfortunately, she was rather profligate with the Argyll inheritance: at Inveraray alone they had 70 servants and 74 dogs.

When Louise and Lorne later became Duke and Duchess, they realised just what state the late Duke's finances were in and there were large death duties too. His family had hoped that Louise might pay for the upkeep of Inveraray but they had forgotten that she was also using her money, at Lorne's request, to save and restore Rosneath. Louise recognised that Rosneath, with 100 rooms, was too expensive to run. To avoid its sale she bought nearby Ferry Inn, intending to turn it into a dream home by the sea so that Rosneath need not be used while it was being worked on, and commissioned Lutyens to build an additional wing and carry out improvements to the Castle. An affair between Lutyens and Louise seems most unlikely, not least because he was an employee and engaged to be married. Certainly, they necessarily saw a lot of each other but while Lutyens found Louise 'witty and downright' in conversation, as his client she was exhausting.

It did not stop his fiancée, Lady Emily Lytton, complaining jealously of the amount of time he spent with the Princess. Lutyens denied any attraction, while acknowledging an easy relationship in which Louise's sense of fun, and his enjoyment of it, were clear. However, while Louise was susceptible to attractive men, there is no evidence of an affair with anyone.

Louise's ambition to live at Ferry Inn was never realised. It was in 1900 that George died and Lorne became 9th Duke of Argyll. Rather than moving into Inveraray Castle as would be expected of the new Duke and Duchess, the late Duke's debts meant they would have to let Inveraray out and live in Rosneath instead. That year, as the wounded from the Boer War began arriving home, Louise turned Ferry Inn into a hospital for them.

The following year, Queen Victoria died and Louise's brother became King Edward VII. She assumed a greater public role while continuing her existing duties, including as first Colonel-in-Chief of the Argyll and Sutherland Highlanders: she allowed them to use her name, which they still bear, and she designed their crest herself. In 1902, Louise designed the memorial at St Paul's Cathedral to the Canadian soldiers who had died in the Boer War, and was delighted to receive an honorary degree from Glasgow University in recognition of her Presidency of Queen Margaret College, the first and only Scottish college to provide higher education for women.

Louise's close involvement with many social causes continued. Her involvement in women's issues had started years earlier with her support for the women's rights campaigner, Josephine Butler, who campaigned against the legalisation of the sex trade and on the taboo subjects of prostitution and sexual morality. Unlike her mother, who did not agree with women entering the professions, particularly medicine, Louise was an admirer of, and visited, Elizabeth Garrett Anderson, the first Englishwoman to qualify as a physician and surgeon in Britain. Anderson was a supporter of women's education and suffrage, and she and Louise railed against the homilies of such men as the eminent psychiatrist Henry Maudsley, who believed that education for women could cause over-exertion and damage their reproductive organs. Louise also worked with Anderson to raise funds for her hospital for women.

In 1907 Louise faced a personally trying time when Lorne's name became linked with the mystery of the theft of the Irish Crown Jewels from Dublin, which have never been recovered. The main suspect was Francis Shackleton, homosexual brother of the explorer, Ernest. Frank was an associate of Lorne's homosexual uncle, Lord Ronnie, and had only a slight acquaintance with Lorne. Nevertheless, an affair between them was hinted at as part of an alleged cover-up in which Edward VII (Lorne's brother-in-law) was said to be involved. No evidence was found which supported either allegation about Lorne, while the King, rather than covering up, had actually ordered an inquiry into the theft.

In 1911, Lorne's health started seriously to decline. He became overweight, eccentric and suffered memory loss. Despite their differences, Louise nursed him devotedly at Kensington Palace, and they became very close again. After suffering double pneumonia, he died on 2 May 1914. Louise's nephew, Kaiser Wilhelm II, not quite yet Britain's enemy, sent a wreath.

In the absence of children, Lorne's nephew became 10th Duke. Louise had a nervous breakdown and suffered from intense loneliness, writing to a friend, "My loneliness without the Duke is quite terrible… I wonder what he does now!!" But she busied herself as always. During the Great War, a terrible time for her given the Royal Family's European relatives, she inspected the Canadian units that came to Britain and prepared Rosneath Castle as a military hospital, while at Kensington Palace she cared for shell-shocked men. In 1918, her nephew King George V awarded her the Dame Grand Cross of the British Empire. Still she continued her work, health permitting, including her associations with her regiments and the building of the Princess Louise Hospital for children in Kensington.

With the social changes that followed the Great War, Louise remained as open-minded and up-to-date as ever, unstuffy and enjoying smoking into old age. On 3 December 1939, she died at Kensington Palace, aged 91. She asked to be cremated, a most unusual request by a member of the Royal Family. Had she died in Scotland, she wanted to be buried next to her husband; if in England, at Windsor near her parents, which is where her ashes lie. Her name lives on, in her art and in the myriad causes with which she was involved. She was, says Eleanor Argyll, a truly extraordinary woman.

Opposite: Josephine Butler.

MAKING A DIFFERENCE:
THE DUCHESS OF MONTROSE

here is a haunting Scottish folksong that schoolchildren once learned:

O ye take the high road and I'll take the low road
And I'll be in Scotland afore ye
But me and my true love will never meet again
By the bonnie, bonnie banks o' Loch Lomond.

It is apt that the song should spring to mind when approaching the home of the Duke and Duchess of Montrose. Even an overcast sky cannot spoil the striking views from Their Graces' house, situated in isolation at the end of a long, narrow track, across to Loch Lomond to the Trossachs mountains in the distance. Despite the dull dampness of a winter's day the countryside around the village of Drymen, 20 miles northwest of Glasgow, still impresses.

James Graham, the 8th Duke, has the distinction – 'the honour', he says – of being the only duke who retains the right through election to sit in the House of Lords following its reform in 1999. Locally, however, he sees his responsibilities less as a duke and more as a landowner, describing himself as a hill farmer, as many of his Graham ancestors were. He is probably better known to the Scots, and to emigrants of Scottish descent all over the world, as Chief of Clan Graham. The Clan's history and its allegiance to various monarchs is complicated and ancient, reaching back to the early 12th century. The Grahams, it transpires, have a connection with that folk song: the Gaelic, if not English, words relate to the Battle of Inverlochy in 1645, on the site of today's Fort William in the Highlands. A significant battle of the Civil War, it was won by the Duke's ancestor, an earlier James Graham, the young Marquis* of Montrose.

Descended from a long line of earls, the Marquis

Opposite: The Duchess of Montrose.

* The Grahams have always used this French spelling of Marquess.

153

was considered a clever and thoughtful man and envied for his good looks and style. By then a supporter of King Charles I, Montrose led his men in the defeat of the forces of his enemy, the Marquess of Argyll, head of the mighty Campbell clan. Further tactical victories by Montrose on behalf of the King and, after his execution, his son Charles II, led to Montrose being regarded as one of the most important figures in British history. Montrose was subsequently betrayed to his enemies. His dramatic execution in 1650, aged 37 – his body hacked to pieces, his head stuck on a spike for 11 years, his limbs distributed to four Scottish cities – add to the romance of this leader, who is still referred to by historians as the Great Montrose. In 1707, the 4th Marquis, again named James Graham, was elevated by the King to the rank of Duke of Montrose as a reward for his services in connection with England's union of the parliaments with Scotland.

Four centuries almost to the day after the birth of the Great Montrose, his descendant, the 8th Duke, who with the Duchess had just hosted a dinner for 80 in honour of his ancestor, welcomed the author into their dark hallway. He is a tall, handsome man; born in 1935, he looks younger than his years. The Duchess, petite and sweet-faced, is six months younger: she says, laughing, that there is a short period each year when he is entitled to boss her about. Born Catherine Elizabeth MacDonell Young in Winnipeg, Canada, she still retains the softness of the accent of her home country.

The Duchess was dressed casually and warmly as befits a country lady on a Saturday morning in the middle of a damp Scottish winter. A person less obviously duchess-like than Catherine Montrose

must be hard to find. But that presupposes duchesses are a type and she makes it clear that she does not approve of stereotyping. Far from grandeur or elevation above others, she is modest in an age when modesty is not a fashionable concept. The Duchess of Montrose is conscious of her duty towards others but less as a duchess, more as a human being. Her commitment seems to derive from a sense of guilt at what she perceives as her own selfishness, her desire to please herself. This started long before she had met her husband, through mutual friends. James was working hard on a family farm in Scotland that had fallen into a poor state, and every now and then was invited to London by his friends.

Married in 1970 when he was the heir to the dukedom, they seem a devoted couple. 'I liked him very much because my idea of someone like that – he was the Marquis of Graham then – was someone who was quite snobbish. He was different, he was unaffected. I thought, "What a very nice person." So that was my first preconception shattered.' Lunch with both of them took place at one end of a long, heavy table in the dark wood-panelled dining room, the furniture unfussy, solid and old. A large window looks out over the top part of the garden. The Duke's family has lived in this area since 1682 but has enjoyed this view only since the 1930s, when the house was built by his grandfather.

Immediately before that, the family seat was Buchanan Castle, built by the 4th Duke in 1854 to replace an earlier building destroyed by fire. Buchanan Castle still stands nearby – but only just. Sold after the Great War as a result of hefty death duties and a weak market in Scottish land, it served as a hospital in the Second World War, with Rudolf Hess as one of its patients, and then as an Army training centre. In the 1950s, it was de-roofed to avoid tax and continues to rot, spectacularly. Today, the castle is a vast Gothic ruin, on the 'at risk' register of the National Trust for Scotland. The Duke would like to build flats around the castle, with the idea of using parts of it as an historical and aesthetic facade. Meanwhile, it continues to have its uses. Those who equate Scotland less with hunting and fishing and more with golf can play their favourite game in its grounds. The Buchanan Castle Golf Club, owned by the Duke and Duchess and which hosted the anniversary dinner for the Great Montrose, has been regarded as one of Scotland's best courses since it was designed in 1936.

The Great Montrose is dramatically captured in oils in the dining room. The Duchess says, 'He wrote poetry about the monarchy like a lover,' while also being 'a great general and one of the first guerrillas. Of course, I don't approve that he took his 14-year-old son with him on a big winter campaign and the son died of pneumonia, but I'm not a man or a general or living in the 17th century! But such was his passion and conviction. He risked everything.' There are also portraits from a couple of centuries later of the Duke's grandmothers by the much-fêted Hungarian portraitist, Philip de Laszlo. The Duchess, an avid reader, had just enjoyed a book about him, 'a real human being from quite a humble family but he got to know them all, the royal houses and my husband's family, and all the little anecdotes about them.'

A simple lunch was prepared and served by the Duchess herself. There is no butler here. Apart from a couple of people employed to work with the Duke on the family farm, they have only a woman and her partner who rent a flat at the back of the house. She does the housework, her partner works elsewhere but when he has time he does odd jobs, like chopping wood. They have been there for seven years. Although there are eight bedrooms and many other rooms, including one that can host receptions for 60, not all of the house is used regularly: the Duke and Duchess are on their own except when they have visitors to stay, such as their three children and two grandchildren. They had a gardener after they married, but he retired. The Duchess tried doing the large garden herself after that but found it 'like the Forth [Railway] Bridge', so she was relieved when she found the first love of the lady who rented the flat was gardening.

It was different in her husband's grandmother's day, she says. The Duke's grandparents built the present house. The 6th Duke of Montrose was inventor of the aircraft carrier in the Great War; his wife was Lady Mary Louise Douglas Hamilton, the only child of the 12th Duke of Hamilton. Born in 1884, she married the then Marquis of Graham in 1906, becoming Duchess in 1925. Mary enjoyed the services of a butler, cook 'and all these things, as they did then.' She also had the garden designed. Her skills make Catherine Montrose aware of her lack of knowledge. 'She was a brilliant gardener, she knew a lot about plants, much more than I do but she had more help than me.' In the grandparents' day the bride of a future duke tended to be aristocratic, as Mary was. Catherine Montrose's father-in-law, the 7th Duke, would not have made such demands.

James Angus Graham became a controversial figure. He had worked to establish a farm in

Scotland, but the Montrose estates had shrunk considerably largely due to death duties and there was little money. In 1931, when he was 24, he went to work in Rhodesia for a subsidiary of ICI. He fought in the war, became 7th Duke in 1954 and, in 1962, was appointed Minister of Agriculture in Rhodesia under Winston Field's government. In 1964, Field resigned and provoked the crisis that produced Ian Douglas Smith's government and subsequent Unilateral Declaration of Independence from Britain.

Ignoring the Queen's appeal to her Rhodesian subjects to obey her Parliament, the 7th Duke retained his governmental posts in Rhodesia. Technically, he was guilty of treason. A Labour MP and Republican suggested that the Duke be banned from Westminster but Prime Minister Harold Wilson would not be pressed. Eventually, differences between the Duke and Smith led to the Duke's resignation but he remained devoted to the idea of Commonwealth and against the idea of a European Union. With his second wife he went to live in South Africa and returned to Scotland in his last days.

When Catherine Montrose became Duchess on the death of the 7th Duke in 1992, she had no need to worry about her mother-in-law's expectations of her or comparisons with what sort of duchess the 7th Duke's first wife, Isabel, had been. Isabel gave birth to her children in Rhodesia but she and the Marquis divorced in 1950. The Marquis remarried in 1952 so it was his second wife, Susan, who became Duchess in 1954. They had four children, half-siblings of the present Duke, with whom he and Catherine are 'on very good terms'.

The Duchess is also part of Scotland's history. Her father's family emigrated to Canada from

Loch Lomond.

Scotland in the 1860s, 'and he was so proud of his Scottish blood and great family trees. I once said to my teacher, "I think we're descended from Bonnie Prince Charlie." She looked at me scathingly and said, "Anyone with Scottish blood says they're related to Bonnie Prince Charlie," so I

never mentioned it again. I was rather mortified by that.'

The Duchess is clearly very proud of the Grahams' part in history and animatedly explains more portraits in the hallway. Above the stairs hangs a massive picture of the execution of the Great Montrose; this one is a copy, for the original hangs in the House of Lords. Yet there is no sense of this house being a showcase. The living room is made cosy by a roaring log fire, comfortable armchairs and hundreds of books lining the walls, with leather bindings, old gilt lettering and intriguing titles. From the window is an uninterrupted view to Loch Lomond. There is a sense of timelessness.

But despite the lack of grandeur, the fact is that

by being married to a duke, the Duchess belongs in the top echelon of the British aristocracy: somewhat ironically, since she has always found the British obsession with class to be fascinating. It took her 'some time to understand how deep and historic class feeling is in Britain'. Having joined the 'system', she also realised how easy it is 'to generalise about a whole group of people – Americans or duchesses and dukes, so I think that anything that dispels this kind of lazy thinking is good'. The class system was 'quite new' to her because she grew up in an academic Canadian family. Her father, Captain Norman Andrew Thompson Young, was an historian who went to university in Canada and then studied at Oxford. He was recruited to teach at Achimota College on the Gold Coast (now Ghana), a highly regarded secondary school based on British public school principles. After marrying Catherine's mother in Canada they returned to Achimota to teach for three years, which they loved. One of her father's pupils was Kwame Nkrumah, who, in 1957, would become Prime Minister of Ghana, leading its first government after independence from Britain.

Back in Canada, her father initiated a school for boys in Winnipeg that has become one of the top independent schools in Canada. In 1929, he was the first headmaster of Ravenscourt School. Catherine, their third daughter and youngest child, was born in 1935. On taking a group of boys on an educational trip to Europe, her father became greatly disturbed by the presence of Nazi stormtroopers that they came across. The view in Canada of his concerns was that 'it would blow over'. As an historian Young predicted it would develop into something more dangerous.

When the war he had foreseen broke out, he joined the Queen's Own Cameron Highlanders of Winnipeg and trained with the Commandos at Fort William. In 1942 he took part in the Dieppe Raid, the disastrous seaborne raid launched by Allied forces on the German-occupied French port. Aged 42, Young was one of those killed, 'which of course was a great sadness for my family, my mother left to bring up four children. I was six, my brother 16, but at the same time we were very proud of him. My mother used to say, "We had 15 happy years," and so she brought us up and saw we got our education.'

The family continued to live in Winnipeg and the children all went to university in Manitoba. Her brother became a respected political journalist. Her uncle, Lester Pearson, was Prime Minister of Canada from 1963–1968. By contrast with others in her family, the Duchess was, she says, not very academic, preferring sports to study. Her favourites were skating and skiing; she also played basketball, did gymnastics and dived for her university.

One of the Duchess's two sisters died in 2010, but the other, a piano teacher, now widowed, lives in California. The sisters keep in close touch despite their very different lifestyles. 'But she has an appreciation of Britain. Our family always have, as we have British relations and we had evacuees during the war who stayed four years with my grandmother.' The Duchess still keeps in touch with them and speaks warmly of the ties her family has always had with Britain and the great affection many Canadians have for England and Scotland. She has always felt at home in Scotland and never homesick.

Opposite: Lester Pearson.

Nevertheless, back in their courtship days, her thoughtful fiancé insisted they marry in her home country. He said that as she would be spending the rest of her life in Scotland, it seemed only fair that she should do something so important in the country where she had grown up. They married in Ottawa, both aged 34. Until then, she first studied English, French and Philosophy at university but did not finish her course. Instead, she undertook a life change. 'I met some people who captured my imagination. They said, "If you want to change the world, the place to start is with yourself." They said to change the world you've got to have a sense of responsibility, that you have a part, that you can do something with your life; that none of us has to feel that we're the victims of circumstance. I was captured by the idea of trying to play an effective part in the world.'

This group of people – known then as Moral Rearmament but now as Initiatives of Change – and Catherine's experiences while travelling with them seem to have laid the foundation of her philosophy of life. The group's international website in 2013, echoed in its UK site, defined itself as 'a world-wide movement of people of diverse cultures and backgrounds who are committed to the transformation of society through changes in human motives and behaviour, starting with their own.'

Catherine's mother had known these people for a long time. She herself had avoided them because she knew there were things in her life that would have to change, 'mainly this basic selfishness of just living for myself, doing what I wanted'. But she considered that it had probably helped her mother tremendously in bringing the family up on her own 'because she'd met these ideas about changing yourself and then asking God – if you believe in God – for help. When I faced these ideas again at 18, rather confused – I found the philosophy course very confusing, all these different theories about existence – I was more ready for them.'

She was raised as an Anglican and became Church of Scotland on marrying but at that time she was not sure whether God existed. When this group told her that God had a plan for her life, she thought she would try it. They told her, "Be quiet and open your mind and see if you get any thoughts, as we believe God is speaking." She tried, and experienced 'a sort of freedom': as the youngest in the family, she was, 'very dependent on what they thought. I wasn't my own person.'

The group invited Catherine to go with them to Asia but this meant not returning to university. Her brother and sister were against it but her mother supported the idea as it had worked so well for her, 'which I'll always be grateful for.' Before she started travelling, Catherine had met a German girl at a conference, about her age, whose father had been killed in the war. 'I thought, "Our fathers have fought each other, maybe our sons are going to – unless we learn a different way." It brought it down to my level as I was 18.' She spent several years with the group, travelling to South America and Africa, meeting people she would never ordinarily have met and having 'all sorts of amazing experiences that I wouldn't change for the world.'

Her aversion to stereotyping people started then, learning to accept them as individuals, even political groups that she had been taught to avoid. 'I'd always been rather afraid of communists but I found they were human beings like me.' Gradually, her faith grew, as did her confidence in 'a guiding person, God or whatever you want to call it, to tell me what to do. Sometimes it's not all that easy knowing what the right thing is, and it takes time to find, but I felt I was on the right track and I've never really looked back.'

The need to examine herself and make changes becomes clearer in the context of the movement. In Brazil, they found crime and corruption among the port workers who were taking bribes and they tried to show the people that they 'couldn't criticise their leaders for corruption if they were corrupt in their private lives'. She spent time in Africa, including Eritrea in Ethiopia, just before the long civil war. She saw people being imprisoned for criticising the government under Haile Selassie; she says it was the people around him who did not want to change things, 'so again we tried to teach them about changing these things in themselves.'

She acknowledges the criticism that the movement has attracted since it started in 1938. 'It will always be a battle because it challenges people to change their ways and anything like that does.' The Duke too has always been a supporter of Moral Rearmament and tries to apply the ideas 'to his life here and in the House of Lords and in building bridges with the Muslims'. Similarly, their youngest child of three, Lord Graham, born in 1975, is a human-rights lawyer who 'has a very strong faith' and has worked with refugees in the Lebanon. He 'has a real conviction about building bridges into the Muslim world'.

The Duchess's faith and her experiences influence her life in a practical way. She is President of a charity called Preshal, Gaelic for 'precious', which helps a community 25 miles away in Govan, one of Glasgow's most deprived areas. Preshal deals

with drug and alcohol addictions in a community where poverty and illiteracy are rife. It was founded in 2002 by May Nicholson, an alcoholic from the age of 15, who asked the Duchess to be its President. She freely acknowledges that her title helps with the fundraising, as does the fact that the Duke's grandmother helped raise funds for that area. 'It continues the family tradition of reaching out.' A new building for the charity was opened in November 2013, thanks to donations.

The backgrounds of the charity's founder and its president could hardly be more different, even before Catherine joined the aristocracy. Although the Duchess lost her father, she considers she had a very normal, happy childhood and education, not lavishly rich but she never suffered materially. By contrast, May Nicholson was one of 13, from a very poor background, who had an experience that changed her and gave her a passion to help similar people. May's point of change, says the Duchess, was alcohol and drugs. Her own was her 'indifference' before she joined Moral Rearmament. She says, 'I didn't care, I was hardly aware of people like her, of their existence. I was only interested in getting what I wanted – my education, my friends. I had to change on that basic selfishness that doesn't really give a darn about her kind of people, and I maintain that's as revolutionary a change as her.'

The contrast between the two women helps their cause in the regular talks they give together to groups. 'It has a certain impact: 'How did these two women become friends? They're from the opposite two ends of the social scale.' But we say we have this in common: we both have faith in God, and we believe that people can change, because we both have experienced change.'

The fact that James Graham had a title did not mean much to her. 'I was just very pleasantly surprised and then surprised I liked him as much as I did, because I had a preconception of a whole group of people which I've since learned is such a mistake. I hear people say Americans are dreadful and I react to that now, because I say if you talk about a whole group of people you must talk about individuals. You mustn't judge a whole group of people, it's just so wrong. And the aristocracy has some wonderful people in it and some not so wonderful people. Like any other group of people.'

The Duchess readily acknowledges her privileged life but sees this emanating from the family into which she was born rather than the one into which she married, although she would not deny that being a duchess carries certain advantages. So what are these? Does she have a ladies' maid, for example? She chuckles, as she does a lot. 'No, but I do have my hair done. If I do it myself, it's hit and miss, and I do think it's important.' Apart from the gardener they had and the couple who live with them now, the only other help she has ever had was au pairs when their children were small. She did not have help with their first child, Lady Hermione, born in 1971, but when their first son, James, arrived two years later, her mother came to stay and said she was not returning to Canada until Catherine got some help. 'We have a river and she had visions of when my back was turned…! So I phoned up an au pair agency in London and a very nice Danish girl came along and I never looked back. We had a series of au pairs until the children were all at school.'

The biggest difference in her life when she married James Graham was going from an ordinary 'Miss' to suddenly being the Marchioness of Graham. Before that, she had not been aware of that title at all. 'I was frightened but because I really loved my husband, that gave me the courage to accept it. But I was clear that I should be myself. I don't believe in putting on airs or trying to be what I think a marchioness or a duchess should be. I think you have to be yourself and not act a role. I think people see through that – and it's such a strain. What works for me is to be myself and to think of the people I'm with, not myself. I'm not an actress. It's just like I could never put on an English or Scottish accent. People say, "Oh, you haven't lost your accent," and I say, "No, I'm Canadian, that's who I am." '

One difference she noticed on becoming Duchess was that some people anticipated that she would have more money. She started getting begging letters 'because people assumed that all duchesses must be rich, so that rather amused me.' She was aware she 'shouldn't let the side down' and felt her new role was more demanding. 'If I felt like giving in to certain things, it was more of a challenge not to. People did expect you to maintain certain standards, and not go around looking sloppy.' It was important to 'give the best you knew and not give into your less than best. That's all you can do.' She says the Scots are more down to earth and 'don't believe in a lot of fanfare over titles': membership of a clan is more important. She joins the Duke when he has to go to America in his role as Clan Chief. They had been to Tennessee the previous summer for the gathering of Clan Graham, where the Duke was guest of honour and many turned up in their kilts: they take the whole thing 'terribly seriously, especially as they get older'.

On the whole she does not feel her life is dominated by being a duchess, 'but there are times when it is important to recognise that title and speak for it.' She thinks it is necessary to be 'flexible', which is seen in the variety of her life. There are not many formal expectations of her role but she is asked to speak, open flower shows and the like. Catherine is, however, the only duchess (other than the Duchess of Norfolk) who remains entitled to attend the historical and splendid ceremony of the State Opening of Parliament, and recalls the first occasion: 'I wore an ice-blue silk dress, full-length, and long white gloves up to my elbows.' On her head she wore a diamond tiara – a family heirloom – which she was careful not to put on until she was in the Duke's office within the confines of Whitehall: his aunt had warned her that one peeress had been mugged in daylight with all her jewellery on.

Seated in a line of ladies who would be nearest to the Queen when she arrived, Catherine was feeling excited, if a little nervous, realising she might not know when to curtsey, as there was no one in front of her to follow. She anxiously asked the more experienced peeress next to her when the right moment would be. 'She replied with great serenity, "You'll know." When the Queen entered the Chamber and ascended the small platform, I took a deep breath as she turned around, and curtseyed. I still don't know if I got the timing right or not!'

She also has her speaking engagements and meetings for Preshal. On the personal side, she and the Duke have board meetings with their golf club and policy meetings about it four times a year. The Duke leaves her every Monday morning to go to the House of Lords, returning on Thursday evenings. Prior to the 2010 General Election, he was Shadow Spokesman for Scottish affairs in the House of Lords. The Duke stays in London during the week, not in a luxurious flat but at the Farmers' Club. She often joins him and loves 'meeting interesting people and learning about things that I'm very hazy about. That I like almost more than anything in the world. I find it really fascinating to meet people who have achieved in some form. It's a huge privilege.'

She goes to French conversation classes every week with a friend and has a book club once a month. She also entertains at home or goes out with friends, while generally managing things in the Duke's absence around the home and in the rambling garden. That day it was drizzling, that light Scottish wetness that is almost imperceptible until you touch your hair. No matter, it does not spoil the view. There is much to see in this garden: no fancy topiary or avenues of pleached limes; no modern sculpture or clever maze. Instead it is a gentle, natural place full of variety and possibility: somewhere to roam or sit, reflect or run. The Duchess confesses to having felt 'overwhelmed' by the garden when they first moved into the house and still thinks she has no sense of vision, so is grateful that her lady has a clearer idea.

Running along the back of the house, underneath the windows, is a large manicured lawn with flower borders, perfect for croquet on a warm summer's day. From there, steep grassy banks run down to a fast-flowing stream and continue on the other side of a little bridge. To the right of the banks is a woodland area. Early-sprouting bulbs flower in the walkways and there are views across to Loch Lomond. It must be glorious in the spring. The garden and the house are well matched, the house painted cream with green paintwork, rustic-looking rather than grand or classical.

Back in the dry, hanging up coats and easing off boots in the sort of casually untidy utility area that country houses always have to accommodate children and pets, the Duchess spoke of how their three children feel about their titles in the 21st century. They hardly sit back idly gloating. Lady Hermione, born in 1971, is a clinical psychologist. Their eldest son and heir, James, the Marquis of Graham, born in 1973, works in alternative energies, while the youngest, Lord Ronald Graham, is the lawyer.

The Duchess sees the future of the aristocracy as being 'like the Roman empire'. She thinks it is important to be honest about its good and bad points. 'I think there are certain things to be proud of in the aristocracy – the sense of history, I think that's terribly important. As my husband said, we care about the ancient institutions of this country and if they can stick to the best of the aristocracy and leave behind the stuff that makes it decay, there is a place for it in the way of setting an example, perhaps, standards.' Moral courage is vital. 'You get such a backlash today if you fight for some of the qualities we hold dear. Somehow I think we must be courageous. That's one of the things I admire in my husband.' If moral standards are allowed to be 'pulled down', then 'that's the way of decay.' She decries snobbery. 'I don't think that gets you anywhere. A lot of the aristocracy did care for the people who worked for them and others were extremely cruel and callous.' If aristocracy ignores the better qualities, then it 'deserves to die.'

Many of the aristocracy are related to each other. In the Duke's family there are also links with European aristocracy. The Duke is the Graham family archivist but the Duchess finds it fascinating: 'Quite difficult to follow but I'm gradually picking it up.' Of assistance is the Duke's aunt, his father's sister, Lady Jean Fforde, born in 1920 and still alive at the end of 2013. Now fond of her, the Duchess used to be very nervous of her: 'She's very forthright. It's that old school.' Jean has written two books about her life, which include the family's connection with the royal family of Monaco. This is via the Hamilton family: Jean's mother, Mary, was daughter of the 12th Duke of Hamilton and married the 6th Duke of Montrose. Mary was brought up in ancient Brodick Castle on the Isle of Arran, in the Hamilton family from the 16th century. When Mary's father died in 1895 without male heirs, his title passed to a cousin and Brodick passed to Mary. After her death, it was given to the National Trust for Scotland.

It is an earlier Hamilton, Anne, the 3rd Duchess of Hamilton, an ancestor of the present Duke of Montrose, who is the Duchess's chosen predecessor. She admires her strength and her organisational skills: as a young woman, initially against the background of the Civil War, Anne had to manage both Brodick and the vast Hamilton Palace. It is not surprising that the Duchess finds such life stories interesting. To Catherine Montrose, it is people who matter.

Opposite: Brodick Castle.

IN HER OWN RIGHT:

ANNE, DUCHESS OF HAMILTON

(1632–1716)

Lady Anne Hamilton, born in 1632, is one of history's rareties: she became a duchess in her own right. As the Duchess of Hamilton, Anne may not be a true predecessor of today's Duchess of Montrose but she is an ancestor of her husband, James: his maternal great-grandfather was 12th Duke of Hamilton. The Hamiltons were one of the most powerful families in Scotland: the current Duke, the 16th, is still its premier peer.

Catherine Montrose says of Anne, 'I was very inspired by her because she had such big responsibilities from such a young age, when I was still turning handsprings. Of course, in those days they had so many staff to execute their plans and very often the financial means, which today, by and large, are simply not available.' Catherine has in mind Anne's greatest legacy: her management of Hamilton Palace, near Glasgow. The Hamiltons' main seat, it was once the largest and most

Opposite: Anne, Duchess of Hamilton.

magnificent country house in Britain, possibly in Europe. Anne's organisational skills, which included her meticulous keeping of household records, has given Britain probably its most comprehensive understanding of life in a 17th-century noble household. That Anne managed to recover the Palace after its confiscation in the Civil War is in itself a testament to her determination.

The Hamiltons had already been established in Lanarkshire for a few centuries before Anne was born; an early Hamilton had been given a barony in the area by King Robert I around 1315. The family would gain other significant lands, including ancient Brodick Castle on Arran – whose image features on today's Scottish £20 notes – and Lennoxlove, their current seat, not to mention lands in London.

In 1474, the Hamiltons became linked permanently with royalty when the 1st Lord Hamilton married Mary Stewart, a daughter of King James II. Their grandson, James, 2nd Earl of Arran, became Regent of Scotland in 1542 to the infant Mary, Queen of Scots; James was next in line to the throne, and the family's power and prominence increased. To reflect his status, James began building Hamilton Palace in 1549. However, in 1579, after his death, Mary's enemies besieged the town of Hamilton and demolished his palace. James' son Lord John began rebuilding it in 1591. In 1599, Lord John was elevated to 1st Marquis of Hamilton by King James VI for services to his mother, Mary.

John's son, another James – 2nd Marquis and grandfather to Anne – became a favourite of the King. He followed the King to England and made his home permanently in London. In 1624, he was made Lord Steward of the Royal Household but died in 1625. While in England he had left the running of his Scottish estates to his wife, the Marchioness Anna; Anne would not meet her grandmother until she was ten years old.

Lady Anne was born in Whitehall Palace, London, to the 3rd Marquis of Hamilton, another James, and Lady Mary Feilding, a niece of the mighty Duke of Buckingham. They had been betrothed in 1620 when James was 14 and Mary just seven. In 1638, when Anne was six, Mary died, aged 25. As Anne's older sister and younger brothers had also died, their father was deprived of a male heir. Only Anne and her younger sister, Susanna, remained. At the time the family estates were not entailed on the male line, which meant that when he died, they would pass to his eldest daughter, Anne.

Although James knew his mother had run the Hamilton estates very ably after his father decamped to London, it was a tricky time politically. Charles I was now King, and James

was his chief adviser in Scottish matters. Charles wanted to introduce an English liturgy to the church in Scotland, but James had been raised as a Presbyterian and was eventually swayed by the Covenanters, those who opposed Charles' changes. James tried to act as a mediator between Charles and the Covenanters, which aroused the suspicions of some staunch Royalists and made James' position difficult.

Although he was close to his daughters, he felt it imperative that the family's interests be represented by a man. James made provision for his only brother, William, Earl of Lanark, to succeed him and inherit everything; William would see that Anne and Susanna married well. That year, 1642, the Civil War began in earnest. James sent Susanna to live with their maternal grandmother in England, Anne to his mother at Hamilton Palace. Aged ten, Anne was separated from her sister and sent four hundred miles away to a country she had never visited, to live with a grandmother she had never met. To cheer her up she was given a new silken gown made from material that had belonged to her mother, and she was allowed to take with her three of her English ladies.

Hamilton Palace was a gruelling two-week coach ride from London and James accompanied them that first time to introduce Anne to her grandmother. Although often said to have been a harsh character, the Dowager Marchioness had much energy, was musical and took pride in keeping meticulous accounts of the Hamilton estates. Fortunately the pair got on straight away. Apart from providing Anne with academic tuition, she took her riding around the vast estates, visiting tenants, dealing with rents,

Engraved for Lambert's History of London.

A Gate belonging to the Old Palace of Whitehall.

Published by M. Jones, N.º 1, Paternoster Row, May 21, 1805.

Whitehall Palace, London, where Anne was born.

supervising their chamberlains – every aspect of estate management.

In 1643, Anne was delighted when King Charles made her father the 1st Duke of Hamilton. But in 1644, James's enemies renewed their efforts to discredit him. This time, Charles listened and imprisoned James, but freed him in 1646. The two were reconciled – Charles made him Hereditary Keeper of Holyrood Palace, Edinburgh and James remained loyal to the King.

Then, in 1647, the Dowager Marchioness died. The following year James led an army for Charles against the English Parliamentarians. At Preston, he was disastrously defeated by Cromwell's troops and imprisoned. He refused to give Cromwell the names of his English allies in exchange for his life. In March 1649, James, 1st Duke of Hamilton, was executed, a few weeks after the King.

Anne and Susanna heard the news of their father's death at their aunt's castle in Fife, where James had sent them. His brother William duly became 2nd Duke of Hamilton and made his will. His only son had died and he had five daughters. In reciprocation for James having favoured him above his own daughters, William did the same for his niece, making Anne heir to all the Hamilton estates. Fatally wounded while fighting for Charles II at Worcester, William died on 12 September 1651. Aged 19, Lady Anne became the Duchess of Hamilton.

Oliver Cromwell.

In theory she was Scotland's greatest heiress; in practice she was almost ruined. Her father and uncle had incurred huge debts as a result of the Civil War. Scotland was part of Cromwell's Commonwealth, and all who had supported the King were punished. The Hamilton lands were forfeited and fines were payable. Anne was also now responsible for Susanna and their cousins. For a while they lived in a barn in the woods next to Hamilton Palace. But it did not quell Anne's spirit;

she is said to have fired a cannon at Roundheads as they passed by but, impressed by her courage, the commander took no action. Anne's favourite saying was 'A given-up battle is never won.'

She even faced a claim to her title by the Earl of Abercorn, her father's second cousin, who challenged her uncle's will. Fortunately by then she had a husband to help her: in April 1656 Anne married Lord William Douglas, Earl of Selkirk. Theirs seemed an unlikely match. Anne was two years older and rather plain; William was good-looking. He was also Catholic: such a marriage was forbidden by her uncle's will, so before the wedding William converted to Protestantism. Whatever the true reasons for their marriage, it would be a long and affectionate union.

They immediately set about raising money to pay the fines demanded by Cromwell's government, selling many of the family's possessions and some of the lands left in their hands. That enabled them to reclaim Hamilton Palace; they could now defend Abercorn's claim, and succeeded. Life improved further in 1660 with the Restoration. Charles II granted Anne's request to make her husband Duke of Hamilton. Following her father and uncle, Anne was 3rd Duchess of Hamilton, and although William was called 3rd Duke, his title would not pass; their descendants would take the title from Anne. Charles II also repaid to Anne a large debt owed by his late father to hers. It was a promising start. The couple made Hamilton Palace their permanent home and began turning it back into a fine house and somewhere to raise a family. The first of 13 children, Mary, arrived in 1657.

It is extremely fortunate that Anne had learned so much from her grandmother in keeping records and that they were preserved, for, in the 1920s, Hamilton Palace was demolished. The destruction is now regarded as one of the greatest losses to Britain's heritage, and a major project is being undertaken to create a virtual world of the Palace, with the help of documents such as Anne's. The changes she and William undertook transformed it into the magnificent building it became.

The Palace had not changed very much since Anne first saw it. It was a substantial stone building laid out over a courtyard with extensive gardens, facing north towards Glasgow. The main wings were three storeys high with steeply pitched slated roofs, and at either side of the north front was a tower. The north front entrance itself was in the style of the previous century; above it a gallery ran along its length. The windows had wooden shutters on the lower half and diamond-paned glass above. Outside were 'offices', like the brew house, bakery, laundry. Inside were dining rooms and drawing rooms, bedrooms for the master and mistress in one wing, other family members and staff in another.

Before the Civil War the walls had been adorned with fine sets of tapestries and paintings; these had had to be sold, although some found their way back. Now, furnishings were replaced and the decor updated. Busy with the family and estate matters, Anne did not take much interest in the minutiae of the running of the household, which had between 30 and 50 servants, almost all men, but she was a competent organiser. She liked to keep up with new inventions: in 1691, for example, she bought one of the earliest mangles for the laundry. Her special interest lay in the extensive gardens, where she loved walking or sitting under the fir trees. William was equally enthusiastic

and planned much of the work himself. Today's Duchess of Montrose might be envious of their achievements but a regular gardener had always been employed at the Palace, and Anne could look to William for design ideas.

Although garden fashions changed with the Restoration, William retained something of the old walled gardens with their profusion of flowers, beyond which lay the Statue Garden and Pond Garden. From the herb garden came culinary and medicinal herbs; from the kitchen garden a surprising variety of vegetables and salads. William introduced and became an expert on fruit trees, especially peaches, apricots and cherries, for which the Palace became famous. For a sport enjoyed by many Hamiltons, he had a new bowling green laid out.

The Duke and Duchess are particularly credited with what is known as their 'Great Design', which they started planning in 1682. For someone of Anne's status, a house like Hamilton Palace meant not only having a family home but one which reflected her position and in which, if required, she could entertain the monarch. As head of the House of Hamilton, she had to pass on the Palace for posterity. By 1682, their surviving daughters were married, their sons – apart from their wayward son and heir, James, the Earl of Arran – were settled in their careers; now they could concentrate on the rebuilding.

They looked to other great houses, some of which William had visited; they read books on architecture and studied plans of great French houses visited by their son James on his Grand Tour. The work began in 1684. Starting with the 'offices', some were altered, others demolished. The north front of the Palace was retained as

Hamilton Palace.

it contained the principal public rooms and the long gallery but the other three sides of the quadrangle were demolished. Two entirely new wings were built. The main entrance was now from the courtyard formed by the two wings, so that the whole building now faced south towards Edinburgh. Its new style was classical, with carved pillars and large plain windows.

As the household had to continue living in the house, the demolition and reconstruction were done over a period of time. Although they used experts, it is clear the Duke and Duchess played a leading part in the planning. But in 1694, before the transformation was complete, the

Duke died, aged 60, following a stroke. Anne was heartbroken. A few months later she also lost her sister, Susanna.

When Anne had recovered sufficiently she tried to draw James into the plans but without much success. Nevertheless, for political reasons she passed her title to him, so he became 4th Duke of Hamilton. Talk of a union with England convinced Anne that the Hamiltons should have a male representative in Scotland's Parliament to oppose it: Anne was a leading figure of the group which opposed a union on the grounds that it would not resolve Scotland's economic problems.

Although Anne passed her title to James, she was conscious of his unreliability, so she retained control of the Hamilton estates. With her mind on posterity, and despite suffering from arthritis, she continued the work on the Palace. The best craftsmen available were employed for the interior. Particularly magnificent was the panelling in the principal rooms, for which a master carver transformed the plain oak panels into elaborate works of art. The new Palace, a glory of its time, was virtually finished in 1701 to much praise.

In the grounds, Anne continued her improvements by laying out avenues of trees, and as always met the present head-on and looked to the future. When James was killed in a duel in London in 1712, she delighted in her ten-year-old grandson, the 5th Duke, who was in her care, and, in summer 1716, sent him to Eton, the first time a Hamilton had been educated in England. Shortly afterwards, on 17 October, Anne died. Born in the reign of Charles I, she lived until the reign of George I. She had outlived her husband, sisters, seven of her children, and some grandchildren.

The Palace remained the principal seat of the Hamiltons for the next two centuries. Its golden age started in 1822, when the 10th Duke enlarged and improved it again, cramming the huge apartments with treasures from around the world. Royalty and the glitterati of the Victorian era were sumptuously entertained there. But the Duke and his successors had caused mounting debts. The demise of the Palace began with a major sale of its treasures by the 12th Duke in 1882; he also leased out mineral rights in the Palace grounds and coalmining began.

The 12th Duke subsequently spent time at Brodick Castle, where his ancestor, Anne, had lived during 1651; as Duchess, she had managed it along with the other Hamilton properties. When the 12th Duke died there in 1895 without a male

heir, his title passed to a distant cousin and Brodick passed to his daughter, Lady Mary Hamilton, who married the 6th Duke of Montrose.

Hamilton Palace served as a naval hospital during the Great War, but mining threatened its stability. The colliery company refused to give up its lease and following a massive sale of contents and fittings, the Palace was sold in 1921 to demolition contractors. It took eight years to completely demolish.

Duchess Anne's legacy lives on elsewhere, too. She invigorated the economy of the poor Isle of Arran. In the town of Hamilton she rebuilt schools and established a woollen industry. She supported poor scholars, provided bursaries and endowed churches. Such was her contribution that she became known in that part of Scotland as 'Good Duchess Anne'. As Catherine Montrose says, she would have no idea how grateful posterity would continue to be.

Portrait of William, Duke of Hamilton.

NORTHERN LIGHT:
THE DUCHESS OF NORTHUMBERLAND

Jane Northumberland can lay claim to at least three 'firsts' since becoming Duchess of Northumberland in 1995. She is the first in that role who is not from the aristocracy; in 2009, she was the first woman to be made Lord Lieutenant of Northumberland (a role dating back to Henry VIII, by which the Queen, on the advice of her Prime Minister, appoints a person to be her representative in each county in the United Kingdom); and at Alnwick Castle, the family seat of the Dukes, she has created the first major garden in the United Kingdom since the Second World War.

'There's an idea that to become a duchess you have to be from an aristocratic background,' Jane says. 'I would say the really important thing, whatever you do in life, whoever you are, is to be yourself.' But it was not a position she had sought or expected. Unlike the role of Lord

Opposite: The Duchess of Northumberland with Fuzzy the dog.

Lieutenant, which she was honoured to accept, that of duchess was greeted less enthusiastically. It had not been anticipated when, in 1979, as 21-year-old Jane Richard, she married Lord Ralph (pronounced 'Rafe') George Algernon Percy, aged 22. Ralph's father, Hugh, was the 10th Duke of Northumberland and Ralph's older brother, Henry Percy, known as Harry, was the heir to the title. The prospect of Ralph becoming Duke therefore seemed remote.

On marriage, Lady Ralph Percy, as Jane became, joined a family dating back to the 9th century, and which during the Middle Ages had been one of the most powerful in England. From one of their castles, Warkworth, given to them by Edward III in 1332, the Percys virtually ruled the north of England and protected it from the Scots; they also had the security of nearby Alnwick Castle, their other great fortress since 1309. Alnwick is one of Britain's most spectacular castles, and the Duke and Duchess live there part of the year.

In 1377, Richard II made his friend Henry de Percy the first Earl of Northumberland. The Earl's son, born at Alnwick, was Harry, nicknamed 'Hotspur' for his speed and eagerness in battle; he would be immortalised by Shakespeare. Father and son later turned against Richard II and supported the man who became Henry IV, until changing allegiance again. After a significant military career Hotspur, and then his father, died in battle but successive generations of Percys have continued to make their mark, particularly on the county of Northumberland. Today, Jane Northumberland is doing just that, most famously as creator of The Alnwick Garden, now a charitable trust of which she is one of the trustees.

In 1988, Ralph's brother, Harry, a godson of the Queen, became 11th Duke at the age of 35. However, Harry suffered poor health and was constantly on medication. In October 1995, he was found dead by his valet in another Percy property, Syon House in Middlesex; the autopsy declared he had died of heart failure. Despite some well-publicised romances, he had never married or had children, so Ralph was now 12th Duke. Although Ralph and Jane had already moved to Northumberland so Ralph could help to run the estates, it was still a dramatic change for the couple. Jane was 37, Ralph approaching 39.

Jane, petite, slim and smooth-skinned, has long since adjusted to the transition to Duchess and, despite a frantically busy life, looks years younger than her age. As a girl she wanted to be a champion figure skater and daily spent hours practising. She is a woman of many interests, one of which is taxidermy. In her flat in one of London's most desirable areas, tall vases of mauve blooms and a big bowl of pink roses are reflected in a huge

mirror, in front of which a marble table displays two large animal skulls and a stuffed hamster: just a tiny sample of her collection.

She and Ralph met at a house party when she was 16, he 18. It coincided with a difficult time in Jane's life; her parents were going through a divorce. 'Ralph was part of a huge family and we were really happy to get married very young and set up our own home.' Her father, a stockbroker, has since died, although he remarried, and her mother – 'a very keen gardener' – has remarried twice. Jane has two sisters and a brother to whom she is close despite living at a distance: one sister lives in the north of Scotland, the other sister and brother live in the Scottish Borders.

When Ralph went to Oxford University to study history, Jane was at a college nearby. He was also very interested in art. 'He loved drawing and painting, and that's a direction he'd like to have taken.' After Oxford, Ralph was 'gently edged into land management' by his father, doing a correspondence degree course at university while working in the estate office at Arundel Castle in Sussex for the Duke of Norfolk's estate.

By then they had two of their four children, Lady Catherine, born in 1982, and the heir, George, Earl Percy, in 1984. They were looking for a suitable house to buy in West Sussex but were enticed up to Northumberland by the Duke. 'We came up to Alnwick for the weekend with two tiny children and we were shown a beautiful Georgian farmhouse.' The agent told them it was becoming available after two hundred years and wondered if they would like it. 'He told us, "You can have it for free but we'd like Ralph to work in the estate office."' She laughs. 'And of course he was thrilled.' Jane, however, was not. 'I couldn't see myself living in Northumberland, particularly leaving friends in Sussex, so I was a little worried.' With hindsight, Jane thinks that, considering Harry spent a lot of time in London, it was all 'obviously a set up! Ralph's a countryman, so it was probably the right thing and he could support Harry in running the Estate.'

Jane is Scottish and was brought up in Edinburgh and, as a child, the Borders. 'You never really went south from Edinburgh, you only went north, so I didn't know anything about Northumberland. I hardly knew where it was!' She wondered what she was going to do 'in the middle of nowhere.' She thought she might commute to Edinburgh and train for something when the children were older, but that possibility evaporated when Ralph inherited unexpectedly in 1995. Yet she knew that 'becoming a duchess in the old sense and just opening things was not something I could ever have done.'

Their first concerns were practical ones. By then with four children, their youngest, Lord Max, born in 1990, they had to move out of their manageable farmhouse into vast Alnwick Castle, now known to the world as the setting for Hogwarts School in the Harry Potter films. It was like living in a museum. She says she and Ralph wanted to create some sort of home within the medieval walls for their family unit, which was very important to them, and also make big changes. 'This wasn't the way we wanted to live and it wasn't the right environment in which we want to bring up our children.' The Duchess, with help from designers, introduced bold colours, striking and cosy soft furnishings, and made a beautiful home for her family which is much admired by visitors during the opening season.

They also needed to look ahead and consider George, the heir to it all. 'In order to have a sense of duty, he had to love the Castle and want to bring his children up in it. That had to happen in his formative years, and we didn't have a lot of time.' They undertook a full restoration of Alnwick, including a new roof, so that George 'can move in there and not have to do anything major for two generations.'

It was also difficult because inevitably there were expectations of her in her new role as Duchess, and comparisons too. Her mother-in-law, Elizabeth, by then the Dowager Duchess, remained much loved in Northumberland until her death in 2012. Jane adored her. 'She did great things but in the old-fashioned way, and she often used to say to me, "You've done so much, I feel I've done so little compared to you," and I'd tell her how wrong she was. Wherever I went I was asked about Elizabeth.' She was the daughter of the Duke of Buccleuch, but her background made no difference to anyone in Northumberland. 'She was loved because she was who she was: she had no delusions of grandeur. She was the same person to whoever she met.'

Jane too seems devoid of any snobbishness but is quite different. 'I think I have been a huge challenge to everyone at Alnwick. I see this as positive rather than negative because I was the first Duchess who, every single job to be done in the castle, I could do myself. I'd cooked for 16 years, I'd run a house, I'd gardened, we'd bought up four children and I wasn't someone who needed to be told what to do.' To her the family was the most important consideration and she decided she must 'just get on and do what had to be done'.

Along the way she learned a valuable lesson. 'If you are married to a duke, you have to develop a very thick skin. You can't worry what people think about you because, as my husband reminded me, you won't win. So just get on and do the job and remember why you're doing it and hopefully, if your values are right, everything else will be right.'

That thick skin has been needed. Restless in her new role, she had to find her own niche. Ralph's suggestion that she restore Alnwick Castle's derelict garden led to her decision to create a new one. Today, many community project groups are involved with and helped by the garden, including those supporting children from deprived areas. Nevertheless, Jane and the project have attracted much criticism over the years for different reasons, partly economic, partly aesthetic; established garden designers have been particularly damning.

At the beginning, Jane did not know what the ramifications would be but a recent Economic Impact Study confirmed that The Alnwick Garden has generated £150 million for the region in the last ten years. When the area was hit by foot and mouth disease, in one year alone 'one hundred farmers applied for planning permission to turn their farmhouses or outbuildings into bed and breakfasts, and the buzzwords at the time were regeneration and diversification. The Alnwick Garden was at the forefront of that. It was a terrible time and The Garden offered a lifeline to many people, completely by chance.'

Apart from boasting one of the world's biggest treehouses, within which is a renowned restaurant, The Alnwick Garden also contains the famous Poison Garden, which inspired Jane to write a series of books called *The Poison Diaries*. They are just one of the businesses that she has started – 'I'm someone who has to keep busy' – which include a clothing range, a

Alnwick Castle, Northumberland.

range of saucy-sounding cocktails, and in 2013 an aphrodisiac marmalade, after discovering an 800-year-old recipe in the dungeons of Alnwick Castle. But as Duchess of Northumberland her life consists of far more than this. She and the Duke are Patrons of more than 160 charities; Jane is particularly involved with fostering and encouraging voluntary and welfare organisations. She estimates that 80 per cent of her time is taken

up with her duties as Duchess, largely because of the charities, and around 20 per cent as Lord Lieutenant. The Duchess was awarded the Variety Club Silver Heart, its highest accolade, for her services to charities in the North East.

Only too aware of the area's economic problems, Jane has the chance to discuss them with local people, not least in her role as Lord Lieutenant. The people of the North East, she says, are wonderful: they care about you and do not mind who you are or what your background is. They are 'straight talking, and I love that.' Some people have told her that if their parents, dyed-in-the-wool Labour voters, could see them sitting down to lunch with her in The Treehouse, 'they'd turn in their grave', while at the same time acknowledging she has done a good job and helped to bring jobs to the area. In November 2013, the Duchess was awarded an honorary degree by Northumbria University in recognition for her significant contribution to the region.

Until 1871, the responsibilities of the Lord

Lieutenant included controlling the military forces of the Crown in the county. Today it involves organising all official Royal visits to the county and escorting the Royal Family member; presenting decorations where the recipient cannot attend an Investiture; and presenting The Queen's special awards. During 2013, Jane's duties included presenting Northumberland residents in a ceremony at Alnwick Castle with the distinguished British Empire Award, for dedicated voluntary work within their communities. In 2011, she gave a huge party at Alnwick Castle and The Alnwick Garden for thousands of unpaid carers and volunteers in Northumberland, to formally recognise the work they do and thank everyone. She was delighted the Queen accepted her invitation to attend: 'It was an important event for the North East.' The Prince of Wales, as Patron of the Alnwick Garden Restoration Project, has visited a few times, and, in 2012, he carried out his first official tour of Northumberland and stayed with Jane and Ralph at Alnwick Castle.

Of the relevance of her title of Duchess today, apart from the impact it must give to the many charities she is associated with, she says that, 'The Castle is what it's all about. With an historical estate like Alnwick it's a focal point, and the Percy flag flies when my husband's home. We're in Scotland half the year when the castle is open to the public.' They live at Alnwick during the winter, and in the summer they commute from their home in Scotland, Burncastle, near Lauder in Berwickshire. 'It is important not to be away too much from Alnwick because otherwise, like an absentee landlord, it never really works.' Their association with the Castle would then become less relevant and become simply a business. She thinks that

people in the area are proud of the Castle and that it gives relevance to community life.

Jane takes note of people's views and is keen to learn what can be done to improve things in The Alnwick Garden. 'I go pretty much unnoticed and I like to sit with a cup of tea in The Garden and watch people to see what's working and what's not and what I could do better.' One day she was sitting in The Treehouse waiting for a journalist to call for an interview. The phone rang, which she answered, only to find it was a man complaining about the service he had received in the restaurant the week before. She asked for his name and phone number and what his problem was. He told her he was a tradesman and used to eat in The Treehouse once a month. On the last occasion service had taken too long, and he did not like the bread. 'He wasn't happy! I listened to him and said, "Someone will call you back." He said, "How do I know someone will ring?" I said, "I guarantee someone will ring in the next hour," and he said, "Can I ask who I'm talking to?" I thought, "Oh dear, he's going to be embarrassed." I said, "Well, funnily enough it's the Duchess of Northumberland and I just happened to be here." The phone went quiet and he said, "I'm so sorry, if I'd known I was going to get you…" I said, "You couldn't have known. I've never picked up the phone before in The Treehouse, and it shouldn't matter who I am – if you have a grievance, we'll deal with it.' When the manager rang him back he told me that the poor man was embarrassed and apologetic to have got me!'

Jane does not stand on ceremony. She thinks the importance of the title of duchess generally is: 'Irrelevant. I think if you're doing what I'm doing it can open a door, but there's a lot of people waiting to knock you down when you get through that door, so it's how you handle things from the minute you enter. In today's world you're only as good as what you do, which is the way it should be. If you do something and you don't do it well, whether you're duchess or not, you've failed.'

Inevitably, where there is a title, especially one that has much wealth to go with it, there is someone waiting to challenge it. Jane estimates they get about three claims a year. In 2009, one was made by a New Zealander, a former Olympic hockey player. He asked the Queen for the exhumation of the 5th Earl, who died in 1560, to see if the DNA matched his. Jane says for years someone has stood outside an Underground station handing out leaflets saying he should be the Duke of Northumberland. A well-known musician born in the area made a claim too. 'We've received several such letters. We'll never know. I'm sure the ancestors were doing all sorts of things they shouldn't have done!' She laughs.

The future of the aristocracy, she believes, is 'about bricks and mortar. I think the aristocracy is nothing without the buildings. Alnwick Castle and Syon House are far more important than any duke or duchess that's in it. The buildings will go on and on.' In 2009, the Duke and Duchess celebrated seven hundred years of his family at Alnwick. 'The people in those buildings will come and go and they are an important employer. That's their major role.'

But owning estates is far from plain sailing. In 2012, heavy rain in the north-east of England caused the collapse of a culvert on land owned by the Northumberland estates. The ensuing flooding washed away land and foundations and caused houses to be demolished. The result for the estates was a repair bill of around £12 million which was found from funds which had been set aside for maintenance of the estates' buildings and projects. To replace the funds, during 2014 the estates are going to sell by auction 80 pieces of artwork and other treasures worth around £15 million from Alnwick and Syon House. The sale will be led by the marble statue of Aphrodite which dates from 41–54 AD and was originally bought by Hugh Percy, the first Duke of Northumberland, husband of Jane's chosen predecessor.

Jane remains concerned to ensure continuation. The Garden at Alnwick is not yet finished and there are plans for further development, including an adventure playground. Contrary to press statements, she is not 'handing over' the gardens in 2015. 'I'm very involved every day with what's going on at Alnwick and you can't carry on like that for the rest of your life – or maybe I can – but what I said was that ideally [by 2015], I'll have finished fundraising and built it.' She needs to raise another £20 million before then. Once it is finished she wants to find the best people to operate it and she will take a back seat. 'But Alnwick's there for life for me, and if ever I see it go wrong I'll step back in immediately. I'll always be a trustee of it.'

Their other major property, Syon House, with its 200-acre park, is the last surviving ducal residence complete with its country estate in Greater London. It, too, is open to the public. Historically used as a summer residence, it has been in the family since 1594 when Henry Percy, the 9th Earl of Northumberland, acquired it by marriage, and stands on the site of Syon Abbey. Favoured by Henry VIII's first wife, Catherine of Aragon, the Abbey became embroiled in the turmoil of his divorce. In 1547, the King's coffin was brought

The Alnwick Garden, created by Jane Northumberland.

to Syon on its way to Windsor for burial. During the night it burst open and in the morning dogs were found licking up the remains; it was regarded as divine retribution for his desecration of the Abbey. The estate became Crown property and then the possession of the 1st Duke of Somerset, before passing into the Percy family. Jane, who designed the courtyard garden, wants to let Syon on a long-term basis: none of the family wants to live in it but someone needs to. She does not mind who it is, as long as it is 'good for the house'.

Continuity of possession of family properties was interrupted in the mid-19th century with the end of the family's ownership of Northumberland House, one of London's great mansions. Situated at the end of the Strand, latterly overlooking Trafalgar Square, it had found itself in the middle of an increasingly commercial area. It was compulsorily purchased by the Metropolitan Board of Works, which wanted to build a new road to the Embankment. It was demolished in 1874; Northumberland Avenue runs there now.

Their house on the Dryburgh estate in the Scottish Borders, known for its fishing, is let out for that purpose. Ralph and their children are keen fishermen, and Jane says she gets many of her ideas in its river, when she has the chance to go there. In Surrey there is the Albury estate, where Elizabeth, the Dowager Duchess, lived, dividing her time between there and Alnwick. 'Our children are in London now and Northumberland is a long way to come for a weekend, so they might all go down to Albury. They're all very close. They make time to go and see each other, which is really nice.'

The children had another reason to meet up at Alnwick in June 2013 when Lady Melissa – 'Missy' – a former professional tennis player and now a tennis coach, was married in the local church. The reception and dinner were held in the castle and a firework display for the town followed in the evening. The groom, Thomas van Straubenzee, is a close friend of Princes William and Harry, who were both guests. The Duchess of Cambridge could not attend, as she was due to give birth. Not surprisingly the occasion attracted huge crowds in the little town.

Security must have been a nightmare on that occasion but it is always important at Alnwick, where a big security team works around the clock. Jane estimates that there are about three hundred staff on the Northumberland estates, but not all in the castle. Additional staff are employed at Albury, particularly for the land, and a few at Syon. The ruin of Warkworth Castle is different because it is leased to English Heritage on a 99-year arrangement.

Jane is not sure what her children's attitudes to their own titles are, but, 'if anything, the problems they've had have been from other people, so I think they keep a low profile and get on with their work.' George, the heir, is not yet married. What would Jane's reaction be if he brought home someone whom she considered unsuitable for the job? 'I don't think the job would matter, if she loved my son. Whoever you are, you want someone to love your children as much as you do. The rest should be irrelevant, because everyone does things their own way.'

When George was a child, his parents took steps to protect him in his extremely privileged position. He was due to inherit a large amount of money when he was 18, but before then they went to court to have the inheritance postponed until he was 25. They thought it wrong for any child to have so much money so young and also feared he might be a target for people with the wrong motives. 'It was an old trust that was set up hundreds of years ago, when life expectancy was much lower. You were considered mature at 14 and you might be killed in battle at 16 or 17. We also thought it could take away the incentive for George to have to go out and work.' She has no doubt it was the right thing to do; she has seen with sadness what too much money, too young, can do to a few of the children's friends.

On the issue of whether women should inherit titles, Jane has some misgivings based on practicalities. She thinks either sex could do the same job as well as the other and considers that women on the whole 'are better communicators than men'.

She refers to her chosen predecessor, Elizabeth, who became the first Duchess of Northumberland in 1766 and who she considers the greatest duchess. The male line of the Percys had died out and she was the surviving Percy heiress. She married Sir Hugh Smithson, a Yorkshire squire, who agreed to change his name to Percy and was made the 1st Duke of Northumberland. The important thing was that it continued the Percy bloodline. 'It was a great marriage and they cemented the Northumberland estates really. You get good dukes and bad dukes, and I suppose it would be the same going through the female line.' Elizabeth was also an inspiration to Jane because through her come the recipes that Jane discovered, including the oldest marmalade recipe in the world. Like Jane, Elizabeth kept very busy. 'How she had time to do what she did I don't know. She noticed everything, was intelligent and caring, and even had time to write diaries, which I don't do. She kept housekeeping notes, the price of bread, how much everything cost. She was a very capable lady.'

It raises the question of how Jane and Ralph manage any time together. She comes down to London every two to three weeks for three days, and has meetings about her businesses or to talk about The Garden. That day she had had two morning meetings, a working lunch to talk about the building and fund raising, then the interview; then there were still two meetings to go. She used have time to shop when she came to London but has not done that 'for ages'.

She is aware she may have grandchildren following her daughter's marriage and realises she will have to put time aside for that, but while she is doing 'probably 50 things at once', it is not easy. Hearing what Jane Northumberland has achieved so far, she is bound to have continued success, thanks to her unwavering determination and positive attitude.

Syon House, Middlesex.

16

THE COLLECTOR:
ELIZABETH, FIRST DUCHESS
OF NORTHUMBERLAND
(1716–1776)

Housed in the Breakfast Room at Alnwick Castle is a fascinating display of items, some of the surviving parts of a collection made by Elizabeth, the first Duchess of Northumberland. Gloves worn by Queen Elizabeth I and a nightcap that once warmed the head of Oliver Cromwell share space with statues, miniatures and all manner of curiosities. Elizabeth was born in 1716 in the reign of George I, and her collection, which she kept at the family's London home, Northumberland House, was one of the very few independently assembled by a woman in the Georgian period. Elizabeth was also a diarist and record keeper, to whom today's Duchess looks with admiration and for inspiration. It was also through Elizabeth that the Percy line continued and during whose lifetime the dukedom was created.

Opposite: Elizabeth, first Duchess of Northumberland, attributed to F Lindo (after Sir Joshua Reynolds).

In 1722 the Percy line became extinct with the death of Elizabeth's grandmother, Lady Elizabeth Percy. Lady Elizabeth's father, Josceline, Baron Percy, the 11th Earl of Northumberland, had died in 1670, aged 25, and his only son had died in infancy so, at the age of just four, Lady Elizabeth Percy became the richest heiress in the country. Her estates included Alnwick, Northumberland House in London, Syon House, Middlesex, and Petworth House in West Sussex.

Despite her riches, life was not always easy for the young Lady Elizabeth. She was pestered by suitors and widowed twice by the time she was 16. Her third husband was Charles Seymour, the 6th Duke of Somerset, nicknamed 'the Proud Duke' because of his legendary eccentric pomposity. As part of the marriage settlement he was obliged to adopt the name of Percy, although Elizabeth released him from this when she reached her majority. Overbearing and snobbish, the Duke did not make an ideal husband for Lady Elizabeth. When she died in 1722, all her Percy estates vested in the dukedom of Somerset.

Of their children, the 6th Duke and his Duchess had only one son, Algernon. With his wife, Frances, he had two children: a son, Viscount Beauchamp, the heir, and a daughter, Elizabeth, who was to become Duchess of Northumberland – a title that was not foreseen. In 1740, when she was 24, Elizabeth married a Yorkshire squire, Sir Hugh Smithson, from a family of modest origins and prepared to spend her life in his family's comfortable, if provincial, setting of Stanwick Hall. There was no reason to suppose that the couple would advance their social status.

However, in 1744, Viscount Beauchamp died suddenly of smallpox, aged 19. His sister Elizabeth thus became heir, after her father, Algernon, to some of the Somerset estates and all of the Percy estates of her grandmother. Her position needed to be protected. Her grandfather, the 6th Duke of Somerset, had objected to her marriage to Sir Hugh Smithson and was upset by the loss of his grandson, the only male heir. The Duke asked the King, now George II, to recreate the earldom of Northumberland; the idea was that he would take the title 1st Earl of Northumberland under a new creation,* with a special remainder to another grandson. This would cut out Elizabeth and ensure that the Percy estates stayed with the Dukes of Somerset. At an audience with the King, Sir Hugh successfully argued against this.

Then, in 1748, the Duke of Somerset died and Elizabeth's father, Algernon, became 7th Duke.

* It was a new creation because the title was restricted to male heirs and so on the death of the 11th Earl, leaving only a daughter, the title had become extinct.

He inherited the Percy estates that had been his mother's, as well as the smaller Somerset estates. He was also created Baron Percy to preserve the name, and persuaded the King to make him 1st Earl of Northumberland under the new creation. The King also agreed that on Algernon's death the title of Earl and the Percy estates would pass to Algernon's son-in-law, Sir Hugh, and subsequently to Sir Hugh's heirs by Elizabeth. The continuation of the Percy line was assured.

Algernon died in 1750. In the absence of male heirs to the Somerset dukedom a distant relative became 8th Duke of Somerset and Sir Hugh duly became 2nd Earl of Northumberland. Elizabeth inherited her father's baronetcy, becoming Baroness Percy in her own right, and by an Act of Parliament Hugh was allowed to assume the name of Percy.

Within ten years of marrying, Hugh and Elizabeth had become Earl and Countess of Northumberland; their social ascent had begun. Inevitably this sudden elevation, particularly of Hugh – Elizabeth was, after all, the daughter of a Duke – caused envy and scorn, due largely to the great increase in wealth he now enjoyed from the Percy estates. The Prime Minister, Robert Walpole, was particularly jealous of Hugh's rise and put it about that his grandfather had been a coachman. Undeterred, Hugh took his seat in the House of Lords in 1750 and in 1753 was appointed a Lord of the Bedchamber to George II and Lord Lieutenant of Northumberland. Made a Knight of the Garter, Hugh continued to enjoy popularity with the next King, George III, to whom he became a Privy Counsellor and his Lord Lieutenant of Ireland.

Opposite: Queen Charlotte.

Elizabeth, too, enjoyed the trappings of wealth that their new status brought. She became a constant presence at social events and in 1761 was appointed a Lady of the Bedchamber to Queen Charlotte, a position she held until 1770. With Hugh she improved the great Percy estates, which had been somewhat neglected. As they held posts within the Royal Household, the couple spent much of their time at Northumberland House on the Strand. One of the largest mansions in London, with around 150 rooms and a garden leading down to the Thames, it was already old, having been completed in 1605. The couple updated it according to contemporary styles into a fashionable urban residence; there Elizabeth hosted official receptions and loved to put on lavish entertainments for which she became famous.

From the beginning, Elizabeth and Hugh were patrons of leading painters and craftsmen and collected art at an extravagant level, including many Old Masters. Contemporary artists also enjoyed their patronage, particularly Canaletto, and the couple became trendsetters in the world of art and architecture. Hugh was one of the chief patrons of the young architect, Robert Adam, and employed him at Syon House and Alnwick Castle. However, it seems Elizabeth always shared with Hugh the choices they made, and she was her husband's greatest source of inspiration and his most vociferous supporter.

In 1761, they used Adam to remodel the interior of Syon House, for which he looked to classical Rome; it is said that the Adam neo-classical style was initiated at Syon. Adam was joined by the landscape architect Lancelot 'Capability' Brown, who laid out Syon's grounds in the fashionable style of the English Landscape Movement. In the 21st century the development of the estates continues under Jane Northumberland, including her refashioning of the courtyard garden at Syon and the creation of The Alnwick Garden.

Hugh and Elizabeth's ascendancy continued. In 1766, Hugh's political ambitions suffered a setback when the posts he had set his sights on, of Lord Chamberlain and the Master of the Horse, went elsewhere. He complained that he had received no mark of favour for his work in Ireland, so the new Prime Minister, William Pitt the Elder, suggested a step up in the peerage from Earl to Marquess. However, the ambitious Hugh rejected the offer and held out for a dukedom. Although he was anxious not to upset Pitt at the beginning of his term of office, the King granted it and thus Hugh and Elizabeth became the first Duke and Duchess of Northumberland.

As shown in the diaries she kept, part of which were published in 1926, Elizabeth was fascinated by pomp and ceremony, dress and jewels, and was said to have travelled with more footmen and coaches than the Queen. Fortunately for history, Elizabeth's fascination with display found an outlet that others could share. Her passion for collecting was fostered by the period during which, as an educated and wealthy aristocrat, she was fortunate to live: the Age of Enlightenment, a time of reason and learning that flourished across Europe and America from around 1680 to 1820.

Collecting was usually reserved for men but Elizabeth's background had nurtured this love. Her mother and grandmother had both been collectors. Her father, Algernon, was President of the Society of Antiquaries and himself a collector. Importantly, in 1753, Hugh became a member of the first board of trustees of the British

Museum. Appointed personally in the will of the Museum's founder, Sir Hans Sloane, Hugh had the responsibility of organising Sloane's collections at the Museum's first home, Montagu House in Bloomsbury. No doubt all this had an influence on Elizabeth's collecting and classification, although the collecting bug had already bitten her well before Hugh's appointment. In 1741, she wrote to her mother that her 'rage of medals' was increasing by the hour.

Elizabeth enjoyed a rich cultural life. Her mother Frances, née Thynne, was a literary patron and poet. Like her, Elizabeth patronised several literary figures. These included Oliver Goldsmith and Thomas Percy (no relation), the eminent poet and later bishop, who dedicated his most important work, *The Reliques*, to her when she was Countess. In 1768, after editing *The Household Book of the Earl of Northumberland in 1512*, a pioneer work of its kind, Percy became Hugh's chaplain and secretary.* Other prominent figures Elizabeth knew included the French philosopher and writer, Voltaire, who made her a present of a (then) exotic melon and rare pineapple. As Lady of the Bedchamber, Elizabeth came into contact with the Queen's cultural circle, which included other female collectors and intellectuals. Queen

Charlotte herself was an avid collector, owning cabinets of butterflies, shells and minerals, and had a large library with collections of prints, coins and medals. George III had a library of nearly 70,000 books, arranged by subject, and he also loved collecting medals.

As Elizabeth's collection grew it was housed in her apartments on the first floor of Northumberland House. In 1770, she resigned as Lady of the Bedchamber when Hugh temporarily moved into political opposition, after which she began to travel around Britain and extensively in Europe, particularly Holland, Flanders and France, where she visited Voltaire at his home at Ferney. She added to her collection and reported everything of note in her diaries, letters and notebooks.

Elizabeth catalogued her collection meticulously and in the 1770s personally put the contents into a nine-volume book called *The Musaeum Catalogue*. As only part of her collection survives, her *Catalogue* is invaluable. The first three volumes referred to her pictures – from miniatures to landscapes, from pastels to wax portraits – and to her prints, medals and coins. In the fourth her ethnographic collection was listed. Here were diverse curios from the Americas and China, including the badge of the Order of the King of Siam, made of precious stones, and the costumes of European religious orders. The fifth contained everything carved or sculpted, such as cameos and statues in ivory, marble and bronze.

Miscellaneous objects that did not easily fit elsewhere were listed in the sixth volume, and included manuscripts, porcelain and glass, the gloves of Queen Elizabeth and a cap made of the hair of Mary Queen of Scots. The seventh volume

---

*The original title included the sideline: 'The Regulations and Establishment of the Household of Henry Algernon Percy, the Fifth Earl of Northumberland.' A few copies were published in 1770 for private circulation to friends of the 1st Duke and Duchess. Wider publication occurred in 1827. The book contained such items as recipes; rules on what foods to be served at which meals; servants' duties; how to seat guests for dinner according to rank; and the occupants of each carriage when the Earl and his family left home. The household book inspired Elizabeth to codify her own Household Regulations.

spoke of 'natural curiosities', such as the skeleton of a sea horse, the 'rattle of a rattle snake' and small shells. A huge collection of different wood samples from all over the world formed part of volume eight, together with mineral specimens: crystals, marbles, gems. Her last volume formed the essential part of every collection of the time – an index.

Elizabeth's collection embraced the whole spectrum of the man-made and natural worlds and was one of the largest private British collections of the second half of the 18th century: an outstanding achievement by a clever woman. By contrast, her diaries were not considered to be very intellectual by the reviewer of *The Bookman* in February 1927, but as, like many diaries, they contained personal thoughts and observations, it is perhaps not surprising. That does not lessen their interest or their humour. For 6 May 1760, she writes: 'Went to Ball; tired to Death. A bad Supper. Miss Townsend drunk.' On 7 August that year: 'I here kissed an ugly Cousin and a sweaty Brother of Ld Belhavens.'

Even the reviewer acknowledges that Elizabeth's entries give unexpectedly human glimpses of lofty persons like the King himself, 'which worshipping historians were too flurried or too dignified to notice.' An entry for 1768, during her time as Lady of the Bedchamber, described the King being woken by his alarm before 5 a.m. getting out of bed, lighting the fire himself and going back to bed until the clock struck five, by which time the fire was ready and 'he rose and dress'd himself.' She also describes listening to

Opposite: A view of Northumberland House (on the right, with turrets).

the King's Speech in the House of Lords when his crown started to fall off and 'sat down upon his nose & misbecame him greatly.'

Significant foreign occasions were also described. In 1770, Elizabeth was present in France for the wedding of the 15-year-old Dauphin and the 14 year-old Marie Antoinette, and described at a pre-wedding dinner the table manners of the Dauphin's older sister, who ate 'with a voraciousness & eagerness I never saw equall'd'. The Dauphin, on the other hand, 'seem'd quite pensive & hung over his Plate playing with his knife.' Perhaps he had some sense of foreboding of what was to come a few years after he and his wife were crowned King and Queen of France.

Elizabeth's love of record-making extended to household tips and passing on recipes, such as those of her four-times great-grandmother, Edith Beale. It is her marmalade recipe from 1576 that is believed to be the oldest in the world and today's Duchess has revived it in her range of jams and marmalades. Tips passed from Elizabeth down the centuries and published in Jane Northumberland's books include how 'To Make a Good Bathe for Women that have Soft Fleshe and Hard Brestes' and 'To Kill Worms in the Handes and Feete'.

Elizabeth died on 5 December 1776 at Northumberland House, aged 60. The Duke did not continue his wife's collecting, although he kept her rooms as an homage to her passion. He also commissioned from Robert Adam the design of a large white marble monument in her memory for the Percy family vault in Westminster Abbey, where Elizabeth lies. The inscription refers to her being 'an ornament of courts, an honour to her country, & patern to the great, a protectress of the poor'. It also mentions the three children she and Hugh had: a daughter, Frances Elizabeth, who died in 1761, and two sons – Hugh, who became 2nd Duke in 1786, and Algernon, the 1st Earl of Beverley.

The inscription also says that the Duke was 'inconsolable for the loss of the best of wives'. It had been a happy marriage, although that did not stop Hugh fathering three illegitimate children. Two were daughters, both born in 1770 and also buried in Westminster Abbey. There was also a son, James Smithson, born in secret in France around 1765, to a wealthy widow and distant cousin of Elizabeth. Hugh never acknowledged the boy as his. A brilliant scientist and a republican sympathiser, James left the fortune he inherited from his mother to the USA to found the Smithsonian Institution.

After Northumberland House was compulsorily purchased and then demolished in 1874, Elizabeth's collection was redistributed between the family's other properties. During the 20th century many objects were sold at auction, but thanks to Jane Northumberland, the diverse legacy of this clever and inspirational woman is remembered for ever.

Alnwick Castle.

LOSS AND LAUGHTER:
THE DUCHESS OF LEINSTER

Having a title in the 21st century can be unexpectedly tricky. When Fiona Hollick met Maurice FitzGerald, then the Earl of Offaly, around 1970 when she was just 17, she thought that having a title was 'rather nice, a bit different'. After their marriage in 1972, she became Countess and addressed as Lady Offaly, and realised people do not always understand titles; they seldom know the history of them and are not sure what to do with them. Since becoming the Duchess of Leinster in 2004 it has not been very different. Sometimes the issue is a practical one: in an age of online form-filling, the aristocracy is not catered for. Just booking an airline ticket can be a headache when the name has to match that on the passport. The usual choice of titles – Mrs, Ms, Dr – do not apply. 'What I've found is if we put our title in the forename bit – so I put "Duchess of" in the Christian name bit – and

Opposite: The Duchess of Leinster.

"Leinster" in the surname bit, it usually comes out reasonably OK.' She was shortly to fly to Ireland, the Duke's ancestral country: 'It'll be interesting to see what happens because I'm "Ms Duchess of Leinster"!' Sometimes she is called Mrs D Leinster, 'because people think "Duchess" is a name!' Most people think she is a pub. Her favourite mistake was when she was Marchioness, her title before Duchess, and someone wrote to her as 'The Martian of Kildare'.

She laughs. Fiona Leinster, a dark-haired, good-looking woman, laughs a lot, a gusty laugh full of delight. Her humour and her zest are all the more remarkable given the sadness and difficulties she and the Duke have experienced; the most tragic was the death of their only son, Thomas, in a car accident in 1997 when he was 23. Yet she is devoid of self-pity. Home with their two adult daughters is a pretty house in a quiet hamlet in the countryside near Oxford. It is a delightful place with much character, but in terms of size it is a far cry from a stately home. Looking out over a beautifully maintained courtyard garden, the light and airy drawing room, adorned with vases of huge pink roses, is decorated not by a top-name London designer but by the Duke. He even made the panelling. The 9th Duke of Leinster can turn his hand to many things. He has had to. In 1918, the family inheritance was gambled away by his grandfather, Edward FitzGerald, the 7th Duke.

It was a devastating episode in a family that had been prominent in Anglo-Irish relations for over seven hundred years. The earliest Maurice FitzGerald played an active role in the capture of Dublin by the Normans in 1170 and was rewarded by being appointed Lord of Maynooth. In 1305, King Edward I created an earldom for Maurice's descendant and heir to the family, John FitzGerald, a reward for helping Edward in his Scottish campaigns. That John grew up to become the 1st Earl of Kildare has been explained by the story of what is known as the Geraldine Ape. When John was a baby, a fire broke out in his family's home, Woodstock Castle in County Kildare. In the confusion of evacuation it was realised that the baby had been left behind. Then someone heard a strange sound from the roof of a tower. Looking up they saw a monkey, kept as a pet and usually chained up, carefully holding the baby in its arms. It had taken John out of his swaddling clothes, licked and cleaned him and wrapped him up again. John would later design his family crest with two monkeys as supporters and a third posing triumphant at the top.

The spirit of the ape seems to have remained with the family in the centuries during which the FitzGerald line has survived and achieved eminence. One of the most important earls was the eighth, Gerald Mór FitzGerald, born in 1456 and known as 'the Great Earl'. At that time the city of Dublin and the area surrounding it, known as the Pale, was ruled by 'Anglo-Normans', who followed English customs and laws. The rest of the country – beyond the Pale (from where the saying comes) – were 'Hiberno-Norman', spoke Gaelic and intermarried with the Gaelic noble families. The FitzGeralds of Kildare remained loyal to the English sovereign and Edward IV rewarded Gerald by appointing him Lord Deputy of Ireland in 1477. On his father's death the following year, he became 8th Earl.

When Henry VII defeated the Yorkists at Bosworth, Gerald retained his position and Henry looked to him to help crush both Yorkist and Gaelic Irish rebels. Gerald took advantage of the situation to rule Ireland independently from 1477 to 1494, disobeying the King when it suited him. Despite being thrown into the Tower of London on suspicion of being a traitor, Gerald persuaded Henry to reappoint him as Lord Deputy. He was killed in 1513 in a campaign against another Gaelic rebellion.

By then the House of Kildare had become a threat to Tudor rule in Ireland. In 1534, Henry VIII imprisoned Gerald's son, the 9th Earl, in the Tower. That Earl's son, Thomas, heard false reports of his father's execution and that the English government intended to kill him and his five uncles. Aged 21, Thomas summoned a Council to St Mary's Abbey, Dublin, and rode there accompanied by 140 horses with silk fringes on their helmets, earning him his nickname 'Silken Thomas'. There he publically renounced his allegiance to Henry VIII as Lord of Ireland

and attacked Dublin Castle. After further hostile acts, Thomas was imprisoned in the Tower for 16 months, and in 1536 was hanged with his uncles. His revolt was a factor in the creation of the Kingdom of Ireland in 1542, when Henry forced Anglo-Norman and Gaelic families to recognise him as King of Ireland.

If Henry thought Silken Thomas's execution meant the end of those FitzGeralds – Thomas's siblings were girls – he reckoned without Thomas's half-brother, another Gerald. Aged 12 and suffering from smallpox, he was rescued by the Bishop of Kildare, then looked after by relatives until fleeing to France, pursued by Henry's agents. Gerald finally made it to Rome, where he was protected by the Pope, educated and returned to England after Henry's death. The family was Catholic at that stage, which pleased Mary Tudor; she restored Gerald to the earldom of Kildare, making him 11th Earl. His scientific interests led to the belief that he had magical powers: he has passed into Irish mythology as the Wizard Earl. The family line nearly died out again in 1620 with the death of the 15th Earl, aged nine; fortunately his teenage cousin succeeded him.

In Elizabeth I's time the family became Protestant, which avoided their lands being forfeited, and they have remained so. Despite having recovered their title and lands under Mary, they did not regain their position at the English Court until the 18th century, when Robert FitzGerald, the 19th Earl, was appointed Lord Justice of Ireland. Robert's son, James, was given various titles by George III and in 1766 was created the first Duke of Leinster; it made him the Premier Duke, Marquess and Earl in the Peerage of Ireland. James married Emily Lennox,

a descendant of Charles II. One of their sons, Lord Edward FitzGerald, despite joining the British army, became a leader of the United Irishmen. Inspired by the French Revolution, their aim was to declare a Republic of Ireland. But Edward's plan to lead the group alongside the French in an invasion of Britain was discovered: betrayed by an informer he was shot and died a national hero in 1798, aged 35.

Edward had been born in Carton House, outside Dublin, commissioned by his grandfather in 1739 and regarded as one of Ireland's finest houses. The family also owned Kildare House, commissioned by James and finished in 1747; on becoming Duke, James changed its name to Leinster House. The family owned it until 1815 when the 3rd Duke sold it to the Royal Dublin Society. Edward would have been delighted to know that today it is home to the Irish Parliament.

Carton House then became the 3rd Duke's main residence. It still stands today and could have remained in the family had it not been for the 7th Duke; instead, it is a luxury hotel and golf course. Although the Dukes of Leinster had not been fabulously wealthy, it was the 7th Duke, another Edward, who caused Carton to pass out of the family. His choice of lifestyle was an unfortunate one and still resonates.

The youngest of three boys, Edward was only a baby when his father, the 5th Duke, died in 1893. His eldest brother, Maurice, became 6th Duke at the age of just six and Edward had another older brother, Lord Desmond. Handsome and adventurous, in 1913, Edward took as his first wife an actress in the musical comedy theatre. They had one son, Gerald, the present Duke's father. Edward fought in the Great War but his gambling habit had

given him huge debts and nothing to pay them with. His brother Maurice was afflicted with a brain tumour that made him incapable of handling the family affairs, so the Leinster fortune was in the hands of trustees who would not advance Edward anything substantial, given his lifestyle. In 1918, he was bankrupted for the first time.

Although Desmond was killed in the Great War, Edward still thought it unlikely he would ever become Duke, and that while Maurice was still alive, his own income from the Leinster estates would be negligible. On that basis, in 1919, Edward took a gamble and sold his reversionary life interest in the Leinster estates to a businessman, Sir Harry Mallaby-Deeley; in return he received £67,000 immediately and £1,000 a year for life. It meant that as long as Edward lived, any income due to him would go to Mallaby-Deeley and his heirs.

But then, in 1922, Maurice died in an Edinburgh lunatic asylum. Edward was now 7th Duke of Leinster and entitled to receive £80,000 a year. He would never see a penny of it: the contract with Mallaby-Deeley was valid and binding. That year Edward and his wife separated and he forbade her to see their son. Gerald was brought up by his father's aunt at a castle in Co. Wexford.

Despite everything, Edward continued to spend and devised increasingly inventive gambling ruses. He was bankrupted twice more and took three more wives. As an undischarged bankrupt he was forbidden to take his seat in the House of Lords or to take part in the coronation ceremonies of 1937 and 1953. He lived in a series of bedsits and council flats and with his fourth wife, a

Opposite: The 1st Duke of Leinster.

housekeeper for local flats, ran a tea shop in Sussex for a while. In the 1960s Edward had to be restrained by police when he entered Gerald's house in Oxfordshire and tried to remove a valuable painting and a tapestry, but, in 1964, he was discharged from the bankruptcies and, in 1975, took his seat in the House of Lords. In 1976, in the tiny Pimlico bedsit where he was living, the penniless 7th Duke of Leinster committed suicide. Gerald had helped his father as much as he could.

Meanwhile, Carton House had been sold. Gerald, as heir to the dukedom, had to give his consent, in return for which he was allowed to live in another Leinster property, Kilkea (pronounced Kilkay) Castle. Kilkea had been in the family since medieval times and is particularly associated with the Wizard Earl. Gerald's sons, Maurice and his younger brother John, were born at Kilkea, where Gerald tried to make a go of farming the estate but it was not profitable. When Maurice was about ten, Kilkea was sold and the family moved to Oxfordshire. There Gerald started a successful aviation business and became chairman of CSE Aviation, becoming 8th Duke on his father's death. Kilkea Castle was run as a hotel until 2009, when it suffered the effects of the Irish financial crisis.

Maurice FitzGerald, 9th Duke of Leinster, loved Kilkea as a boy. A huge grey fortification, it looks like a medieval castle should look. Fiona's father-in-law moved to England 'for the best reasons'. He thought his sons' futures lay there, 'and I think there was a lot of anti-British feeling [in Ireland], though I think the FitzGeralds over the years really championed the Irish cause'. The Irish government told Gerald that no foreigner could buy Kilkea – 'I think there was a German or Dutch buyer in the pipeline' – and the government effectively bought it for next to nothing. 'I think my father-in-law thought they were going to knock it down and use it for road building or something and then they sold it on, of course, at huge profit. So I think there was actually a lot of bitterness in his heart and you can understand why. Maurice has been back to Kilkea a few times and he's almost wept. They've cut down all the trees. He said it was like a fairytale castle, you could barely see it from the road. I think he's very sad about that.'

Maurice never knew Carton, which Fiona believes was probably a good thing. She would have loved the chance to live in it. 'People say, "Oh, you don't want to be running a house like Carton." I wouldn't mind! It's not like Blenheim, it's a much smaller version. Yes, the rooms are big compared to this but you could make it into a family home – it's not enormous.' She and Maurice stayed in Carton when it became a hotel, and the then owners gave them the Ducal Suite. 'This house would have fitted into it three times!' The gardens were lovely too. 'My husband drew the curtains back onto the rose garden and I said, "I suppose this is the view previous duchesses had every morning!" His reply was, "Yes, but I bet it wasn't the duke who brought her tea in bed!" It's big obviously by ordinary standards but by stately home standards quite small and quite modest. Elegant. A lovely library but quite small and an organ in the salon. Lovely French windows going onto steps. The landscaping is quite simple, a nice lake and boathouse, and the shell cottage.'

Fiona met the 7th Duke once and found him 'rather dull. He was eccentric, no doubt about that. He was very old at that stage, in his eighties. I think obviously he'd had great charm. It's rumoured he had an affair with Wallis Simpson but we don't know that. I think latterly women probably wanted to mother him. I was disappointed. I thought I was going to meet someone quite charismatic. I thought, "I want to wring your neck because you're so dissolute, just thought of yourself."' However, it now seems it may not have been entirely his fault: 'There was a lot of bad advice given to the family and a lot of the fortune would have gone at some stage, probably. Every time we go to Ireland we're finding out more.'

But the Duke and Duchess are not ones to dwell on what might have been, certainly not on something as comparatively trivial as property when they have lost what was most precious to them. Their son Thomas was in Ireland with his girlfriend, on the way to her parents' house for the weekend, when he was killed. It was his sister Pollyanna's birthday and he had rung to wish her happy birthday. 'Amazing really, that he remembered! But thank God he did and he was in good spirits. I didn't speak to him that day. I'd spoken to him three days earlier, and I could so easily have been telling him off – one does, as a mother: "Why didn't you go and see so-and-so?" so thank God it wasn't like that.' He rang his sister at about six o'clock, set off with his girlfriend and never made it. He had not been drinking or taking drugs, nor was he speeding. He skidded at a notorious accident black spot and was propelled into oncoming traffic, dying almost instantly. His girlfriend sustained leg injuries; she remained a family friend.

Their situation supports the argument for the inheritance of titles by women. On Maurice's

Opposite: The 7th Duke of Leinster.

death the title will pass sideways to his younger brother, John, who has a son, Edward, so at least the line will continue. Fiona acknowledges that at least the title is not passing to some distant relative who has no connection with Ireland, but 'no disrespect to my brother-in-law or his son but I think things should change in this day and age.' Coincidentally, Edward's sister does have a link: she is a professional golfer and spends time at Carton golf club, which has sponsored her. Nevertheless, it annoys Fiona that her eldest daughter, Lady Francesca, cannot take on her brother's title because she is a girl. 'To be honest, I don't think she's that bothered but she would do it for her brother.'

She says, 'People frequently ask Maurice, "Who's your heir now?" It's bad enough losing a child. But when it's rubbed in the whole time… and I'm afraid we do rather get that when we go to Ireland.' They named their son Thomas partly because there had not been a Thomas since Silken Thomas, 'and I think they were similar characters, rather hotheaded,' although Silken Thomas is now thought to have been a shrewd operator. There were other similarities. 'His father was the 9th Earl and Thomas's was the 9th Duke.' Both were the same age, with blond hair and blue eyes.

Out of Thomas's death has come some good. Like his father and sisters, he suffered from dyslexia. Fighting his disadvantage he had trained as a chef and was about to start a business course, with a view to opening a delicatessen. After his death, Fiona and Maurice set up a charity, the Thomas Offaly Memorial Fund, the TOM Fund for short, which provides assistance to dyslexic sufferers. Additionally, for over 30 years, Maurice has been President of the Oxfordshire Dyslexia

Association. 'When he took it on we were still fighting to have dyslexia recognised in the state system. And even in private schools – all three of our children are dyslexic to some degree, Thomas being the worst – we were quite limited as to which private schools had a teacher on board who knew what they were doing.'

When they realised their youngest, Lady Pollyanna, was dyslexic, Fiona decided to study for a qualification to work with dyslexic children so she could better understand the condition and help her daughter. After tough training by a woman who started the Unicorn School for children with Specific Learning Difficulties, Fiona received a diploma and became one of Unicorn's one-to-one support staff. After other experience she was approached by and now works for an independent boys' school three days a week. There are no barriers with the other staff in the support unit just because she happens to be a duchess. They get on very well and share laughter: 'You need a sense of humour when you're teaching little boys!'

The boys call her Duchess. 'I think some of the boys think it's a nickname, and that's fine! I don't mind.' When working at Unicorn, she was Marchioness – Maurice became Marquess when his father became 8th Duke – and was addressed as Lady Kildare, 'and to be honest, people need to realise that we're not all sitting on committees doing good works and going out to lunch. Some of us are working – I'm sure a lot of us are. There's no shame in their knowing I've got a different name. I'm very proud of it.'

One day a week she collects Francesca's two children from school and looks after them. She does some work daily for the TOM Fund, which is run by volunteers and kept small to keep costs down. The applicants for the charity's funds are means-tested by a professional trustee: 'It's mind-blowing how some people exist, many on benefits.' She says it is not easy raising money for dyslexia because it is not something you can see: one has got to have been affected by it to understand it. Their initial target of £100,000 has been reached. 'We're paying for the specialist tuition for these children but we didn't realise demand would be so high. I think we'll be running out of money at some stage but I think we've helped a generation of local children. I feel that even if we can't carry on for ever, we've helped give some children a brighter future than they'd have had otherwise.'

The Duke works too, as a self-employed landscape gardener. His dyslexia, so inadequately catered for in his youth, limited his qualifications and choice of work, and there was no estate left for him to run. He was an excellent horseman, having spent much of his childhood at Kilkea on a horse, and had worked in training racehorses, but gardening was his passion.

The couple met in Wargrave, an affluent village by the Thames in Berkshire where Fiona was brought up. Her family was not particularly wealthy but they were well connected. In Norman times the head of her mother's family, the Purcells, had been Hereditary Usher to the King's Bedchamber for over a century until Henry II. Later they joined Maurice's ancestors in the invasion of Ireland and were quietly influential, although they lost their lands there eventually. A 19th-century ancestor was Sir Richard Westmacott, Professor of Sculpture at the Royal Academy. He was proposed as its President but declined the post. Family legend has it that he was not given a peerage as Queen Victoria was

scandalised at the lack of clothing on his famous statue of Achilles at London's Hyde Park. Fiona's mother's cousin was Lord Audley, an old barony whose title, somewhat topically, he inherited through the female line. Fiona is also related to Maurice by marriage through Sarah Lennox, later Napier, sister of her chosen predecessor Emily, the first Duchess of Leinster.

Fiona was privately educated but says that in the 1960s it was still possible to go into certain professions without having a degree. Her father was a solicitor and they considered her going into the law, but she didn't know what she wanted to do. She took an Alliance Française exam in a language college abroad and when she returned she was 'packed off to secretarial school because it was considered a useful thing to do. I absolutely loathed it.' Her mother wanted her to 'do the Season'. She herself had done it, 'but it was in the days when you got presented at Court. She was presented to Edward VIII – she must be one of the few. She said he just looked thoroughly bored – unless it was someone particularly pretty, then his eyes lit up!' Fiona's academic brother, who still cannot bring himself to address her and Maurice as Duke and Duchess, said the whole process was 'just a marriage market'.

Fiona decided he was right and rebelled against her mother's wishes, feeling there were other ways of meeting people. One day an acquaintance asked her mother if her son was back from university abroad. 'My mother said, "No, but Fiona's back. Why?" and she said, "I've got this Maurice Offaly staying and he doesn't know anyone young and I want him to meet someone." That's what happened then: people don't do that so much now.' Her mother threw a dinner party and invited

Maurice, who was lodging locally while training in landscape gardening. Fiona was 17, he 23. He told her later that he knew within ten minutes that he was going to marry her. 'I can't say I felt the same. I was introducing him to my friends, trying to pair him off but it wasn't working terribly well. Then after about six months, I thought, "Hang on, maybe I'm barking up the wrong tree!" I made him work quite hard for me.'

Maurice was then the Earl of Offaly: his grandfather was still 7th Duke and his father was the Marquess of Kildare. When Fiona first met the Marquess and Marchioness she was 'terrified of them. Not so much because they had titles because I was quite used to that – my parents had lots of friends who had minor titles – but you know how terrifying it is when you're going out with someone. I was very young and also I'm not particularly horsey and I thought I'd put my foot in it and say the wrong thing.'

As for her fellow students at secretarial college, 'When I got engaged it was in the paper and they were all over me like a rash when they realised he was an Earl. I thought that was quite interesting and I didn't like it.' Their traditional wedding in 1972 was held at her parents' local church, with the reception for the three hundred guests in a marquee in their garden. After marrying, Fiona temped for three weeks at Oxford Airport for her father-in-law's business, but says she was 'a disaster'. The typing was fine but she kept cutting people off on the phone.

The children arrived between 1974 and 1982, when she was in her twenties. Fiona believes that the birth of Thomas, whose title then was Viscount Leinster of Taplow in the County of Buckinghamshire, meant that for the first time in the family's history there were four male generations alive. When the children were young, Fiona worked as a receptionist for a neighbour who was a dentist and trained in decorative paint techniques, taking commissions. Maurice started his own landscaping business and later got a job as head gardener and group adviser to Robert Maxwell, the media tycoon, looking after his Oxfordshire manor house and the roof garden of the Mirror Group building in London. He was also in charge of Mrs Maxwell's garden in France, although he never had to go there. It was a happy eight years, until Maxwell's death. Maurice was made redundant and also suffered loss of pension following the Maxwell scandal. He found other gardening work but had a minor breakdown after Thomas's death and resigned. Fortunately, he managed to get back on his feet, with his wife's support.

Fiona has helped the family through that and other problems, their often tight financial circumstances meaning that she is a stranger to benefits that some other duchesses enjoy. When Fiona was pregnant with Francesca in 1976, Maurice was starting his business and Fiona did his secretarial work; later, when Pollyanna was barely five days old, he needed Fiona's help again. At that stage they took on a girl to help with the three children in the mornings so Fiona could assist Maurice. Their life is not what people anticipate. 'I think generally if you have a title people expect things – they have a preconceived idea of how you are.' However, she thinks that 'people are much more open-minded now about titles and realise you're not really very different but in the old days…' She recalls the time when she was Patron of a breast cancer charity run by local doctors and was asked to present prizes.

A famous actress known for her left-wing views was invited as a crowd-puller. When Fiona spoke to her she sensed her hostility. 'I thought, "If only you knew… OK, I've got the title but I'm probably working just as hard as you are, if not harder – I wash my own kitchen floor, put it that way!"'

Once people discover she is a duchess, they still tend to think she must have 'two black Labradors, a Range Rover and green wellies. And it makes you want to do the opposite!' They often think she must have money and she finds it embarrassing when she is approached by charities for that reason. If she lived at Carton, she says she would be only too pleased to let it be used for charitable purposes. On the leisure side she has been a keen ballet dancer from childhood, and had the opportunity as an adult to dance with a former member of the Royal Ballet in a production for the Newbury Operatic Society; she still takes dance lessons.

Despite the family's difficulties, there are highlights when the FitzGeralds are remembered and lauded. Every year she and Maurice try to spend at least a week in Ireland where one of his half-sisters lives. It is a bittersweet experience for them but they enjoy it. 'In Ireland we are treated like royalty by those who are really interested.' In 2011, they were invited by the Speaker of the Irish Parliament to visit the Duke's ancestral home. In a press release, the Speaker said it was 'truly humbling' to tour 'the hallowed hallways of Leinster House with direct descendants of its first occupants'. They had 'the most fabulous day', and were shown the National Library and the Masonic Hall, because the 3rd Duke was Grand Master for over 60 years, the longest time anyone has done it. 'He was a bit of a good egg, I think.'

Maurice still has friends near Kilkea who entertain them: 'The Irish are wonderful, they're very hospitable.' They have a good contact in historian Colette Jordan, who is an expert on Duchess Hermione, wife of the 5th Duke. In March 2013, Fiona was delighted to be invited as the modern Duchess to a lecture in memory of Hermione at Alexandra College, Dublin, a Church of Ireland Girls' School set up in the 19th century to educate girls to university standard; Hermione was a major benefactor. Maurice's niece, Hermione's namesake, went with Fiona to the event, which was opened by the Archbishop of Dublin. Fiona presented the Inaugural Hermione History of Art Prize, and gave a short speech.

It upsets her when someone makes uninformed comments about the FitzGeralds' history. 'They really cared about the Irish. They were very well thought of and I have to say when we go over there we are made to feel quite important, whereas over here, no one knows where Leinster is! Unless they are rugby fans! We have won the Heineken Cup three times in the last four years. But we still don't get free tickets!' She laughs.

She realises that as a duchess she is not in demand today in the same way as celebrities are but she sees the aristocracy as an integral part of Britain's heritage. 'I think sometimes we forget about our history and I'm proud of the title. I married into it, but I'm proud of my mother's history too. I'm proud of what they've achieved, what they've done in the past, even though sometimes they were very naughty, but it's all part of our history and wouldn't life be poorer without some of those stories?'

They are often reminded of that history. In 2014, there is a lunch at the Tower of London, a place with which Maurice's ancestors were only too familiar, in aid of the preservation of the chapel. In September 2013. they attended a symposium in Trinity College, Dublin, to mark the 500th anniversary of the death of the Great Earl. Another ancestor was a founder of the Red Cross; on its 150th anniversary they were invited to Westminster Abbey, together with Princess Alexandra, its Patron, with dinner at the Foreign Office afterwards. That was very special, although there was no tiara for Fiona to wear if she had wanted to: both her mother's and her mother-in-law's tiaras were split up. There is very little family jewellery belonging to Maurice's family left. 'Most of what I wear is my mother's stuff.'

Maurice's family is not entirely bereft of heirlooms. Some interesting portraits from the old houses survive, although many subjects are unknown and some were badly damaged by a fire, when or where nobody knows. The majority of the possessions were sold before they got to Maurice. A few remaining items are from Carton: Maurice's father discovered 24 hours before the house sale that the contents were being sold too, and tried to recover what he could. There is a rumour that William Randolph Hearst bought a lot, which is 'sitting in crates at his place in California'. The owner of Carton went out there to see if he could discover anything but without success. 'There may be a lot of Leinster stuff just sitting in boxes somewhere. The maddening thing for us is that every so often things come up for sale and we find out about it usually fairly late and I'm always outbid.' They did manage to buy back some silver bedchamber sticks. Just before their fortieth wedding anniversary an old family fishing gaff came up for sale. As Maurice is a keen

fisherman, Fiona thought it would be ideal for him, especially as it was inscribed 'Presented to Maurice' – the 6th Duke – 'by the staff at Windsor Castle'. Again they were outbid.

Despite the family's lack of wealth today, perhaps it is their eminent history that has encouraged one vigorous and persistent claim to the title, which began when Gerald became 8th Duke. The claimant is an American builder who, based on a deathbed confession by a relative, claims he is the rightful heir. He first asserted that he was related to the 6th Duke, saying that he did not die in the asylum but escaped, and then changed the story to being related to Lord Desmond, saying that (despite the many witnesses to his death in the war) he escaped to Canada. Every time he has emerged the family has had to spend considerable sums to oppose the claim, quite apart from the emotional strain of it.

But Fiona has coped with it. It is not surprising that her choice of predecessor is Emily, née Lennox, the first Duchess: 'She was a girl and a half!' Emily had 23 children and, like Fiona, lost her eldest son, as well as her rebel son, Lord Edward. 'She was a very strong woman and wanted Rousseau to tutor her children and then she went off with the subsequent children's tutor and created a great scandal. She married him after the duke died. She'd already had one child by him and she had two more when she was actually married.' Focused and determined, just like Fiona.

Opposite: King Edward I created an earldom for Maurice FitzGerald.

THE CLEVER MOTHER:
EMILY, FIRST DUCHESS OF LEINSTER
(1731–1814)

When in 1747 the newly married Emily, Countess of Kildare, arrived at Carton House, her husband's mansion near Dublin, she declared herself disappointed. It was not just a sulk of the 16-year-old she was, for it was not yet finished. Emily's husband, James FitzGerald, the 20th Earl of Kildare, had inherited it in 1745 and had started a redecorating project but it had some way to go. When over two hundred years later Fiona, Duchess to the 9th Duke of Leinster, stayed at the hotel that had been Carton House, her disappointment was for a different reason – that such a lovely house had never been hers.

Emily was used to large houses, having been brought up in the splendour of Goodwood House in Sussex and Richmond House, Surrey. Emily and her sisters, especially Caroline, were avid correspondents and a huge cache of letters about their and their brothers' lives has provided a

Opposite: Emily FitzGerald when Countess of Kildare by Sir Joshua Reynolds.

detailed insight into their extraordinary lives and times. Born in 1731, Emily was the second of seven surviving children of Charles Lennox, 2nd Duke of Richmond, and his wife Sarah. The children were also great-grandchildren of King Charles II through his mistress, Louise de Kéroualle.

The successor to Nell Gwyn, Louise gave the King one of his many illegitimate children. Charles made their son the 1st Duke of Richmond and gave him, as well as other titles, a substantial annuity and a slice of the Crown's tax revenue from mining and manufacturing. It was a healthy start to the riches of the Lennox family. Although the 1st Duke nearly squandered his inheritance by gambling, the family fortune was saved when he married his son and heir, Charles, to the daughter of the Irish Earl of Cadogan. It was an inauspicious start to a marriage. Charles was 18, Sarah 13, and the first time they met was their wedding day. Sarah was horrified. Charles thought her dowdy and went off to do the Grand

Tour. On his return three years later, while delaying calling on his wife, he was besotted by a beautiful woman at the theatre. On introduction, he discovered it was Sarah. Theirs became a marriage of deep love and devotion, especially by Georgian standards.

When Emily was born her parents were courtiers to George II. She was their favourite daughter and much indulged. Very pretty, she had brown curling hair, light blue eyes and a tall, well-proportioned figure. When she was 14, the Earl of Kildare, aged 23, proposed to her. Her parents had already had a tempestuous time with her older sister, Caroline, who had eloped with the much older Henry Fox, an ambitious Whig politician. Despite his political ascendancy they disapproved of Fox, and they and Caroline were estranged for years.

The Duke and Duchess of Richmond initially also opposed Emily's marriage to Kildare, despite his wealth and the prominence the FitzGeralds had enjoyed in Ireland for centuries. His nationality was an issue for them, and not just because the Duchess did not like being reminded of her own Irish roots. Kildare was an Irish Protestant nationalist: he wished to protect Ireland from control from Westminster over Irish finances. He was an important figure in Irish politics, controlling a large group of MPs in the Irish House of Commons at a difficult time; Irish Protestant nationalism was at odds with the interests and rights of the Gaelic and Catholic Irish.

Emily's parents knew Kildare regarded marriage to her as being politically advantageous to him. He did not yet have a title or lands in England that would give him a seat in the House of Lords; he

also wished to have an alliance with Henry Fox. Yet it was clear they were in love, and after much discussion about marriage settlements they were married at Richmond House in February 1747. The King made Kildare Viscount Sterling, and there was talk of his being made a Duke to ensure he would always be premier peer of Ireland.

By June the couple were living in Ireland, where towns like Dublin were enjoying prosperity while the Gaelic-speaking inhabitants experienced terrible poverty in the countryside. In Dublin the nobility were busy establishing themselves in grand houses, among them Kildare's newly built Kildare (later Leinster) House. Carton was only a couple of hours' drive from Dublin, so when Emily tired of the countryside she would shift to the town, staying in Leinster House, for the culture Dublin offered. When Emily was pregnant, which was often, she moved there during her confinement.

Emily, like her siblings, was extremely well read with a lively mind and kept up to date with the latest news, views and literature. She also enjoyed socialising, which was even more important from 1761, when George III made Kildare 1st Duke of Leinster. However, Emily was also fond of gambling, running up huge debts from card games that her besotted husband always paid. Such was Emily's sexual power over him that he did not demur when she asked for money, whether for gambling or to buy the latest stockings, which he wrote to say he liked to imagine her wearing. His borrowing arrangements kept Dublin's bankers happy, too. The result of the Duke and Duchess's appetite for sex and spending was that by 1773 they had 19 children and debts of £148,000.

The earlier refurbishment of Carton and its running costs, with a household of around one hundred permanent staff, had not helped. Emily told James that she hoped their plans for redecorating Carton would make it like London houses, 'pretty and smart and well furnished'. Emily had a passion for improvements. Her plans included walls hung with Chinese prints and bedrooms upholstered in silk. It was her husband's redesign of Carton's park, including an artificial lake upon which Fiona Leinster would later gaze, that really impressed Emily, moving her to compare him lovingly with the most celebrated landscape gardeners. Emily loved Carton's grounds, especially being driven around in the evenings in her one-horse chaise.

Like today's Duchess, Emily lost her eldest child. George, Lord Offaly, was born when Emily was 17. George and his much younger brother, Edward, were considered the brightest of the children. In 1756, when he was eight, George and his seven-year-old brother William were sent to school in England. George and their cousin, Stephen Fox, both started at Eton, while William and the precocious Charles Fox* attended an academy in Wandsworth. During the holidays, Caroline took charge of Emily's boys and the two sisters corresponded frequently.

In the summer of 1765, when George was 17, Emily was pregnant with her 13th child, although such a number did not diminish her love for each one. George had finished Eton and was in London, waiting for a commission in the army. Emily's sisters Louisa and Sarah had been in Paris, and on

* Charles Fox became the most famous opposition politician of the 18th century.

returning to London found George behaving like a typical young man about town. However, by the beginning of September he had been confined to Richmond House with a consumptive fever. His aunts kept Emily informed by letter and stayed with him until he died, on 26 September.

Emily's brother, Charles Lennox, by then the 3rd Duke of Richmond, in whose house his nephew had died, had to make the prompt decision as to where he should be buried. He decided upon St Martin-in-the-Fields, London, where their grandfather lay. Emily heard the news of the death and burial from her brother's letter the next morning. George's brother, William, became Marquess of Kildare, their father's heir.

In the months that followed, when grief was mixed with the tiredness of pregnancy, Emily told Louisa she wished her existence in the world would end. She recovered her gaiety but became less satisfied with life. After their new son was born in 1766, she turned her attention to transforming a labourer's house in Carton's park, which they called Waterstone, later known as Shell Cottage. Emily modelled it on the shell grotto she had loved as a child at Goodwood, although it became the site and expression of her grief for George. Emily and family embedded rocks and thousands of shells on the walls and in the domed roof. Today a tourist attraction, it served in the 1990s as the rented home of the singer Marianne Faithfull.

Emily now developed a real interest in politics and became something of a radical, more so than the Duke, whose main position was opposing control from Westminster, rather than being a reformer. Emily started to question the relationship of monarch, Parliament and its people

and what would happen if a government became despotic or unjust. She also wanted civil rights for different groups, such as access to offices, courts, information and religious emancipation. She never praised the British monarchy, nor would she ever openly express regret about the execution of the French royal family in 1793, as most of her contemporaries did. She and her son, Lord Edward Fitzgerald, born in 1763, would come to have much in common.

Edward and his younger siblings enjoyed a different kind of education to the older children. Strongly influenced by the educational theories of the philosopher, Rousseau, and after the death of George and the prolonged illness of her son Charles, Emily resolved not to send her children away to school but to have them educated by a tutor. In 1766 the Duke converted a bathing lodge at Black Rock, on the coast south of Dublin, into a house to be used as a school. Rousseau, who happened to be in England, declined Emily's invitation to be tutor in return for an elegant retreat.

Disappointed, they engaged William Ogilvie, an awkward but clever Scot who came with an excellent recommendation. Although other tutors were employed, Ogilvie was in charge and occupied the children in non-academic subjects too, like gardening and swimming. As the journey from Carton was possible in a day, Emily would visit once a week. Meanwhile, Ogilvie wrote to her regularly with news of her offspring, who were clearly very happy with him, and he would pass on to Emily their affectionate wishes. It soon became obvious to Emily that his letters included his own

Opposite: Marianne Faithfull *c.* 1994, in the Shell Cottage, Carton.

affectionate messages to her, disguised in double meanings. By 1771, they were in love. Who made the first move is not known, but it seems Emily did not even tell her sisters of the illicit affair to start with; she only told two of her maids and paid them to keep quiet.

In April 1773, Emily had another son, Lord George Simon Fitzgerald. In November, the Duke died of kidney failure, aged 51. William, 24, became 2nd Duke of Leinster and Emily the Dowager Duchess. Despite her relationship with Ogilvie, she and the Duke had enjoyed a happy marriage. Her husband's death left Emily vulnerable to the exposure of her affair with Ogilvie. Also the Duke's fertility had disguised Emily's adultery: it is highly likely that baby George was Ogilvie's. But Emily refused to do what convention – and rumours – demanded, which was to give up Ogilvie after her husband died. In 1774, she took Ogilvie and the younger children to France where they were married, although it was kept quiet and the date imprecise.

It was a brave move. No duchess had ever married her children's tutor, someone who was not only socially inferior but who had been in the pay of her husband. Emily was determined Ogilvie should have a political career: after all, her sons had enjoyed political influence by virtue of their birth. William, as Duke of Leinster, made his mother happy by bringing Ogilvie into the Irish House of Commons as an MP for one of the boroughs under his control.

Meanwhile, as Edward Fitzgerald matured, revolution was in the air, although his conversion to republicanism was gradual. Short and solidly built, with closely cropped hair and a pock-marked face, he joined the British army in 1780,

aged 17, and soon left for America, where he fought 'against the cause of Liberty': the Wars of Independence had started in 1775. When they ended, Edward became an MP in the Irish Parliament under his brother, William. In 1788, the year after the French Revolution began, Edward went to Nova Scotia; impressed by the native Indians, his republican sympathies grew. In 1792, the year the French monarchy fell, he went to Paris, renounced his titles and married Pamela, the illegitimate daughter of the Duc d'Orléans, a Prince who supported the Revolution.

Edward wrote to Emily about his republicanism and was confident she shared his views. Until 1794, she did: she wanted Parliamentary reform, disliked a strong monarch and liked Edward's views on democracy. However, that year the United Irishmen, originally a legal movement with whose members Edward had been in contact since 1792, was forced underground. Nevertheless, Edward joined them and left the Irish Parliament. Between 1795 and 1796, a United Irish movement emerged; the Duke, although opposed to Westminster as their father had been, seemed moderate compared with the movement. Emily realised with concern that Edward's republicanism now meant rebellion and violence. He became a target for government spies monitoring his secret activities. Fearing his letters were being read, Edward stopped writing to Emily about politics.

The Irish situation became more complex, with different factions emerging and merging. Catholics and Protestants who mistrusted each other found

Opposite: Artist's impression of the arrest of Edward FitzGerald.

themselves in agreement in the language of universal rights, while Catholic defenders merged with the secular, republican United Irishmen. In 1796, Edward was in Hamburg and Switzerland with the movement, pressing the French to send an invasion force to Ireland that would begin an Irish revolution. After an abortive French expedition that year and outbreaks of violence throughout Ireland, the Lord Lieutenant moved against the United Irish leadership; by June 1797, many leaders were behind bars. Papers stolen by informers incriminated other leading radicals, including Edward. By plotting the downfall of the Irish government, he was committing treason. Emily tried in vain to talk him out of it; by then she was based in London with Ogilvie, distanced from Edward geographically and by the censor.

In the spring of 1798, there were rumours that the French were preparing another invasion fleet for Ireland. Responsibility for rebellion now lay with the United Irish leaders in Dublin, including Edward, but they were divided about the timing and course of any rebellion. Then one of the leaders was arrested in England on his way to France. Edward went into hiding in Dublin, dodging arrest often dressed as a woman. In March, martial law was imposed throughout Ireland and a violent time followed. Terrified United Irishmen looked to Edward for an announcement that he would lead an immediate rebellion, while still hoping for a French invasion in May.

But in May, Edward was discovered in the house of a feather merchant. He was reading in bed and resisted arrest violently. Shot in the shoulder, he was bundled off to Dublin Castle and then to the gaol. The man he had fought with died, so manslaughter was added to the charges. Initially, the real version of Edward's arrest was concealed from Emily. His family was not allowed to see him. Emily petitioned the Prince of Wales and his brother, asking them to intercede with the King on Edward's behalf. While he waited for trial, Edward developed septicaemia, which locked his jaw, causing spasms and delirium; passers-by could hear him screaming. On 4 June 1798, aged 35, Edward FitzGerald died, for many a national hero.

Emily was never told of the extent of the dementia Edward experienced at the end, believing that, despite a little rambling, he died at peace. She did not mention his death in letters for months but found some consolation in his young son. By September, the rebellion had been crushed. The outcome was a Union with Great Britain.

Emily died in 1814. Ogilvie, who nursed her tenderly through her last years, died in 1832, aged 92. They had had other children together; Emily suffered several miscarriages but two girls survived into adulthood. When Mimi, the youngest, was born in 1778, William was by then 29 and Emily 47. Perhaps it was her modern attitude to pregnancy and childbirth that ensured that, during her marriage to the Duke, only one of their 19 children died in infancy.

Emily had been born into tremendous privilege and married the highest peer in Ireland, during a time of great change. It was also a period when, despite her advantages, she enjoyed no political power. Although she could be emotionally demanding, and may have set a poor example in her financial management, those flaws were outweighed by her application of intellect in other areas of her life. By providing her children with a loving upbringing and a wide education, she helped to develop their confidence and curiosity; she equipped her sons for the world, encouraging them to think for themselves, and her daughters to excel in those skills which that era valued. Together with her capacity for love, for the Duke, for Ogilvie – her determination to marry him disregarding the conventions that governed their lives – and for her many children, Emily is a woman that history cannot ignore.

Hers is a story that Fiona Leinster can understand.

Opposite: Charles Lennox, the second Duke of Richmond.

COMPASSIONATE CREATIVITY:
THE DUCHESS OF ABERCORN

Until she met her future husband in 1965, young Sacha Phillips had never been to Ireland. Staying with family friends on Islay in the Hebridean isles, she would look out to sea, to 'a glimmer of a form, a shape in the mist', which she thought looked fascinating. 'Little did I know a major part of my life would be here and all we've lived through over these years.'

Since marrying in 1966, when the Duke was still the Marquis of Hamilton, the Duchess has spent most of her time in Northern Ireland, at the family seat, Barons Court in Co. Tyrone. The estate, with its 18th-century house, is in a tranquil and secluded location and offers some of the best fishing in the country: an ideal spot to get away from the world. For the visitor it is easy to forget that Omagh, where the horrific car bombing by the Real IRA took place in 1998, is just down the road, while Belfast, with its history of troubles and

Opposite: The Duchess of Abercorn at Barons Court.

continuing unrest, is only an hour's drive away. But for the Duke and Duchess of Abercorn, each closely involved with both places, recent history is constantly present.

To those who associate dukedoms with places in England or Scotland, the title of Duke of Abercorn may be unfamiliar. The family surname, Hamilton, may be more recognisable, but it is not to be confused with the *Dukes* of Hamilton, a Scottish title whose family surname is now Douglas-Hamilton. To further complicate matters, the head of the House of Hamilton is the Duke of Abercorn.

The link between the dukedoms in Ireland and Scotland comes from a common ancestor: the 2nd Earl of Arran, Governor of Scotland and second only to the Crown in power, who in

Introducing the Duchess of Abercorn

1542 was appointed Regent to the infant Mary, Queen of Scots. One of the Earl's grandsons, James Hamilton, was created 1st Earl of Abercorn in 1606. The earldom took its name from the family's lands of Abercorn in what was then called Linlithgowshire, now West Lothian, in Scotland. In 1610, James was granted lands in Co. Tyrone in Ireland,* including the estate of Barons Court; the first castle there was built around 1620 by his brother. The title of Duke of Hamilton proceeded down another family line, along which is found one of the rare instances of a woman becoming a duchess in her own right.**

Over two centuries later, in 1868, Queen Victoria's son, the Prince of Wales, and his wife, Alexandra, were entertained at Barons Court by (another) James Hamilton, the Marquess of Abercorn (as the title had become) and his wife, Louisa. That year, the Queen made James 1st Duke of Abercorn. Today's Duke – almost inevitably, James Hamilton – the fifth, is the only nobleman to hold titles in the three peerages of Ireland, Scotland and Great Britain (rather than England – some peerages were specifically created after the Act of Union of 1707 and before that of 1800). Born in 1934, the strikingly tall James (as he prefers to be addressed) also holds the title of Duke of Chatelherault, which had been given to the 2nd Earl of Arran in 1549 by the French king, Henri II, who wanted to secure his alliance against Elizabeth I.

Between them, the Duke and Duchess of

Abercorn have ancestry which is exotic and complex, an example of how the nobility has intertwined through the centuries and across nations. James is even connected to his wife's family. His great-grandfather was the 1st Duke of Westminster, so he is related to the current (6th) Duke, to whom he is also godfather, and to whom Sacha's sister, Natalia, is married.

The Duchess of Abercorn OBE, also tall and looking younger than her age, has a broad smile and a gentle voice. As she opens the front door into the spacious Front Hall with a polished wood floor and large fireplace, the eye is drawn to several large portraits. Opposite the door is a pretty young woman with long, flowing hair and a pensive air. It is Emma, Lady Hamilton, mistress of Lord Nelson and, through her marriage to Sir William Hamilton, an ancestor of the Duke.

In a large and comfortable library where coffee is served, there are family photographs and some small paintings, one by Sacha. She was born Alexandra Anastasia Phillips in 1946 in Tucson, Arizona, where her part-Peruvian father, Lt-Col. Harold 'Bunnie' Phillips, had been sent to recover from tuberculosis. Her parents had met during the war. Towards the end of it her father worked under Sir William Stephenson, known both as 'the quiet Canadian' and by his codename 'Intrepid', a major figure in wartime intelligence. 'He was one of the great leaders of the time against the Nazi build-up in countries, particularly South America, so my father, who spoke Spanish, was sent to Argentina and Chile to do counter-espionage work.' Not long after marrying he discovered he was seriously ill with

---

* This was part of the Plantation, the organised colonisation of Ulster by Protestant Scots and English during the reign of James I.

** Anne, 3rd Duchess of Hamilton, chosen predecessor of the Duchess of Montrose.

Opposite: 1st Duke of Abercorn.

tuberculosis. By then he was based in Washington DC and, as there was no drug for TB at that time, he was sent to a sanatorium in Tucson. The only cure 'was to be totally immobilised for six months. I was on the way and my mother was quite happy to sit in the desert waiting for me!'

Through her mother Georgina ('Gina'), née Wernher, Sacha is by descent one of the Romanov family, a great-great-great granddaughter of Tsar Nicholas I of Russia. She is also a great-great-great granddaughter of the legendary Russian poet, Alexander Pushkin. Sacha's maternal grandmother was born Countess Anastasia Mikhailovna de Torby, known as Zia, a daughter of Grand Duke Michael of Russia. She was not born in Russia but in Baden Baden in Germany, 'because her parents were pushed out of Russia before the Revolution.'

Sacha explains. 'Grand Duke Michael Mikhailovich, grandson of Nicolas I, married the Pushkin granddaughter.* That was not a royal marriage, so they weren't allowed to stay in Russia and they were sent out to Germany. My grandmother, my great-aunt and great-uncle were born in Germany. Then, eventually, after all the difficulties of the Revolution in 1917, I think King George helped them, gave them some funds and a house in England.'

The family gradually established themselves there. Her grandmother married Harold Wernher and had three children: Gina, Myra and Alex, who was killed in the war. 'I have a very eclectic mix of blood which, like a chameleon, helps you to fit in anywhere! Wherever you go you have a little touch of this or that!'

---

* Countess Sophie de Torby, daughter of Pushkin's daughter, Natalya.

When Sacha's grandparents married in London in 1917, it caused a sensation. Zia, being a daughter of the exiled Grand Duke and related to most of the royal families of Europe, was glamorous and fascinating, while Sir Harold Wernher was extremely wealthy; his German-born father, Sir Julius Wernher, was one of the pioneers of the Kimberley Diamond Mines in South Africa with Cecil Rhodes and Alfred Beit and was one of the richest men in the world. Julius was also an avid art collector. 'He built up an amazing collection which then was housed at Luton Hoo.' Julius had bought the Luton Hoo estate in Bedfordshire in 1903, the original house designed by Robert Adam.

After Julius's death in 1912, Sir Harold inherited Luton Hoo and its art collection, 'and my grandmother brought in a lot of things from the Russian side, so it was an interesting mix.' Among them were exquisite pieces by the court jeweller, Fabergé. Much of the collection is now permanently on public display at Ranger's Lodge in Greenwich.

During the Second World War, Sacha's grandfather, Sir Harold, by then Major-General, played an important role in the Mulberry Operations (huge floating harbours to provide port facilities for the invasion of Normandy in 1944), and Luton Hoo was commandeered by Eastern Command. In 1947, Princess Elizabeth, as she was then, and Prince Philip spent part of their honeymoon there. The root of the family's relationship with the Queen and Prince Philip is partly Sacha's great-aunt, the Countess Nadajda ('Nada'). She married George Mountbatten, 2nd Marquess of Milford Haven and a descendant of Queen Victoria. George and his younger brother,

Luton Hoo Estate.

Lord Louis Mountbatten, 1st Earl Mountbatten of Burma, were uncles of Prince Philip. Also, Sacha's mother and the Queen were lifelong friends and shared a love of horse racing.

On the death of the widowed Lady Zia in 1977, the Luton Hoo estate jumped a generation to Sacha's brother, Nicky, born in 1947. Their parents had returned to England from Arizona when Sacha was about three months old. Her godfather was Earl Mountbatten and her godmother was Princess Marina, a first cousin of Prince Philip and the wife of Prince George, Duke of Kent.[*] Marina's mother was part of the Russian Royal Family; her father was Prince Nicholas of Greece and Denmark.

The Phillips family (Sacha's parents) first lived

[*] It was at Marina and George's wedding in 1934 that Elizabeth and Philip first met.

in Leicestershire, in 'a lovely old house [Thorpe Lubenham Hall] that belonged to the Wernher family that they gave to my mother.' They had another four children. In her teens, Sacha went to a boarding school in Wantage, Oxfordshire: St Mary's, an Anglican school run by nuns. Her parents then sold the house and moved to the Chilterns to avoid the weekend travelling to the children's schools all around the Thames Valley. Sacha was happy here as well as in Scotland, where her parents spent the latter part of their lives. There they had 'a lovely little property in Aberdeenshire, so holidays were in Scotland, which we all loved.' After Bunnie died in 1980, Gina remarried and became Lady Kennard.

Although Sacha says the nuns who ran St Mary's 'were wonderful, wonderful people', she was not happy there. Her experiences, together with inspiration from her ancestor, Pushkin, would become the driving force behind her deep involvement with the education of children in Ireland. 'I didn't flourish academically. I hated school! I didn't appreciate the way we were taught to learn, stuffed with facts and figures, so I was taken away at 16, and with a friend we went to Westminster Tutors in London because the nuns said, "She won't get her A-levels."' Within a year she had taken three A-levels which would have taken her two years at St Mary's, and passed them 'with flying colours. Suddenly I realised I was not a dunce. The school had made me out to be completely hopeless at everything because I wasn't good at exams, but with interesting tuition and real love of a subject which these tutors had, suddenly the spark was lit' and confidence was restored.

Bunnie took each of his four daughters travelling

in their youth, 'on wonderful visits to all the places he loved, most especially to South America.' At 19, Sacha was sent to St James's Secretarial College, which she did not find very inspiring. During that time she met James at a wedding. He was 31. 'I think my parents knew James, as they'd been together in Kenya that winter.' They all met up again at this wedding and introduced Sacha.

It was 1965 and James 'was very involved in becoming an MP, fighting for a seat in Fermanagh and South Tyrone.' He had become Ulster Unionist MP for that area in 1964 and wanted to hold his seat in the forthcoming 1966 election. James invited Sacha to visit Ireland; it was her chance to discover the mysterious island. 'It was a Bank Holiday, a beautiful sunny May, and was quite magical, which it is anyway, but it was even more beautiful then, and James said, "Yes, it's always like this"! I have to say that's a slight exaggeration! So we went to Donegal and had a wonderful drive along the Atlantic coast, and he said, "Wouldn't it be great if we got married?"' She agreed. 'So we literally got engaged there and then! I must have been just 20. These things often happen when you're least expecting it, don't they?'

They married in October 1966, in Westminster Abbey. The Queen and Prince Philip attended, as did her godmother, Princess Marina. The Queen Mother also attended 'because my mother-in-law, Kathleen Abercorn, was Mistress of the Robes to the Queen Mother and they were great friends. Prince Andrew [aged six] was a page, amongst a retinue of others.' It was, she says, an 'amazing' occasion.

After her marriage, Sacha, now the Marchioness of Hamilton, divided her time between London and Northern Ireland. But Northern Ireland in 1966 was not an easy place to be. That April Belfast had seen a major commemoration by northern Catholics of the Easter Rising of 1916. The core message was an end to British rule in Ireland. James managed to keep his seat in the election that year. However, it was a very tough time. The head of the Ulster Unionist Party was Terence O'Neill, Prime Minister of Northern Ireland, recognised for trying to reconcile different sectarian divisions. 'He was a very moderate man and James was one of his supporters, but you couldn't be a moderate at that time. You had to be an extremist of one sort or another and if you weren't, you fell between the Devil and the deep blue sea.' In 1970, O'Neill lost his seat as MP and James lost his too, about which Sacha was 'glad because he could not put a foot right. It was impossible to be a moderate in the centre: the ground didn't hold.' O'Neill's successor in Parliament was Ian Paisley and control of the UUP passed to harder-line elements.

After his political career, James put his energies into helping small businesses to start up in rural areas in Northern Ireland and then became chairman of the Laganside Development Corporation, a scheme for regenerating Belfast. Now he is on the board of Titanic Quarter Ltd, which is energising Belfast's waterfront and former shipbuilding land.

Sacha, meanwhile, had experienced huge changes in her life and direction since marriage. First, she had to come to terms with having a title: this was before the cult of celebrity diminished the impact of the aristocracy. Opening events and making speeches was 'something I was simply not trained to do. I was really terrified getting up

there and saying platitudes. It was so alien to me.' Eventually, she learned that if there was something she wanted to say that really came from herself, it was very different. Until then, she knew she just had to get on with it.

When they first married and James was still in politics, they had a flat in London and went back and forth to Northern Ireland. It was now that she came to realise what their age difference meant. 'My husband being 12 years older meant all his friends and his career were in another world compared with the teenage world that I was just emerging from.' She loved being with 'such interesting and broad minded people' but she missed people of her own age.

However, the most difficult experience was having children in Northern Ireland during the Troubles. 'My eldest son, Jamie, was born in 1969 – literally as Belfast was ablaze, with bombs and incendiaries. The whole place was in complete mayhem and I remember thinking, "What is going to be the future for this little child coming into the world at this time? You just have to take each day at a time and live through it." When Sophie was born in 1973, Sacha became really worried. 'Sophie was having nightmares and deep anxieties about the Troubles, about the family being attacked and invaded – it was complete terror, and I thought, "What are we to do if a child is suffering that much at this age? Is she going to carry this on into the future?"'

Sacha agonised about all children in the country at that time, afraid that they would suffer into the future if the issue were not addressed. 'I didn't know at that point what to do.' As a result of her questioning an answer came, 'but at the time it was very, very grim. People were terrorised and that's a very corruptive energy to carry. If not transformed, it becomes another bomb, another bullet. It makes people perpetrate the same horrors on others.'

She found the answer in Pushkin. At Luton Hoo, in 1986, her brother hosted a commemoration of the poet's life, bringing together many different ideologies and backgrounds. 'We had people from the Soviet bloc, from the White émigré community, from all kinds of different mindsets, but all gathering together at Luton Hoo for something inspiring and uplifting. It was Pushkin who lifted us from what I would call tribal separations and differences to a level where we were totally connected on a universal plane with the love of being alive.' Pushkin could bring them together 'in a way that 70 years of diplomacy had certainly failed to do. There was no way people were going to meet together through politics but the realm of the artist is the place of transformation.'

Inspired by what she had witnessed, she wondered how she could 'bring a little bit of the spirit of Pushkin into the life of a child here in Ireland', and bring Catholic and Protestant voices, north and south, together. The chief executive of the Education Board helped her to find four Catholic and four Protestant schools, four from Northern Ireland and four from the Republic. Sacha realised that she would have to find a way to explain to the schools about what she wanted to do in the name of her ancestor Alexander Pushkin. As Pushkin's works include *Eugene Onegin, Boris Godunov* and *The Queen of Spades*, which have all become operas, she knew that talking to children aged nine to 13 – the focus group – would be 'a big challenge'.

Sacha wanted to help children to find their inner voice and not be inhibited in their writing by poor grammar or spelling. She remembered that Pushkin as a child was told stories about his land by his nanny, Arina Rodionovna, 'a wonderful old Russian-speaking woman. Of course, his entire imagination came to life through fairy stories and the folk tales of Russia.' Fairytale would be the natural link, for children in Ireland likewise come from a land of storytelling in the Celtic tradition: 'It's in the DNA.' Teachers liked the idea. Soon the charity, the Pushkin Trust, was formed.

With the help of writers and artists in other mediums, children are encouraged to express themselves through all art forms. They also work with environmentalists in the natural world by way of their five senses. Even those who are not very academic have flourished once they discover they are valued. 'Suddenly a little switch turns on, they become curious, confident, motivated – in fact, lifelong learners.' Sacha is conscious of her own school experience. 'It's given me more joy than anything to see children flourish who would otherwise have become failures in our system thanks to this lop-sided focus on exam results.' She delights in seeing children who have become enthusiastic. 'If you light the spark within, your life will take off and you will find what it is you have to do, no matter what.' In 2008, she was awarded an OBE, about which she is delighted but characteristically modest.

Sacha became Duchess in June 1979 and the following month she had her youngest son, Nicholas. She considered the role deeply. One aspect of the word 'duchess' is, she considers, 'something which comes out of the fairy tale world' and is based on the fairy-tale composition of kings and queens: 'a hierarchy of beings, if you like, and it means the fairy tale resides in us all as a deeply felt imprint.' When she visits schools the children are often disappointed that she is not wearing a long dress and tiara; the drawings they make show 'a picture that's deep within ourselves, an archetype'. It means that 'the role of any of us bearing such a name is fundamentally an important one, if it's seen in the right light.' It is not about being self-important. On the contrary, 'the archetype of hierarchy is to be seen in service to humanity. It has immense possibility to help the greater good, and that's the way I see it.'

Having a title is a privilege that carries with it certain but 'joyous' responsibility. She realises that it has 'a magical power to open spaces and it's very important that that space is tended in the right way so that the right things come out of it.' Crucially, she believes that the word 'nobility' is misused. 'Everyone has that noble spirit in them and that's what I'm searching for in Pushkin: the nobility of the human being within us all.' She believes it has been badly damaged by a brutalising 'love of power' but 'the possibility of greatness is within us all.'

During the late 1970s, Sacha discovered the work of the Swiss psychoanalyst, CG Jung. She found that the world of depth-psychology spoke to her at an important crossroads in her life and subsequently helped her understand the crisis and challenges other people were facing at that time in Northern Ireland. After the Omagh bomb in 1998, she joined the Northern Ireland Centre for Trauma and Transformation as the Honorary Secretary. She had learned that it is necessary to understand and befriend the traumas of life that humans experience. 'We brush them away because we don't know how to handle them.'

After the bombing a friend started up the trauma centre and invited her to be a director. She agreed, provided that the word 'transformation' be attached to it, because, from her own experience, 'trauma doesn't have to be the end of the world. We can wake up and be transformed and start to live in a new way.' The centre, which now holds a significant archive on working with trauma, is connecting to many countries worldwide, as it did with the Police and Fire Service in New York after 9/11 and now with the huge problems in Syria. In 2006, Sacha was honoured to receive, from Prince Albert of Monaco, the Princess Grace Humanitarian Award of the Ireland Fund of Monaco.

She too has experienced personal loss. On 27 August 1979, her godfather Lord Mountbatten and several others were killed when his boat was blown up by the IRA on the coast at Sligo, not far from the Abercorns. 'We'd been on that boat, *Shadow Five*, many times.' Mountbatten had been staying with them beforehand. His grandson, Nicky Knatchbull, aged 14, was among those killed; he was Sacha's godson. His twin brother, Timmy, was critically injured but survived. In 2009, his award-winning book about rebuilding his life was published. 'He's a remarkable human being. He truly has come through such a challenge, such a trauma, in the most unembittered way.'

Then, in 1991, Sacha's brother, Nicky, died 'very suddenly, very sadly'. He was 43. 'We don't know the real cause of it all but he was low and not well and had all sorts of problems.' The press reported that he had been found dead in a fume-filled car following money problems. Today, Luton Hoo House is owned by a leisure company, although the estate, where his widow, an Austrian countess, still lives, remains in the family and is managed by her son.

Sacha still visits Luton Hoo: the previous year she had attended her nephew's wedding there. 'We all stayed in what had originally been the garages, which was a strange feeling!' She remembers with delight her 'coming out' party there. Thrown by her grandmother, Zia, 'a great hostess', it was 'an amazing dance, which possibly was the last of the white tie and tails and tiara evenings.' Although by then debutantes were no longer presented to the Queen, it made little difference because she attended anyway, with Prince Philip. After dinner, Joe Loss played the music in the ballroom and guests from all generations mingled in the 'magical' floodlit gardens. 'It was lovely and so many people said it was the most beautiful thing they'd ever been to.' She laughs that her grandfather regarded it as a waste of time and money because she did not meet her husband at the party, 'which he said was the only reason he had given it!'

Sacha tries to balance her charity work with other activities, including visits to Russia and seeing their three grandchildren: Jamie's two sons and their son Nicholas's daughter. Sophie had been married to a prominent war correspondent: it was not an easy life and had ended in divorce, although she now has a new partner. Although Barons Court is not open to the public it hosts many events: charitable, business, horticultural. At weekends guests visit who have a professional

interest in the house, 'and we often discover things we hadn't found out before.' There are always people around. As a result, 'I do find the need for a little retreat.' In the grounds she has built the Pushkin House. 'I built it really for my work, for the teachers in the Pushkin schools. It's a wooden house, it's built like a dacha in Russia with a lovely hearth and a fire, and when I'm not working I often go up there where I have my own sitting room, and it's wonderful. I just have a corner that I can call totally my own.'

Their staff at Barons Court is 'small compared with how many once upon a time ran this huge house, although the house itself has been reduced over time.' There are two floors and 12 bedrooms. Daily ladies come to help and there are estate staff, 'just a few people who are wonderful at their job.' Sacha thinks her sister Natalia must have met her future husband at Jamie's christening at Barons Court. Gerald Grosvenor was brought up in the adjacent county of Fermanagh and came over for the event. 'I don't think they noticed each other too much but we've seen photos of both of them at the christening!'

Sacha and James have enjoyed the opportunity to be involved in significant State occasions. James was Lord Steward to the Royal Household from 2001 to 2009. On visits to Britain by heads of state, 'his job was to introduce the foreign guests to the Queen and he, with the Lord Chamberlain, would lead the Queen and her guests into the banquets at Buckingham Palace or Windsor Castle.' Made a Knight of the Garter* in 1999, he was appointed Chancellor of the Order of the Garter in 2013. This involves 'helping the

* The Most Noble Order of the Garter is the oldest surviving Order of Chivalry in the world, founded by Edward III around 1348. Its purpose was to reward past honour and to bind the warrior to the Sovereign in an allegiance of friendship and honour: it ensured the Knight could be called upon to fight for his King and country when needed.

Opposite: At home with the Duke.

Queen to find new Knights, explaining how the ceremony works, and introducing the new knight to the Queen in the very formal setting in the chapel at Windsor.'

They had been to such a ceremony the previous week. 'It's truly wonderful. You see these splendid Heralds in their tabards and the Military Knights with great plumes in their helmets. The music and the bands and the whole ritual is something from another world and yet it still has a fundamental meaning. Basically, these knights are the Queen's spiritual warriors; they are there symbolically to defend her spirit. It is the most extraordinary ceremony, quite magical.' For her it epitomises 'the archetypal power of a true monarch, someone who is there by destiny.' To have been a part of the ceremony, even as spectator, is 'profoundly moving. It transforms people, they are touched; they are different because of it.'

Before the reforms of 1999, when the Duke was still in the House of Lords, Sacha took part in the State Opening of Parliament – 'another occasion of amazement' – when Jamie, aged about 14, was the Queen's page. Sacha proudly shows a photo of him in the role. However, although watching the procession was moving, it was also nerve-racking, as Jamie had to manage the Queen's train safely down a huge flight of steps.

The future of the monarchy and the aristocracy is hard to predict, she says, because the House of Lords has already been diminished. She compares it with a great 'tapestry' out of which they have torn the threads and 'don't know what to weave back into it.' If they put in some new threads, 'it could be a wonderfully new tapestry from which a new picture might emerge but I don't think the present incumbents have any idea of what they are

doing.' She thinks it may collapse unless someone is brought in who can see it from what she calls 'a symbolic point of view' and could 'carry people psychologically'. However, she does not think there is anyone in Britain's current leadership who can do that. 'I believe only the Queen and Prince Charles have a true understanding of it.'

As for the nobility, 'it doesn't have to be aristocrats – it has to be people of nobility of spirit who will be part of the fabric of society, of civilisation.' She believes our children 'are saying wonderful things. Let's listen to them and find inspiring educators to lead them on, to enable them to become whole human beings and to help them reclaim their birthright.'

The inheritance of non-royal titles by women is not something on which she has yet reached a conclusion. She supposes that if the girl is the eldest, it is right that she should be given the title – 'the first-born should carry what comes their way' – but she is concerned about the continuation of the line: on the girl's marriage, the name would change and the situation could lead to estates being broken up, to the great houses becoming museums.

Her children 'are perfectly happy to be who they are with the attachment of "Lord" or "Lady" but they don't use it as such. I don't think it's made a big thing of, it's just there. They accept it as part of them and I hope that they carry it – and I think they think they do – in a way that gives dignity to it.' When Jamie becomes Duke, she thinks he would 'just accept it in a very natural way. He doesn't dismiss it but it would just be

Opposite: Once the ballroom, now a family room of many treasures.

part of how life unfolds. And that of course we can't see, can we?'

Lunch with Sacha and James is served in a striking modern dining room with views of the grounds. James was taking a short break from working in his office upstairs; Sacha had a meeting that afternoon at their other property, Belle Isle at Lough Erne. That estate, which contains a 17th-century castle, includes a hotel and self-catering complex, of which Sacha is a director. The previous week the G8 summit had taken place at Lough Erne and the press had stayed in their hotel. A couple of months earlier the Russian ambassador, sent to inspect the summit's location on behalf of President Putin, came to lunch. He was 'a most friendly and interesting man', says Sacha, who has tried learning Russian but did not persevere.

Sacha's choice of predecessor is the 1st Duchess, born Louisa Jane Russell in 1812. 'She had 14 children and she was loved by everybody. She lived until 93, she was completely clear in her mind and her body, only her eyesight was starting to let her down. She loved theatricals. They used to do the most entertaining shows – we once found some costumes in baskets in the attic. A terrific sense of humour and she used to walk on stilts. Her great-grandson at some point was having trouble getting up on his little stilts, and she in her eighties was seen trotting along the terrace here on her stilts, showing him how to do it! Here's her family tree. I think she had 169 direct descendants.'

Two familiar names are immediately evident – Bedford and Buccleuch – as well as many other old families. 'She was the real matriarch in the right sense of the word.' The Duchess would mix 'a wonderful bottle' and take it to anyone ill on the estate. 'The cures that were wrought through this bottle were unbelievable – they say it was probably just the whisky that did it!' Newborn babies received clothes she had knitted. 'She loved people and was concerned for their well-being.'

Portraits and photographs of Louisa's descendants and objects from Sacha's family adorn a lovely room running from front to back. The Long Gallery is 92ft long. In the centre of the house is a stunning rotunda, with a painted domed ceiling in exquisite grey and white plasterwork and cabinets of Sèvres china. The modern colours were chosen by the late designer, David Hicks, son-in-law of Earl Mountbatten. But despite the treasures it is very much a family house. Beneath the portraits in the Front Hall it is hard to resist climbing onto a large, friendly-looking rocking horse, which Sacha has restored and says the children love.

She opens the door onto a bright afternoon, with trees fringing the lake. 'It's a joy being able to go for a walk here and there's no vibrations, no rumblings. Here it's just peace and quiet and beauty.' Yet living in such a place does not mean forgetting the outside world, as the Duchess of Abercorn so compassionately shows.

Memories of Barons Court…

Opposite: Sacha Phillips is a descendant of Tsar Nicholas I of Russia.

THE GOLDEN LINK:

LOUISA JANE, FIRST DUCHESS OF ABERCORN

(1812–1905)

Even the USA was interested in Louisa Jane, the first Duchess of Abercorn, when she celebrated her 82nd birthday. Under the headline A Remarkable Duchess, the *New York Times* of 5 August 1894 described the birthday gathering, over which she presided at Montagu House in London, as 'probably absolutely unique'. Yet it was not just the longevity of the great-great grandmother of the present Duke of Abercorn that was worthy of note: it was the fact that helping her to celebrate were her 101 descendants. Through her the line of many aristocratic families continues; some members of today's Royal Family are descended from the Duchess, including (through Diana, Princess of Wales) Princes William and Harry. Louisa's position as matriarch of such a dynasty, together with her humanity, endear her to Sacha Abercorn.

At the time of her birthday celebration she was Dowager Duchess: the Duke had died in 1885

Opposite: 'Portrait of Louisa' by Edwin Landseer.

but it had been a long and happy marriage. Lady Louisa Jane Russell was 20 when she married 21-year-old James Hamilton, then 2nd Marquess of Abercorn, on 25 October 1832 at Gordon Castle in Moray, Scotland. James, born in 1811, had come into his titles early. His father, Viscount Hamilton, died in 1814, leaving his wife, Harriet, with three small children. The eldest, James, took his father's title.

In 1815, James gained a stepfather when Harriet married the Tory politician (and future Prime Minister) George Hamilton-Gordon, 4th Earl of Aberdeen, himself a widower. When James's grandfather, the 1st Marquess of Abercorn, died in 1818, seven-year-old James became 2nd Marquess, inheriting considerable estates in England and Ireland which were held in trust until he came of age.

James's wife was also of the nobility. Louisa's parents were John Russell, 6th Duke of Bedford, and his second wife, the pretty Lady Georgiana 'Georgy' Gordon. In 1803, they too had married at

Gordon Castle, Georgy's birthplace. Her father was Alexander, 4th Duke of Gordon, her mother Jane Maxwell, a beautiful, socially ambitious woman, who was determined her daughters should marry well. Despite the Gordons being staunch Tories and the Russells fervent Whigs, Jane engineered a match between Georgy and John Russell, who was both recently widowed and unexpectedly Duke of Bedford on the death of his brother.

By the time of Louisa's wedding, Georgy had developed a very close friendship, widely believed to have been an affair, with the Scottish artist Sir Edwin Landseer, 21 years her junior. The Duke, by contrast, was 15 years older than Georgy. Their nonetheless happy marriage produced ten children, of whom Louisa, born in July 1812, was the seventh and the second of three daughters. Louisa had three half-brothers, the youngest of whom would twice be Prime Minister, and the eldest the next Duke of Bedford.

Although Louisa was baptised in the grandeur of Woburn Abbey, the Bedfords' family seat, she did not spend all her childhood there. Her parents preferred the cosier Endsleigh Cottage, which they had built in Devon in fashionably rustic style. At Endsleigh, the children could sail their toy boats and visit the model dairy. At Woburn they put on plays; one room was permanently fitted out as a theatre where every winter Georgy and the children performed, often joined by a leading comic actor. Louisa loved to take the lead role and enjoyed theatricals all her life; she also retained a very sweet singing voice. The Duke adored their children, writing in a poem to Georgy:

The merry girls, and jumping, sporting boys,
Make the old Abbey echo with their noise.

Louisa was a beautiful child. On 1 January 1824, she and her siblings attended a children's Ball given by King George IV at Brighton Pavilion. Another guest, Countess Granville, wrote to her sister: 'The King was engrossed with the Bedford children … The youngest Bedford girl [Louisa] beautiful, exactly like what Lady Georgiana Gordon was.' Indeed, the King told Louisa so himself and praised her solo performance of the Spanish shawl dance. He asked if he could do anything for her, whereupon she requested a plate of ham sandwiches and 'a glass of port wine negus', which the King obediently fetched himself. No wonder the tall, imposing young Marquess fell in love with her; the fact that he was marrying into a great Whig family, quite at odds with his Tory politics, did not matter to him.

James's family had always owned estates in Ireland and England. While attending Harrow School, he lived with his mother and stepfather at The Priory at nearby Stanmore, the largest English estate the family ever owned. After marrying, he and Louisa lived there for a short time, and then leased it to Dowager Queen Adelaide, consort of William IV. There were London properties, too, although Louisa disliked London, both physically – believing the air affected her lungs – and socially, apart from meeting friends.

Louisa's real love lay in country life. The Abercorns' main seat, Barons Court, was set in Ireland's beautiful countryside. James initially spent much money remodelling and extending it for his growing family: Louisa had their first child, Harriet, in 1834, and three months later was expecting again. However, the changing circumstances of their lives meant that for years they would make only brief visits to Barons Court.

Louisa was part of the early Evangelical movement in England. Large families were believed to be pleasing to God, which perhaps explained her having 14 children. The first three children were girls, born 12 to 13 months apart; James, the necessary heir, arrived a year later. The others, four girls and six boys, arrived at intervals of around 18 months to two years, the last one in 1858. Meanwhile, James bought the large Dale Park estate near the sea in Sussex for the family and their many staff. The cost of that purchase, together with the expenditure on Barons Court, caused something of a financial problem for James, who had to sell The Priory.

Fortunately, James's career was in the ascendancy. In 1844, he had been appointed Lord Lieutenant of Donegal, a post he would hold until his death, and already made a Knight of the Garter. Then, in 1846, he was appointed a Privy Counsellor and Groom of the Stole to Prince Albert, a position he held until 1859 and meant he was effectively head of the royal bedchamber. Louisa became a close friend and confidante to Queen Victoria, who in 1841 wanted to make her Mistress of the Robes, the highest position a lady could hold at Court. Traditionally it was the only post to be held by a duchess; as Louisa was then Marchioness, Prime Minister Sir Robert Peel declined to agree.

Such was the relationship between the Abercorns and the Royal Family that in August 1847, when Victoria and Albert made their first visit to the Scottish Highlands, they stayed for ten days at Ardverikie, a shooting lodge built by James at the head of Loch Laggan. Victoria enthused in her diary about its location and their 'comfortable' house, with walls on which the Abercorns' friend Landseer had made 'beautiful drawings of stags'.

Despite the honour, the visit was not without its stresses for the hostess. When Louisa prompted Lord Claud, aged four and dressed smartly in his kilt, to bow to Her Majesty, he was still so cross that he'd had to give up his room to the royal children that he stood on his head instead. Victoria was not amused. Then the Queen decided to give a Ball. There was no time for Louisa to request dresses be sent for her eldest daughters, so, ever resourceful, she had gowns made up from the muslin curtains in the drawing room. Fortunately, Louisa had an irrepressible sense of humour, so no doubt appreciated the funny side later.

Louisa and the Queen corresponded frequently. Coincidentally, in April 1853, they both gave birth within days of each other. Prince Leopold was delivered safely but Louisa's 12th child, Cosmo, died. These sensitive matters were surely discussed between the two women; such was the personal nature of their letters that in her will Louisa stipulated that they must never be published.

Louisa's life took another direction in 1866, when James was appointed Lord Lieutenant of Ireland, the Queen's representative there, during a difficult period. By now their family was complete. The youngest, Ernest, was eight; the eldest, Harriet, was 32 and the Countess of Lichfield by marriage. Louisa and James moved, with their younger children, to Dublin. For most of the year they lived in the Viceregal Lodge in Phoenix Park and from January to March at Dublin Castle, where as Lord and Lady Lieutenant they were obliged to entertain, often at their own expense.

Louisa's son Fredric wrote that her faith meant that 'though in this world, she was not of the world', but that circumstances meant she had

Queen Victoria.

to 'take her place'. That was certainly the case in Dublin. By Christmas 1866, disaffection among radical Irish nationalists, who opposed British rule in Ireland, had increased. The Lodge was given special security. In March 1867, the Fenian Rising began and a plot was discovered for nationalists to capture the Lodge and take the children hostage. Three of them, convalescing there after measles, were urgently returned to Dublin Castle, where the gates were closed for the first time in living memory.

Despite the grave danger to the family, Louisa was determined to show that she and James were not afraid, and they drove in their carriage through the poorest quarters in Dublin without any special security. Louisa's courage was widely praised, as was that of the constabulary who defended their barracks against attack. In the 21st century a descendant of the Chief Constable would write proudly about the day the Marchioness of Abercorn awarded his great-grandfather a medal for bravery.

In November 1867, the Abercorns' lives were disrupted when, after a short illness, their son Ronald died, aged 18. He was in the English spa town of Great Malvern, taking the 'water cure'. Louisa and two of his older siblings were with him when he died. But life had to go on. In April 1868, Louisa helped James entertain the Prince and Princess of Wales at Dublin Castle during a long visit to Ireland. After the death of his father Prince Albert and his marriage to Alexandra, the future Edward VII had started to appear in public life. He publically praised James for performing a very arduous task as Lord Lieutenant during a troubled period. On 10 August that year, James was delighted to be created first Duke of Abercorn.

Now the Queen's letters to Louisa addressed her warmly as 'Dearest Duchess'.

Ten days later, still savouring the honour, Louisa and six children boarded the Irish Mail train from Euston to Holyhead to catch the boat back to Ireland. As the train approached Abergele it collided with wagons from a goods train that had been left on the line. They were loaded with petroleum drums. Louisa must have thanked God for guiding her family to the back of the train. The ensuing explosion incinerated all 33 passengers in the front carriages. With others, her eldest son, James, uncoupled the rear carriages to avoid the fire spreading and then collapsed. During the hour it took for doctors to revive him, his family thought he had died. Afterwards, the Duke received many letters expressing relief at his family's escape.

No wonder he gave Louisa a very special present: the most famous pearl in the world, La Peregrina. With an exotic history spanning five hundred years, it remains one of the largest pear-shaped pearls in existence. James had bought it from his friend, the future Napoleon III, during his exile in England. Although beautiful, it worried Louisa because its weight caused it to fall from its necklace setting: she nearly lost it at a Ball at Buckingham Palace before spotting it in the velvet folds of a lady's gown, and then down a sofa at Windsor Castle. An excellent raconteur, Louisa probably recounted those anxious moments later with amusement. The pearl remained in the family until 1969.*

As a mother of many children during the

---

* It was bought at auction by Richard Burton for Elizabeth Taylor.

Victorian era, it was perhaps inevitable that Louisa should experience grief as well as joy. She had already lost two sons, when, in 1871, their daughter Beatrix died, aged 35, three days after the birth of her 13th child. James, having resigned as Lord Lieutenant upon a change of government, began another term in 1874, and Louisa prepared herself for more duties. But that September, their daughter Katherine died suddenly, aged 34. It was too much and Louisa suffered a severe nervous breakdown. With the Queen's permission, their only unmarried daughter took Louisa's place as Lady Lieutenant. During 1875, Louisa convalesced in the South of France, writing to the Duke, who was unhappy in Dublin despite his popularity. Unforeseen circumstances would lead to his resigning.

In 1869, their daughter Albertha had married George Spencer-Churchill, Marquess of Blandford and heir to the 7th Duke of Marlborough. Although they had four children, Blandford was having an affair with a socialite, Edith Aylesford. Lady Aylesford wrote to her husband, who was abroad with the Prince of Wales, saying she wanted to elope with Blandford. When the Prince openly condemned Blandford, his brother, Lord Randolph Churchill,* defended him and reminded the Prince of his own friendship with Lady Aylesford and of letters he had sent her. Churchill threatened to make the letters public, saying they would ensure the Prince never sat on the throne.

Not surprisingly, Victoria was angry and upset. Disraeli ensured the Prince's letters were retrieved and burned, and arranged for the 7th Duke of Marlborough to have the post of Lord Lieutenant in Ireland, taking Lord Randolph with him. To his relief, therefore, the Duke of Abercorn was able to resign in 1876. Albertha became Duchess of Marlborough in 1883 but, shortly afterwards, the marriage was annulled upon her petition. Despite her true title, Albertha always referred to herself as the Marchioness of Blandford.

Following James's resignation, Barons Court was refurbished and became their permanent country residence. Now there was more family time. Even after celebrating their golden wedding, Louisa and James still sang the duets of their youth and played chess every evening. They still enjoyed dancing and held energetic barn dances every Harvest and Christmas. Following James's death in 1885, when Louisa was 73, she moved to Coates Castle, a manor house in Sussex. There she visited all her less fortunate neighbours as she had done in Ireland, taking with her the redoubtable mixture called 'Her Grace's Bottle', comprising such ingredients as ginger, red lavender and – probably mostly – whisky. Son Frederic described her character as 'a blend of extreme simplicity and great dignity with a limitless gift of sympathy for others'.

Louisa's vitality and health were remarkable. She loved fishing, taking a footman who would bait the hook, unhook the fish she caught, then put it back in the water. Louisa attended the coronation of Edward VII in 1902 and, until she was 90, all her descendants' weddings, including that of Albertha's son, John Spencer-Churchill, the future 9th Duke of Marlborough, to the wealthy American, Conseulo Vanderbilt.

Opposite: Elizabeth Taylor wearing La Peregrina.

* Father of Winston.

Like all Louisa's descendants when they got engaged, John took his fiancée to receive the blessing of 'Grannie'. Louisa never criticised people unkindly, 'obstinately' (according to her youngest son, Ernest) refusing to see their failings. Consuelo described in her book *The Glitter and the Gold* their first meeting: 'The Hamiltons were a formidable clan headed by the Dowager Duchess of Abercorn, who was proudly conscious of her family and their alliances.' Consuelo said that Louisa's children 'had all been ordered to marry into the peerage and no one beneath an earl.' They did indeed marry well. After one daughter became Duchess of Buccleuch, Queen Victoria appointed her Mistress of the Robes, the position she had wanted to give Louisa.

On visiting an eye specialist, Louisa was assured that her difficulty in reading small print by lamplight was hardly surprising as she was 90. However, her antics sometimes worried her family, not least the stilts demonstration that amuses today's Duchess. One day, her children organised a rat hunt. The 90-year-old Dowager Duchess could not be found. Eventually, she was discovered inside a barn with a stable boy, both of them armed with sticks, eyes fixed on a rat hole into which he had inserted a ferret.

Louisa survived her friend Queen Victoria by four years, dying on 31 March 1905 aged 92. She left 169 direct living descendants, ranging from her ten surviving children to great-grandchildren. Among them were two current dukes; two future dukes; a future marquis; two current earls; and two future earls. As the *New York Times* said admiringly, Louisa was always a 'très grande dame and was for fifty years a prominent figure in the very best and most exclusive English society.' Ernest said she was 'the one golden link that held together some 50 families scattered here and there about the United Kingdom'. Sacha Abercorn would readily agree.

HAUNTED HISTORIES…

Many of the grand houses featured in this book have led lives of their own throughout centuries of non-royal dukedoms. A few were strongholds during some of the most tumultuous decades of British history, while others were home to some of the most intriguing figures of our time. From strange goings-on in the Chinese Room of Belvoir Castle, to the sounds of a child crying in a far off corridor in the depths of Inveraray Castle, the homes of the Duchesses tell more than the stories of the living.

 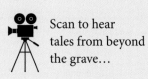

Scan to hear tales from beyond the grave…

SOURCES

GENERAL

Brian Masters, *The Dukes,* London, Pimlico 2001

www.thepeerage.com (accessed variously during 2013)

http://en.wikipedia.org (accessed variously during 2013 and 2014)

CHAPTERS 1 AND 2 (SOMERSET)

The Duke and Duchess of Somerset

Burton Latimer, *Winter Distress League,* www.burtonlatimer.info/churches/wdl-review1932-3.html (7 January 2014)

Every Woman's Encyclopedia, 'Duchess of Somerset', www.chestofbooks.com (30 December 2013)

Goldonian Web, Founders Day 1920, www.goldonian.org/barkingside/images/open_day_1920 (7 January 2014)

King's Royal Rifle Corps Association, *History,* www.krrcassociation.com (3 January 2014)

M.N. MacDonald, *Indigo Planting in India.* Article in *Pearson's Magazine, Vol. 10,* 1900

Mackinnon family website, *The Shankbone newsletter, Fall 2009, Recipes from the Duchess Susan's Cookbook,* editor Jen Webberson, www.themackinnon.com (30 December 2013)

Norway Heritage, *Allan Line,* www.norwayheritage.com (7 January 2014)

Opening the kitchen in Nov 1920 from Wikipedia entry for Lady Muriel Paget, citing Court circular from *The Times,* Monday 15 November 1920 (25 January 2014)

HSH Riddell, *The Red River Expedition of 1870,* Morrin Centre, www.morrin.org (30 December 2013)

Joan and Peter Shaw, *Burton on the Wolds village hall,* Wolds Historical Association website, www.hoap.co.uk/who/burton04.htm; also www.hoap.co.uk/who/burton05.htm for *The Seymours at Burton Hall* (30 December 2013)

Somerset estates, www.duchyofsomerset.co.uk and www.english-heritage.org.uk (10 June 2013)

Mrs Algernon St Maur, *Impressions of a Tenderfoot,* accessed at https://openlibrary.org (various dates)

Strath Family Search, www.familysearch.org/ learn/wiki/en/Strath,_Inverness,_Scotland (4 January 2014)

Wiltshire Council, *Wiltshire Community History* (Tedworth and Edward Studd), http://history.wiltshire.gov.uk (2 January 2014)

Minden J. Wilson, *History of Behar indigo factories; Reminiscences of Behar; Tirhoot and its inhabitants of the past; History of Behar Light Horse Volunteers,* Calcutta General Print Co. 1908, https://openlibrary.org (30 December 2013)

CHAPTERS 3 AND 4 (ST ALBANS)
The Duke and Duchess of St Albans

Donald Adamson and Peter Beauclerk Dewar, *The House of Nell Gwyn,* London, William Kimber, 1974

Charles Henry Ashdown, *Paper on Salisbury Hall, read at excursion to Salisbury Hall, in July 1902,* www.stalbanshistory.org (7 April 2013)

Bestwood Male Voice Choir, www.bestwoodmvc. org.uk (6 November 2013)

Coutts Bank, *Our History,* www.coutts.com/ about-us/history (6 December 2013)

Friends of Tring Church Heritage, *Henry Guy,* www.fotch.childassociates.co.uk (6 December 2013)

Nottinghamshire County Council, *History of Bestwood County Park,* www.nottinghamshire. gov.uk (7 April 2013)

Nottinghamshire History, *The Great Houses of Nottinghamshire and the County Families: Bestwood,* www.nottshistory.org.uk (7 April 2013)

Royal Bank of Scotland, *Harriot Coutts,* http://heritagearchives.rbs.com (7 May 2013)

Royal Navy, *HMS St Albans,* www.royalnavy. mod.uk (4 January 2014)

Royal Stuart Society, www.royalstuartsociety.com (6 December 2013)

St Albans City & District Council, *Mayor views refit of HMS St Albans,* 23 August 2013, www.stalbans.gov.uk (4 January 2014)

Telegraph obituaries, www.telegraph.co.uk/news/ obituaries, *The Dowager Duchess of St Albans,* 15 March 2010 (7 April 2013); *Ursula Davidson,* 9 July 2001 (5 November 2011)

CHAPTERS 5 AND 6 (BEDFORD)
The Duke and Duchess of Bedford

BBC Beds, Herts & Bucks, *People – Not just a Flying Duchess,* 15 August 2008, www.bbc.co.uk/ threecounties (12 December 2013)

Bedford Estates, *History,* www.bedfordestates. com (11 September 2013)

The British Journal of Nursing, "The Woburn Abbey Base Hospital", 27 February 1915

PID (Political Intelligence Department), Marylands, http://clutch.open.ac.uk (12 December 2013)

The Parish Church of St Mary, Woburn, www.woburnparishchurch.org.uk (12 December 2013)

The Picket Line, *Distraint on a Duchess,* 25 April 2011, www.sniggle.net (13 December 2013)

The Women's Library @ LSE – Featured Collections. Oral Evidence on the Suffragette and Suffragist Movements; the Brian Harrison interviews – interview with Maude Kate Smith, 14 January 1975 (Record 8SUF), www.lse.ac.uk/library/collections/featuredCollections/home.aspx

Scottish Birds, the J*ournal of the Scottish Ornithologists' Club,* Summer 1966, "Ornithology in Scotland" re. Mary, Duchess of Bedford, www.the-soc.org.uk/scottish-birds-onlinethe-journal-of-the-soc (7 November 2013)

Woburn Abbey website www.woburnabbey.co.uk (11 September 2013)

Woburn Abbey, *The Flying Duchess,* adapted and edited by Tim Jennings from the notes by John Gore based on Duchess Mary's diaries

Woburn News, *Moth Magnificence at Woburn,* 22 August 2013, www.woburn.co.uk/news (12 December 2013)

CHAPTERS 7 AND 8 (RUTLAND)
The Duchess of Rutland

Aegis Trust, www.aegistrust.org (18 April 2013)
Bell's World of Fashion, 1 January 1829, www.onelondonone.blogspot.co.uk (9 September 2013)

Belvoir Castle, website www.belvoircastle.com (9 September 2013)

Bottesford Living History Project, www.bottesfordhistory.org.uk (8 December 2013)
Cheveley Park Stud, www.cheveleypark.co.uk (8 December 2013)

Cricket Without Boundaries, www.cricketwithoutboundaries.com (26 September 2013)

The Duchess of Rutland with Jane Pruden, *Belvoir Castle: A Thousand Years of Family Art and Architecture,* London, Frances Lincoln Ltd, 2009

The Gentleman's Magazine, December 1825, www.onelondonone.blogspot.co.uk (9 September 2013)

Elizabeth Grice in the *Daily Telegraph*: "A Thoroughly Modern Duchess", 16 July 2012, and *The Duke and Duchess of Rutland: it's one wing for him and one wing for her,* 18 September 2012, www.telegraph.co.uk (18 April 2013)

The National Horseracing Museum, Newmarket, Suffolk, www.nhrm.co.uk (11 December 2013)

Emma Rutland in *MailOnline* www.dailymail.co.uk 16 September 2012 (13 September 2013)

Sue Steward, *Belvoir Castle's Towering Ambitions,* www.telegraph.co.uk/gardening 23 April 2005 (8 May 2013)

CHAPTERS 9 AND 10 (BUCCLEUCH)
The Duke and Duchess of Buccleuch and Queensberry

Paul Boucher, Montagu Music Collection, www.paulboucher.co.uk (10 January 2014)

Boughton House, www.boughtonhouse.org.uk (6 May 2013)

Buccleuch Group, www.buccleuch.com (29 September 2013)

Jack Campin, *Dalkeith Palace and the Scotts of Buccleuch (Music of Dalkeith)*, 2001, www.purr.demon.co.uk/dalkeith/Scotts (10 January 2014)

Deene Park, www.deenepark.com (16 January 2014)

Electric Scotland, *The Scotts of Buccleuch*, www.electricscotland.com/webclans/families/scotts.htm (10 January 2014)

English Heritage, *The National Heritage List for England*, http://list.english-heritage.org.uk (16 January 2014)

Gareth Fitzpatrick, MBE, Buccleuch Living Heritage Trust

William Fraser, *Scotts of Buccleuch*, Edinburgh, 1878 (ebook)

Robert King, notes on *Handel: Fireworks Music & Coronation Anthems-CDA66350*, 1989, www.hyperion-records.co.uk (10 January 2014)

Oxford Dictionary of National Biography, on Henry Scott, www.oxforddnb.com (10 January 2014)

National Archives, family and estate details, www.nationalarchives.gov.uk (10 January 2014)

Crispin Powell, Buccleuch family archivist

Survey of London: Volume 13, Chapter 19: Montagu House, British History Online, www.british-history.ac.uk (4 September 2013)

Victoria and Albert Museum, *18th-Century Opera*, www.vam.ac.uk (16 January 2014)

CHAPTERS 11 AND 12 (ARGYLL)
The Duke and Duchess of Argyll

The Argyll and Sutherland Highlanders (Princess Louise's), history of first Colonel-in-Chief, www.theargylls.co.uk (6 September 2013)

Josephine Butler Memorial Trust, *A Brief Introduction to the life of Josephine Butler*, www.josephinebutler.org.uk (6 September 2013)

Cadbury, *The Story of Cadbury*, www.cadbury.com.au/about-cadbury/the-story-of-cadbury.aspx (16 August 2013)

David Wilson Fine Art Ltd, on Boehm's bust of Gladstone and Princess Louise, www.davidwilsonfineart.com (23 November 2013)

John Charles Dent, *Canadian Portrait Gallery Vol. I*, pub. Toronto, John B. Magurn, 1880, http://www.gutenberg.ca/ebooks/dent-portraitgallery2/dent-portraitgallery2-00-h-dir/dent-portraitgallery2-00-h.html (6 September 2013)

Girls' Day School Trust (GDST) and Predecessors, www.archiveshub.ac.uk (9 September 2013)

Greenwichtime.com, *Greenwich Polo Club preps for royalty*, 14 May 2013, www.greenwichtime.com (16 August 2013)

Helensburgh Heritage Trust, *Rosneath's Princess*, 2012, www.helensburgh-heritage.co.uk (5 September 2013)

Inveraray Castle brochure and website, www.inveraray-castle.com (19 August 2013)

Iona History, *The Abbey: Restoration*, www.ionahistory.org.uk (20 August 2013)

Mapping Sculpture, *Her Royal Highness the Princess Louise Duchess of Argyll,* http://sculpture.gla.ac.uk (5 September 2013)

National Archives, *The Theft of the Irish 'Crown Jewels',* www.nationalarchives.ie/topics/crown_jewels/ (24 November 2013)

Quilt Museum, *The Ladies Work Society,* www.quiltmuseum.org.uk (9 September 2013)

Rosneath Games, *Rosneath Peninsula Highland Gathering,* 2013, www.rosneathgames.co.uk (6 September 2013)

St John's Wood Memories, *Places of Worship, Canon Duckworth,* www.stjohnswoodmemories.org.uk (6 September 2013)

Victoria and Albert Museum, *Left Hand of Princess Louise,* http://collections.vam.ac.uk (6 September 2013)

Jehanne Wake, *Princess Louise: Queen Victoria's Unconventional Daughter,* London, Collins, 1988

CHAPTERS 13 AND 14 (MONTROSE/ HAMILTON)

The Duke and Duchess of Montrose

About Aberdeen, *Brodick Castle,* www.aboutaberdeen.com (13 January 2013)

BBC History, *The Dieppe Raid,* www.bbc.co.uk (19 January 2013)

Buchanan Castle Golf Club, www.buchanancastlegolfclub.co.uk (19 January 2013)

Initiatives of Change UK, www.uk.iofc.org (20 January 2013)

Overview of Hamilton Palace – Gazetteer for Scotland, www.scottish-places.info/features/featurefirst7709.html

Preshal Trust, www.preshaltrust.org.uk (25 November 2013)

Rampant Scotland, *Buchanan Castle,* www.rampantscotland.com (20 January 2013)

Rosalind K. Marshall, *The Days of Duchess Anne: Life in the Household of the Duchess of Hamilton 1656–1716,* Scotland, Tuckwell Press, 2000

Scotland Magazine Issue 38, April 2008, "The Clan Graham", James Irvine Robertson www.scotlandmag.com (10 December 2012)

St John's-Ravenscourt School, www.sjr.mb.ca (19 January 2013)

South Lanarkshire Leisure and Culture, *History, Hamilton Palace,* www.slleisureandculture.co.uk (25 November 2013)

Trossachs, *Drymen Village,* www.trossachs.co.uk (12 January 2013)

Virtual Hamilton Palace Trust, *Rediscovering the Palace,* http://hamilton.rcahms.gov.uk (25 November 2013)

CHAPTERS 15 AND 16 (NORTHUMBERLAND)

The Duke and Duchess of Northumberland

About.com, Washington, DC, *James Smithson, Founding Donor of the Smithsonian,* www.dc.about.com (29 December 2013)

Adriano Aymonino, *The Musaeum of the 1st Duchess of Northumberland (1716-1776) at Northumberland House in London: An*

Introduction, in S. Bracken, A. M. Gáldy, A. Turpin (eds.) *Women Patrons and Collectors,* Newcastle upon Tyne, 2012, www.academia.edu (18 December 2013)

Alnwick Castle website, www.alnwickcastle.com (18 December 2013)

The Bookman, *Diaries of a Duchess,* Feb 1927, www.unz.org (18 December 2013)

British History Online, *Northumberland House and its Associations,* www.british-history.ac.uk (18 December 2013)

The Duchess of Northumberland, *The Duchess of Northumberland's Little Book of Poisons, Potions and Aphrodisiacs,* Stroud, The History Press Ltd, June 2013

Northumberland County Council, *Four Northumberland residents receive British Empire medals,* 24 September 2013 www. northumberland.gov.uk (7 October 2013)

Oxford Dictionary of National Biography on "Hugh Percy", www.oxforddnb.com (18 December 2013)

St Anne's Cathedral, Belfast, *Thomas Percy,* www. belfastcathedral.org (21 December 2013)

Syon Park, website www.syonpark.co.uk (19 December 2013)

Westminster Abbey, *Elizabeth, Duchess of Northumberland,* www.westminster-abbey.org (19 December 2013)

CHAPTERS 17 AND 18 (LEINSTER)
The Duke and Duchess of Leinster

Ask About Ireland, www.askaboutireland.ie/enfo

The Wizard Earl (1 October 2013); *The Great Earl of Kildare* by Donough Bryan, Dublin and Belfast, the Phoenix Publishing Company Ltd, 1933 (30 September 2013); *The Earls of Kildare* by the Marquis of Kildare, Dublin, Hodges, Smith & Co, 1862 (30 September 2013)

Carton House, *History of Carton House,* www. cartonhouse.com/history.html (30 September 2013)

County Kildare Heritage, *Carton House* www. kildare.ie/heritage (30 September 2013)

Houses of the Oireachtas, www.oireachtas.ie/ parliament, *Press Releases, Duke and Duchess of Leinster 'Come Home',* 2011 (3 February 2013); *Leinster House: A Tour and History* (30 September 2013)

Irish Castles, *Kilkea Castle,* www. britainirelandcastles.com (30 September 2013)

Telegraph obituaries, *8th Duke of Leinster,* 7 December 2004, www.telegraph.co.uk (11 November 2012)

Stella Tillyard, *Aristocrats,* Great Britain, Vintage, 1995

CHAPTERS 19 AND 20 (ABERCORN)
The Duke and Duchess of Abercorn

Clive Aslet, *The English Country House,* London, Bloomsbury, 2008.

Bath Chronicle, Belfast Newsletter and other regional newspapers on death of Lord Ronald Hamilton, November 1867

BBC blogs Wales, *Abergele Railway Disaster,* 19 September 2013, www.bbc.co.uk (12 February 2014)

Bedford Estates, *6th Duke of Bedford*, www.bedfordestates.com (23 January 2014)

Denbighshire archives, *Abergele Train Disaster*, www.denbighshirearchives.wordpress.com (12 February 2014)

Every Woman's Encyclopedia, "Women in Great Social Positions". *Ladies Who Serve the Queen*, www.chestofbooks.com (24 January 2014)

Gordon Castle, *Gordon Castle Estate*, www.gordoncastle.co.uk (24 January 2014)

History Ireland, *Fenian Attack on Kilmallock Barracks, 1867*, www.historyireland.com (13 February 2014)

London Gardens Online, *Bentley Priory*, www.londongardensonline.org (24 January 2014)

Lord Ernest Hamilton, *Forty Years On,* New York, George H. Doran, 1922, accessed from https://openlibrary.org (12 February 2014)

Lord Frederic Hamilton: (1) *The Days Before Yesterday,* New York, George H. Doran, 1920; (2) *Here, There and Everywhere,* New York, George H. Doran, 1921; (3) *The Vanished Pomps of Yesterday,* London, Hodder & Stoughton, no date. All accessed from https://openlibrary.org (12 February 2014)

Hon. F. Leverson Gower (ed.), *Letters of Harriet Countess of Granville 1810–1845,* London, Longmans, Green and Co, 1894, accessed from https://openlibrary.org (30 January 2014)

James Macaulay, *Speeches of Prince Albert 1863–1888*, London, John Murray, 1889, accessed from The Project Gutenberg eBook of Speeches and Addresses of HRH The Prince of Wales, www.gutenberg.org (31 January 2014)

Jewellery of Today's British Royalty, *La Peregrina* www.thetudorswiki.com (30 January 2014)

Parks & Gardens UK, *Dale Park, Madehurst,* www.parksandgardens.org (31 January 2014)

Public Record Office of Northern Ireland, *Introduction to Abercorn Papers,* November 2007 (30 January 2014), and Letters between Duke and Duchess, www.proni.gov.uk (8 February 2014)

Queen Victoria's diary, from www.electricscotland.com (30 January 2014)

Windsor Castle, *Pilgrimage Background Notes re. Order of the Garter,* www.stgeorges-windsor.org (3 December 2013)

LIST OF ILLUSTRATIONS

INDEX